It is said that big things come in little packages. On reading the book *Ashutosh Baba: The Memoirs of Acharya Ramananda Avadhuta,* one arrives at the same conclusion. In fact, this book is the repository of little stories that reveal big secrets of the Lord's divine play.

The central theme of these stories is that the simplest and easiest way to please Parama Purusha is through devotion. But devotion comes when seekers of spiritual attainment are willing to risk everything for their ideal. Baba Himself risked His own life and suffered inexplicable ignominy and torture for the ideal he preached to others.

These stories are educative, inspiring and absorbing. The language is lucid and simple. The book contains an immensely readable account of the author's spiritual journey and the first-hand experiences he gathered as an Ananda Marga monk and Personal Assistant to Baba from 1971 to 1984.

R.D. Singh, former editor of *Prout Weekly*

The book *Ashutosh Baba,* written by Acharya Ramananda Avadhuta, is a dedicated exposure of a great hidden treasure and a sincere expression of a devotee's subtler experiences. I personally feel that Baba's devotees will like reading it and get completely lost in the realm of Divine Panorama.

May Baba bless us all .

Acharya Svarupananda Avadhuta, Principal, Ananda Marga Degree College, Anandanagar

It is with great joy that I offer some remarks about *Ashutosh Baba,* written by Dada Ramananda, who has been a good friend for a long time. I don't recall when exactly I first met Dada, who was Baba's personal assistant for many years. Perhaps it was in 1978 after Baba had been released from jail. I became very fond of him because of my own self-interest. He was a VIP in my eyes because he controlled access to Baba, who attracted everyone, especially his disciples, like a magnet.

Whenever I visited India, I would be eager to see Baba in his room and prostrate myself at his feet. And I was able to do this with Dada Ramananda's help. But that is not why I have relished reading Dada's memoirs. Many margis have offered their fond recollections of the time they spent with their sadguru, Baba Anandamurti Ji, and I have enjoyed reading them all. But Dada Ramananda's recollections are in a class by themselves. In them Baba's omniscience, magnificence, compassion and above all his vast love for humanity shine with great effulgence.

Dada Ramananda was Baba's personal assistant for more than a decade. He was an eyewitness to a lot of what Baba did for the world. His account is a treasure trove of material for historians and future devotees of God. Baba's undying legacy to humanity comes alive in what Dada has offered to his friends and readers. His memoirs, I think, rival Naginaji's amazing book, *Ananda Katha*. The fact that Baba appointed Dada as his personal assistant speaks loudly of the greatness of Acharya Ramananda Avadhuta.

Ravi Batra, prize-winning economist and the author of *The Downfall of Capitalism and Communism*

Exquisite writing. Exquisite story telling. And, fortunately, for the reader, Dada Ramananda has an amazing memory. This book is a true gem. One cannot put it down. What impressed me most was the focus on detail: when Dada Ramananda writes of Laldhari, the cowherd in Patliputra Colony, we are transported there. When he recounts that he is no longer able to hear the flute sound that had been giving him bliss for decades, we feel his pain. When P. R. Sarkar — Baba — blesses him to hear the sound of divinity again, we are there in the room. When Baba tells Laldhari why he lost the ability to hear Krishna's flute — cavorting with politicians to gain employment for his children — the narrative becomes more than an evocation of bliss, it becomes a story of what is right and what is wrong.

Dada Ramananda uses his text not just to inspire, not just to transport us to other worlds, but to teach us, to help each one of us inquire into our own life's journey, to reflect on what is the true path, the path of bliss.

There are also humorous stories. For example, when Baba returns to his childhood home of Jamalpur, a throng of hundreds greets him outside of the plane. In their bliss, they begin to wash his feet with cow's milk. Lost in devotion they do not give Baba enough time to remove his shoes. Baba remains smiling as milk splashes everywhere.

While Ramananda remains ever the serene storyteller, what counts most is the view of the person whom he is writing about. In one story, Jaganath, who has come to learn microvita sadhana, is instructed to have his lessons reviewed. Time after time, he goes to do this, but with no luck. Finally Baba asks him how he meditates. He responds: "Baba, I just remember you. You are my mantra, you are my lessons. I just think of you and that is why I am always happy." We see the world from Jaganath's eyes and are changed.

But there is something else that Ramananda gives us. The stories certainly establish Sarkar's divinity, but they go much further than that; they demonstrate Baba's humanity: his care of the weak, the disempowered, his willingness to speak truth to the powerful and to use his spiritual power to spread the waves of bliss throughout the planet and the cosmos. It is Sarkar's interaction with real people that makes this book no ordinary book, no ordinary memoir. We are lifted toward the extraordinary as microvita dance around us.

Sarkar, of course, is extraordinary. Dada Ramananda's text shows that he is too. Hopefully *Ashutosh Baba* can make us all extraordinary. Permanently.

Sohail Inayatullah, author of *Situating Sarkar: Tantra, Macrohistory and Alternative Futures*

Respected Acharya Ramanandaji Avadhuta has done a great service to the future humanity by penning his first-hand account of his life with beloved Baba and what he witnessed during his many years as Baba's personal assistant. He had the rare fortune and privilege to experience and observe the life of a Mahakaula, a Mahasambhuti Sadguru, from the most intimate of quarters. His stories of Baba become a part of the historical record of Baba's life. They are special because they give us a direct glimpse into the divine play of Lord Shrii Shrii Anandamurtiji.

Acharya Shambhushivananda Avadhuta

Ashutosh Baba

Ashutosh Baba

The Memoirs of Acharya Ramananda Avadhuta

Ananda Marga Publications

Anandanagar • Ranchi • New Delhi

Interviews recorded and edited by Devashish

ISBN 978-81-89718-60-2

Published by:
Ac. Sampurnananda Avt.
Publications Secretary (Central)
Ananda Marga Pracaraka Samgha
Anandanagar P.O. Baglata, Dist. Purulia (WB)

Camp: Madhu Manjusa
Ananda Marga Pracaraka Samgha
Hchal Ratu Road, Ranchi 834005

Acknowledgements:

I would like to thank Devashish, Prabhakar, R. D. Singh, and Acharya Iishvarakrsnananda Avadhuta for their kind assistance in the various stages of the preparation of this manuscript.

The proceeds of this book go to social service projects in different parts of the world

Dedication

This book is dedicated to the revered memory of my loving guru, Shrii Shrii Anandamurti, whom we affectionately call Baba. May his grace be with us all.

Contents

Foreword

*I*FIRST MET DADA Ramananda in August of 1977 in the Ananda Marga office in Patna. He had just returned from Bankipur Jail where he went every morning to attend to Baba's needs, and he was gracious enough to invite me to his room for a chat. I was twenty at the time, newly arrived in India, and listening to him talk about Baba was an unforgettable experience, one that seems as fresh today as it did then. I remember staring wide-eyed as he told me that Baba had given him a special mantra that morning for him to use whenever he didn't get time to complete the complicated lessons of Vishesh Yoga due to the pressures of being Baba's personal assistant, lessons he had learned directly from Baba himself.

After many years and many pleasant memories of other encounters with Dada whenever I went to India to see Baba, I had a chance to reprise that first chat in the fall of 2007 when I stayed with him in Anandanagar for four days and listened to him tell stories of his experiences with the master—this time with a digital recorder at my side. It was during those few days that Dada requested me to come back to India for a longer period of time to help him write his memoirs. It took four years before I could make good on my promise, but finally, in October 2011, I was able to spend several weeks with Dada in Anandanagar, recording his experiences each morning and evening. As always, it was a privilege to be able to enjoy his company, to witness first-hand the depths of his devotion and the extent of his profound commitment to Baba's mission—despite his poor health, Dada never let a single moment go by without doing Baba's work, especially the relief activities to which he has devoted his life. It was not easy to pull him away from those activities for a few precious hours each day to record his experiences but I am grateful that I was able to do so. He had a unique relationship with Baba and a unique perspective on the master's life, serving as Baba's personal assistant for thirteen remarkable years. It would have been a shame had this treasure lode of memories been lost to the rest of us, who through Dada's book now have a chance to relive the drama of Baba's earthly incarnation and in this way draw closer to the guru.

— Devashish

Preface

*T*HERE IS A *shloka*, or poem, in Sanskrit that describes the impossibility of a devotee's attempt to describe the infinite attributes of the Lord:

> *Asitagirisamam syát kajjalam sindhupátre,*
> *Surataruvarashákhá lekhaniipatramurvvii.*
> *Likhati yadi grhiitvá Sáradá sarvakálam,*
> *Tathápi tava gunánámiisha páram na yáti.*

"If we use the Himalayas as an ink-tablet, the largest ocean as the ink-pot, the branch of the biggest tree of heaven as a pen, and the entire lithosphere as paper; and with this paper, ink, and pen, if the goddess of learning writes for an indefinite period, even then it would not be possible to write all the attributes that he possesses."

Though it is not possible for me to do justice to Baba's greatness with mere words, I hope my small book will give the reader a glimpse of his divine personality.

The White Lotus

*I*N THE FALL of 1963, when I was nineteen, I had my first opportunity to accompany Baba on field walk. When I reached the Jamalpur *jagriti*, Baba's PA (personal assistant), Dada Abhedananda, told me that I would be in the first group that evening, the group that would accompany Baba from his house to the tiger's grave. In those days there were three groups. The first group would accompany Baba to the grave and leave him there. The second group would wait for Baba on the grave and would sit with him until he was ready to go back. The third group would come later to accompany Baba back to his house.

There were two other margis in the first group that evening. One of them was Ram Bahadur Singh, a police superintendent whom I knew quite well. He was a staunch devotee and a scrupulously honest man who would not accept bribes and was therefore transferred frequently by his immoral bosses. After I prostrated in front of Baba's door, Ram Bahadur explained to me that there was a rule that we should wait outside the gate, rather than outside the door. When I asked him why we needed to wait so far from the door, he explained that Baba lived there with his family—the rule was to protect his family's privacy.

When Baba came out a few minutes later, he asked me straightaway, "Did Abhedananda not tell you about my rule? It is not permissible to do sastaunga pranam inside the gate, as you have done. Anyhow, you didn't know about the rule, so you are excused."

Baba then started walking in the direction of the field and we followed after him. As soon as we set off, I started noticing a strong fragrance coming from Baba's body. It was the natural fragrance of a flower that I couldn't recognize. It was very distinct and very intoxicating, almost overwhelming. Now, it was Baba's habit to walk very fast. We almost had to run to keep up. While I was hurrying to keep pace, I asked Ram Bahadur if he smelled anything unusual. "Yes," he said. "Such a beautiful fragrance is coming from Baba's body, it is driving me mad. I can hardly think of anything else."

We started talking about the fragrance, which to us seemed a kind of miracle, and by the time we reached the railway bridge we had fallen a little ways behind. Baba stopped for a moment and called out to us. "Where are you? What kind of conspiracy are you hatching back there?" When we caught up again, he asked us why we had fallen behind and what we had been discussing.

Ram Bahadur was very bold by nature. He said, "Baba, ever since we started our walk we have been aware of a beautiful fragrance. We were enjoying that fragrance and talking about it, and that is why we were delayed. It is coming from you."

"I never use any fragrance," Baba said. "I only use lifebuoy soap and coconut oil, only the simplest natural things. How could there be any such fragrance coming from me? Are you not imagining it?"

"No, Baba, we all smelled it."

Baba resumed walking. After a few moments he said, "Okay, if you are all sure that you are smelling some beautiful fragrance, then each of you tell me which flower you think it is—unless you think that it is an artificial fragrance?"

"No, Baba, it seems to be the fragrance of some flower."

"Then which flower is it?"

But none of us could say. We could only tell Baba how beautiful the fragrance was. At the end of the bridge, he turned to us and said, "Who is the youngest among you?" They both pointed to me. Baba nodded and asked the two of them to try to name the flower they were smelling. One by one, they guessed different names, such as queen of the night, rose, and so on. But Baba kept saying, "No, it's not that; that's not right either," and as they named different flowers Baba talked about their respective fragrances, giving various details to show why it could not be those flowers. Finally, he turned to me and said, "Yes, he seems to be the youngest. Neither of you could tell me which flower it is, but I think this young boy will be able to tell me the correct name. Since you insist that this fragrance is coming from my body, even though I don't use any fragrance, we will conduct a test. Come here, my boy, stand here."

I came and stood just in front of Baba.

"I will place my hand on your head and after ten seconds you will see a bud, but you will not recognize the flower. After fifteen seconds it will begin to blossom, and after forty-five seconds you will be able to name it. As soon as you identify the flower, I will remove my hand. If I keep my hand there any longer, your attention will be diverted and you may not be able to remain on your feet, so I will only give you forty-five seconds."

Baba placed his hand on my head and I started seeing the bud of a flower.

"Can you see it?" he asked.

"Yes, Baba."

"You will be able to see it whether your eyes are open or closed, it doesn't matter. Continue to concentrate on the flower."

"Has it bloomed?" he asked.

"Yes, Baba. It is fully bloomed."

"Do you recognize the flower?"

"Yes, Baba. It is a white lotus."

Baba removed his hand from my head and the vision disappeared.

"Yes, you are correct. It is a white lotus. I am very fond of the fragrance of the white lotus and I love to sit on it. When you learn the process of *dhyana*, you will understand the significance of this."

As we resumed our walk, Baba began talking about the botanical characteristics and history of the white lotus. The scent continued for the duration of the field walk, some two and a half hours.

1963

I Become a Worker

W HEN I HAD my personal contact with Baba he didn't punish me, nor did he point out my mistakes. He just told me that he wanted me to become a noble human being. Then he asked me if I wanted to dedicate myself to the mission. I said yes, but it took me several months before I followed through on my decision. I returned to my studies at Buddha Degree College in Uttar Pradesh. Then in February of 1964 I got a letter from Abhedananda saying that Baba wanted to see me. So I took the monthly allowance that my parents gave me for my studies and went to Jamalpur. This was when Baba showed me the white lotus. Again I returned to my college but a few weeks later I got another letter from Abhedananda informing me that Baba wanted me to come to Jamalpur. When I showed it to my acharya, he told me how lucky I was that Baba was calling me personally. Then I made up my mind once and for all. I left without telling my family and I never went back. On March 4, I entered the training centre in Anandanagar to become a dedicated worker.

When I completed my training and went to Jamalpur for my acharya exam I couldn't reply to any of Baba's questions. I could only weep, thinking that Baba knew everything and I knew nothing. There were six of us and I was the only one who couldn't answer any of Baba's questions. The next morning, when Baba came to the jagriti, he declared that I had passed and the other five brothers had failed.

1964

Raipur

*A*FTER I COMPLETED my acharya training in Anandanagar, I was
sent to the Darbhanga school and then to the school in Madhubani
for fifteen-days field training. When I finished my field training I was
sent to Raipur in Madhya Pradesh to start a school. It was a difficult
assignment but I was able to start the school, and in time it became
one of the best in India. I began by renting a house and organizing the
margis. At that time there were three family acharyas living in Raipur:
Acharya Ram Lal Dani, Acharya Narendra; and Acharya Kailash Balla.
The first student I enrolled was the son of one of these acharyas. Soon
I had so many students that I found it difficult to manage. Even the son
of the local commissioner started attending, as well as many other non-
margi children. Since I was the principal and had little help, the entire
burden fell on my shoulders. Apart from giving classes, contacting the
people, and paying the bills, I also had to do the shopping, the cooking,
and the cleaning. As a result I hardly had time to sleep.

The school soon earned a good reputation, and after some three or four
months these three acharyas decided that they should go to Jamalpur to
request Baba to send a new principal—an English-speaking principal,
since it was an English-medium school. They also wanted to invite him
for DMC. Their intention was good, no doubt. They wanted what was
best for the school but Baba didn't see it that way. When they put their
request, Baba became furious. "You nonsense people!" he told them. "This
boy knows English better than you. Do you know how sincere he is, how
hard he is working? How dare you put this request! Get out of here this
minute, the three of you!" I did, in fact, know English at the time, but I
had no experience teaching in English medium. After some time, they
were able to calm Baba down, but when they invited him for DMC, he
was completely unreceptive. "DMC cannot be held in Raipur," he said,
"unless the principal recommends it. And why should he recommend

it? You are not helping him with his work. He is suffering and instead of helping him you are criticizing him. Your request is denied."

After receiving this chastisement, they returned to Raipur and started helping me with the school. At first I wondered about their change of heart, but then after Sunday Dharmachakra they explained what had happened when they went to see Baba. They apologized and begged me to go with them to Jamalpur to invite Baba for DMC. "Unless you ask him," they said, "there is no way Baba will agree."

I agreed to go with them and Baba kindly accepted my petition. Baba stayed in my room in the school and the DMC program was held in the Giridhara Bhavan Dharmasala. Not long afterward I was reposted to Anandanagar as central relief in-charge, and Acharya Shraddhananda was sent to Raipur to take over as principal.

1965

Chandradeva Varma

*I*WAS STILL IN Raipur when Acharya Chandradeva Varma was transferred there by his employer, All-India Radio. He was a man of
strict principles and keen intelligence who used to organize regular
Renaissance Universal meetings. In fact, he was so strict regarding his
conduct that he even used to correct the other acharyas whenever they
did anything wrong. Shortly after his posting to Raipur, he began having
problems with his boss. This man was envious of Chandradeva's good
reputation and was inconvenienced by his high standard of rectitude,
so he became determined to get him transferred. One day Chandradeva
came to my school to talk to me—his daughter was attending the school.
He told me that he needed to go to Jamalpur to talk to Baba about the
situation and he requested my help finding someone to look after his
wife and daughter while he was gone. I went to talk to Narendraji and
the others and made the arrangements.

It was morning when Chandradeva arrived at the Jamalpur jagriti. It
just so happened that on that morning Baba passed by the jagriti before
going to the office. When Baba saw him, he called him to his room and
asked him to tell him what was the matter—in those days it was much
easier to meet Baba.

"Baba," he said, "I have no one else in this life to whom I can confide
my problems. You are my father and my mother, my everything. Things
have gotten so bad in my work that my *sadhana* is disturbed. I need
your advice."

"You have no need to worry, Chandradeva," Baba told him. "Return
to your job and everything will be set right."

Once Baba said this, Chandradeva's confidence returned and his
mood lightened. Baba inquired about me and the work in Raipur, and
Chandradeva gave him a detailed report. When he returned to his office,
he learned that his boss had been diagnosed with a bad heart condition

and could no longer continue in his position. A new man was sent in his place and he was so charmed by Chandradeva's personality that he quickly became his great supporter.

1965

Baba Donates One Thousand Rupees for Relief

*I*N 1966 AND 67 a severe drought affected Bihar, as well as some parts of Madhya Pradesh, Bengal, and Orissa. Baba formed a committee for our relief efforts and specified that some worker should be included. Important margis got involved, such as Shashi Rainjan, who opened a relief office in his quarters, and the government cooperated with us by donating rice and other foodstuffs. Jaya Prakash Narayan, who was directing the relief efforts for the state of Bihar, gave us a lot of wheat. Other foodstuffs we purchased with the money donated by margis and other well-wishers. We distributed these materials, and once the worst of the disaster was behind us we started a food-for-work program so that the local people could feel that they were responsible for their own recovery rather than being the recipients of aid programs. Together with the people we constructed roads and opened cheap kitchens and dug wells.

In October of 1967, severe floods began to ravage the Bengal coast in the area of Contai. I did not speak Bengali at the time, but since I had experience in relief work Baba sent me there to help the flood victims. He even taught me a few Bengali words and expressions before sending me to the constituency of Samar Guha, a close associate of Netaji who knew Baba. There were a few margis in that area, including Bamkin Chandra Bera, and they helped me to collect materials and foodstuffs. We opened up a kitchen for the victims and distributed the materials we were able to collect. I was unhappy with our efforts, however. The devastation was tremendous; hundreds of thousands of people were suffering and we were only able to feed some five to six hundred people a day. I felt as if I had failed Baba. Then I learned that he was coming to Medinapur for DMC, about three hours from where I was working. I knew that I was required to attend the DMC, but I didn't feel that I could face Baba and admit how little I had been able to do for the people. So I decided not to attend. But early one morning Nirmalananda showed up at my door with orders from Baba to bring me to Medinapur. I was meditating at the time, enjoying a very good meditation, when I heard his voice: "Ramananda, where are you? What are you doing? Baba sent me to bring you to the DMC. Leave whatever you are doing and come with me." It turned out that when the workers arrived in Medinapur, Baba had asked where I was and when he learned that I was absent he chose Nirmalananda to go fetch me.

"How can I go," I told him. "The margis are working very hard to help the people. I can't just leave them like that."

"The margis will take care of the work while you are gone. My orders are to bring you with me no matter what you are doing—eating, sleeping, working, it doesn't matter. You have to come with me, right now."

So I accompanied him to Medinapur, sure that Baba would scold me.* Throughout the journey I tried to prepare myself mentally for Baba's displeasure, though I knew that I had worked to the best of my capacity. If Baba scolded me, I decided, I would accept it as his grace.

We reached the house where Baba was staying just after lunchtime. Baba was walking his hundred steps, his regular routine after lunch and dinner. When he was informed that I had arrived, he called me into his room. I did sastaunga pranam and when I got up he told me to sit in the corner. "If you sit in the middle of the room," he said, "it will get in the way of my walking." He walked for another ten or fifteen minutes and then sat on his cot. Then he told me to call whatever margis and workers were there in the house. I thought it odd because Baba was wearing a lungi and a T-shirt. He never received margis or workers like that, in such informal dress, but it was his order, so I went and called everybody into his room. When everyone was inside—there must have been at least a dozen people, including three or four workers—Baba told me to bring him his Punjabi shirt. Ah, I thought, he has remembered that he is not wearing a proper shirt. But when I went to hand him the shirt he said, "No, I am not going to put it on. Just hold it out in front of me as if I were going to put it on." Now I was really curious. By this time I had realized that Baba was not going to scold me. When I held the shirt up in front of him, he said, "Ramananda, I have a specific system for my belongings. That way I always know what is in the right pocket and what is in the left. Now I will take out what is in the right pocket."

---

*   Baba's scolding was an expression of his love for his disciples, like a father correcting his son or daughter for their own improvement.

Baba put his hand in the right pocket and drew out an old-style Indian wallet with a zip. He opened the wallet, took out the money that was in it, and then put the wallet back in the pocket. Then he told me to return the shirt to its hanger.

As I was putting the shirt back, he started counting out the bills that he had removed, counting them out loud. There were ten bills, ten one-hundred rupee notes. When he finished counting, he said, "You know, this boy was weeping this morning because he had so little funds. He was pained because he could do so little for the victims of the flood. No one is helping him but at least I am able to contribute one thousand rupees. This is my physical contribution. Ramananda, come here. From now on I assure you that you will not lack for money or materials for your relief work. This is my pledge to you. Come, take this money."

I started crying. How kind Baba was to me! After that, the margis who were gathered in the room started helping. They collected a great deal of funds for the work and I was able to expand our relief efforts many-fold.

September 1967

Breaking Danuka's bow

*I*N THE SUMMER of 1968 the Brahmaputra River in Assam flooded and thousands upon thousands of people were left without shelter or resources, most of them stranded on the banks of the river. I was working for the Ananda Marga Universal Relief Team (AMURT) at the time and Baba sent me there to do relief. At the time there were very few margis in Assam, and AMURT was without funds, but I had already learned from Baba that if there was good work to be done you should jump right in and he would help.

When I arrived in Guwahati, I went to the quarters of one margi who worked for the railway company. He agreed to put me up and help me with my work. I called a meeting of the local margis and explained what I wanted to do and what help I needed. Above all, I needed materials and money so I could begin distributing food and blankets to the refugees. The margis themselves had no money but they were enthusiastic about helping. At first we went into the streets trying to collect money but the response was meagre and I became desperate. People were suffering and time was of the essence. After two days, the margis suggested that I approach one Marwari businessman, Mr. G. R. Danuka, who was reputed to be one of the richest men in the entire state. He was also said to be a religious-minded man who led a principled life.

We went to see him that very same day. But there were a lot of hoops to jump through. He was a very important man in Guwahati, the head of a large organization. You could not simply walk up and get an appointment. At first his people told me that he wasn't there. But we persisted and eventually someone agreed to take a note to him. I wrote the note and he sent back a message that he was busy at the moment but that we could come to see him the next morning.

Early the next morning, after finishing our spiritual practices, I and five margis went to see him. He had finished his morning prayers when we arrived, and when he was informed that we were there he asked us to be let in at once. He was very gracious and well mannered. He brought chairs for us and asked us how he could help.

"My gurudeva has sent me here from Ranchi to do relief work," I told him. "Thousands of people are living on the riverbank under miserable conditions, without any food or shelter. I want to help them."

I was surprised by his response. He agreed to help us without any hesitation whatsoever. "Tell me what you require," he said, "and what you plan to do. I will give you all the help I can."

"What the people need most urgently," I said, "is food: rice, pulse, potatoes, molasses."

"Then do one thing," he said. "I have one lakh of rupees with me now. Take it and start your work. If you need more later, then come back and see me."

I felt like Baba was speaking through this man's mouth. I told him that instead of giving us money it would be better if he bought the supplies, since he was a businessman and was far more experienced in these matters. If he could also supply some trucks, I said, then our people could accompany those trucks and begin the distribution.

He was impressed by my suggestion. "Then I will give you twenty thousand," he said, "so that you don't have any difficulty moving around and getting your work done. I have my contacts in Dhubari and other places. I will tell them to give you everything you need, including twenty trucks and enough assistants to help you load and unload them. Even if it is more than one lakh, it doesn't matter. Select the places where you want the materials delivered and I will make sure they get there. I will also place a house at your disposal for you to use as your centre."

I was stunned. Twenty trucks full of relief materials! We were only five or six margis but everything was taken care of for us. We selected five or six places as distribution centres, with one margi to oversee the work in each place, and when we reached those places the trucks were already waiting for us under the banner of AMURT. From there we started distributing the materials, mostly on boats since access to the people was difficult by any other means.

Later, when I met Mr. Danuka again, he told me that the money had not been his. It had been sent to him for the flood victims by his friend Hanuman Prasad Poddar, the owner of the Gita Press in Gorakhpur. "I wanted to give it to some religious society, "he told me, "but I couldn't decide which until I saw you. The moment I saw you and saw how sincere you were, I had the feeling that the money had been sent specifically for you."

Our relief operations lasted for one month. We had great success and garnered much attention from the media. When I returned to Ranchi, Vishokananda, Baba's PA, sent me right away to Baba's room to give him the good news. After doing sastaunga pranam, I told Baba the whole story, especially how Danukaji had helped us. Baba asked me to use his full name. I said it was G. R. Danuka. "No," Baba said, "this is an abbreviation. What is his full name?" But I had never learned his full name. Then Baba told me that it was Ganapati Rai Danuka. "So, have you broken Danuka's bow?" Baba asked. Danuka was the name of Rama's bow and when you break somebody's bow it means that you have defeated him—in this case I had succeeded in convincing him to help. He said it in Bengali, *tumi danukar danush benge diyecho*? Baba used to speak to me in Bengali so that I would learn the language.

August 1968

Saving Indira Gandhi

*I*N 1968 THE river Tista in North Bengal underwent severe flooding, creating great devastation. Property and livestock were washed away by the flood and many people died, so Baba gave us instructions to go there immediately and begin relief activities. Myself, Raghuvir Prasad, and Shashi Rainjan flew to Bagdogra airport near Siliguri, and from there we went by car to Jalpaiguri, from where we conducted our relief efforts. Mother Teresa and a team from the Ramakrishna Mission came with us on the same plane.

The flood was declared a national disaster and political allegations abounded, accusing the central government of failing to respond adequately to the situation or to earmark sufficient funds and other resources. In response to these concerns, Indira Gandhi paid a visit to the flood-affected area and the governor organized a meeting in Jalpaiguri so that she could meet with the various relief organizations. Myself, Dada Viragananda, and Shashi Rainjan attended as representatives of AMURT—Shashi was the chairman of the AMURT relief committee. At the conclusion of the meeting, Indira pledged that her government would increase the aid they were sending to the area. This was a public meeting, and when she sat down again after her speech the crowd grew unruly. They started pelting her with stones and shoes and shouting slogans and accusations that she was cheating the people and doing nothing for them. They may have been instigated by the local communist government, taking advantage of the widespread dissatisfaction with the central government, which was in the hands of the congress party. In the melee, the prime minister headed for the stairs so she could get to her helicopter, but none of her security people were near her. I was standing on the dais next to the governor of Bengal, Mr. Dharmaviira. With the crowd surging toward her, I knew I had to do something to shield this woman from harm. I was in uniform, of course, with a dagger in my belt and a sturdy bamboo *lathi* in my hand. So I held out my *lathi* to hold back the crowd and asked the governor to lend me a hand. Indira took advantage of the corridor we created and was able to get to her helicopter, after which she flew back to Delhi.

A few weeks later, Shashi Rainjan, who was a Member of Parliament and a friend of the Gandhi family, and Raghuvir Prasad, who also knew her well, arranged for the three of us to meet her at her residence in Delhi. There we briefed her on AMURT and the work we were doing, and she remembered how I had helped her to escape unharmed from the meeting at Jalpaiguri. When she asked us how she could be of help, we explained to her that the other relief organizations had packed up and left but the people were still suffering from a shortage of food, medicines, blankets, and so on. We were keeping three large centres open there but in order to keep them going we needed help. She responded by allocating 125,000 rupees from the prime minister's relief fund. Earlier the governor had also given us ten thousand rupees.

October 1968

Baba Helps a Needy Cause

*B*ABA USED TO give personal donations to poor people and needy institutions out of the money he would get from the royalties of his books. He would receive a certain percentage from these sales and he would earmark those funds for the very needy. One day in Ranchi, Baba was reading the newspaper—it was only in later years that we would send people into Baba's room to read the newspapers to him, after his eyesight deteriorated due to the poisoning. There was a notice in the paper that day about a school run by the Brahmo Samaj that was in dire straights. The school building was falling apart to the point that classes could no longer be taught in many of its rooms; thus the society was soliciting funds to help with its repair.

The next morning Baba took his royalty money with him, the money he received from the sales of his books, and asked his driver and security personnel to take him to that school before proceeding with his morning field walk. When Baba entered the premises, the principal and staff were astonished to see him and his entourage. He was taken to the principal's office, given a seat, and offered some refreshments. When they asked him to what they owed the honour of his visit, Baba said that he had seen the notice in the paper and felt that he should help. Then he handed the principal an envelope and said, "I think this should be sufficient to repair the classrooms. You are an honest person. I know you will utilize these funds properly."

Baba would regularly contribute to good causes in this way. He did not pay any attention to the group or affiliation. If the cause was good and the need was great, he was always ready to help.

1969

Ratnesh Bhatt

*T*HERE WAS ONE senior family acharya in Lucknow by the name of
Ratnesh Bhatt. He ran a printing business and was a man of sunny
disposition, always laughing. He was an educated man also, of fair
complexion, who had grown up in the mountains of Himachal Pradesh.

At that time he was having some family problems but he was hesitant
to disclose them to Baba—he was a high-caste Brahmin and both his
wife and his son and daughter continued to practice idol worship in the
house. They would keep their images of the gods and goddesses on the
same altar where he kept his photo of Baba, and if at all he said something they would tell him that his Baba photo was no different than their
idols. They also criticized him for having removed the sacred thread.
Two or three times he went to Baba, thinking to broach the subject, but
each time he could not bring himself to tell him. Finally Baba himself
brought it up. He described his problem and told him exactly how to
approach his family. "You are an acharya," Baba said. "If you talk to them
in a psychological way I am sure you will convince them to give up their
idol worship. Talk about sadhana, tell them that the Lord is infinite, and
in a few days you will find that they will give you no more problems in
the house. They themselves will remove the idols and images without
your having to ask. Don't worry. Because you love me and because I also
love you, it is my duty to solve your problem for you."

Ratnesh followed Baba's instructions. He quoted one of Veda Vyasa's
shlokas to them, as Baba had suggested, a shloka that speaks out against
idol worship. At first, they were not receptive. But each day they listened
a little more to what he had to say. "I am not telling you that you should
stop your idol worship," he told them, full of the confidence that Baba
had given him. "You are adults. You must make your own decision. But
I am in contact with such a personality as you will not find anywhere
on this earth. He knows our family problems without my having to tell

him anything. He knows what is in your mind also. That is why I keep his photo on the altar, to remind me that such a personality exists."

Each day they listened to him talk about Baba, and on the third or fourth day they began removing the statues and paintings of the various gods and goddesses, until only Baba's photo remained. Though they were not margis yet, they began to feel a great attraction for Baba's photo. After that, the atmosphere in the house became very vibrated, very spiritual, and the conflict disappeared of its own accord, just as Baba had said it would.

There is another story of Ratnesh that I would like to relate. This happened in 1969, most likely, in Varanasi when he was sent there for SPT (sadhana, *piitha*, training). I was also there along with Shashi Rainjan. Every day for a week or ten days the three of us would go out to beg for food, as per the rules of SPT. We could not talk when we were begging. All we could say was *hari om tat sat*. It was very interesting what happened. Shashi Rainjan was a rich man but he never received any food when he went out to beg. Every day Ratnesh and myself would come back with our bowls full and he would come back empty-handed. We would have to share our food with him.

Now at that time Ratnesh had a weakness for tobacco, which he would mix with lime and keep in his mouth under the tongue, as many people do. It was a bad habit, but he was unable to overcome it. Every day when we went out to beg, a certain man would offer him tobacco. Each day we would go to a different village but the same man would appear and offer him some tobacco. And every evening when we came back he would tell us the same story: "I was tempted to take it but the moment he offered it I felt as if Baba were looking directly at me, waiting to see if I would succumb to the temptation or not. So I couldn't accept it."

By the time the SPT was over, Ratnesh had left his chewing of tobacco once and for all.

It was around this time that Baba sent me to the Andaman and Nicobar islands for prachar. I was with Baba in the Patna airport when Dr. Ramesh expressed his concern that we had yet to do prachar in those islands. So Baba sent me there. I was the first pracharika to go to the Andaman and Nicobar islands. Now we have twenty-five schools there.

1969

Rupan Kaul

*R*UPAN KAUL WAS a friend of R. Prasad's wife, who inspired her to take initiation. She and her husband are from Kashmir but they were living in Delhi since he was employed in the central excise department. After her initiation she changed her way of life and started sitting regularly for meditation in the morning and evening. She also went for Baba's darshan whenever he visited Delhi or nearby areas. But her husband and grown son were not happy with the change. She began inviting the dadas and didis to her house and helping them in their missionary work in whatever way she could, and her husband began to object to their presence in his house. But her sadhana made her very strong, to the point that she began scolding him for his lack of hospitality. "It is your personal choice whether you respect them or not," she would tell him, "but it makes me very sad to see your attitude. They live for Baba's mission and Baba's mission alone. They deserve your respect. You don't know how important they are to me and how much I treasure their company." Prasadji would also meet Mr. Kaul from time to time and try to persuade him to change his attitude but Kaul was intransigent. "I respect you and your personal choices," he would tell Prasad, "but you are wasting your time trying to get me to change my mind."

One day Baba came to Delhi for a visit and Rupan Kaul got a chance to prepare his food—she had been doing sadhana some six or seven months by then. She prepared a number of Indian dishes with great love and affection and served them to Baba. While he was eating, Baba asked her about her family situation, and she told him about her problem with her husband and son. I was also there at the time. "Don't worry," Baba told her. "It is quite natural to face such clashes when you begin meditating. Many sadhakas are tempted to leave their sadhana when this happens but you should consider these clashes to be a blessing in disguise. You are doing well. Continue with your practices and these samskaras will gradually get exhausted. You will see: in a few months your entire family situation will change."

And that is exactly what happened. She trusted in Baba's word, and rather than say anything to her husband or son, she simply continued doing her practices sincerely. Little by little she noticed a change in them. Her husband started sitting quietly nearby when she meditated. After a while he grew to respect her convictions so much that he told her that she should go and see Baba whenever she wanted and that the dadas and didis were welcome in his house; there would be no restriction from his side. The son was the same way. So the atmosphere in the house became very pleasant and she was able to work for the mission without any impediment. Whenever any worker would ask her for help they would never go away with empty hands. I remember when I was PA that she was always on tour with Baba helping the dadas and didis, and Baba was always happy to see her. After a few years she convinced her husband to take initiation and he also became an asset to the mission. He even allowed her to live in Calcutta so she could be near Baba during the last days of his life. She remained in Tiljala for two or three years after Baba's mahaprayana. Then she went to live with her family in Hyderabad.

If she is still alive she must be eighty or eighty-five by now. A very soft-spoken woman who got along well with everyone she met. When you met her you immediately felt that she was a noble personality. There was no blemish in her mind.

1969

Baba's Urdu Exam

ONCE IN RANCHI, before Baba sent me to Bangladesh for relief work, he told me a story about an Urdu exam he took when he was a grade school student. His teacher gave him a grade of 101 and when this was brought to Baba's father's attention, Lakshmi Narayana Sarkar got upset. He thought that the teacher was cutting a joke at his son's expense, so he went to the school and complained about it to the principal. The principal called Baba and his Urdu teacher to the office so Lakshmi Narayana could talk to the teacher directly. "Why are you making a joke of my son's exam," Mr. Sarkar asked. "Is there any such grade as 101?"

"Sarkar Babu," the teacher replied, "I am sorry if I have upset you but I cannot joke when it comes to this boy. The grade I gave your son is the correct grade. There was not a single error on his exam. I could not even touch his paper with my pen. Some of his answers went beyond my knowledge even. I was so pleased by his effort and by his talent that I honoured him with a bonus number that I was keeping in my pocket."

"When my father came to the office he was angry," Baba told me, "but when he left it he was pleased."

1971

Personal Contact

*T*HERE ARE A few amusing stories about PC that I heard from Baba before I became PA. One time in Ranchi, Baba gave PC to a Bengali-speaking margi. Baba asked him his name, the name of his acharya, when he was initiated—all the usual questions. Then Baba started recounting the mistakes he had made in his life. After a long list of misdeeds, Baba said in Bengali, "You have committed many mistakes in your life. Place your hand over your heart and make a pledge that you will never commit such mistakes again." In Bengali the expression "place your hand over your heart" is *chati diye dhore*. The word for "umbrella," however—*chatri*—is quite similar, and this brother misunderstood what Baba was asking him. There was an umbrella hanging on the wall near Baba's cot and he thought that Baba had asked him to grab the umbrella. So he went over to the wall and caught hold of the umbrella.

"What are you doing!" Baba said. "I didn't tell you to grab the umbrella. I told you to place your hand over your heart. You are an educated person. You shouldn't make such a foolish mistake."

Baba was scolding him but actually he was quite amused by his error. Afterward he told us what had happened and he had us all laughing.

There was another PC in Ranchi that is worth mentioning. It was the first PC of the day, just after Baba came back from field walk. Normally, when Baba went for field walk, we would take advantage of his absence to send somebody into his room to clean it. On this day that person was still cleaning his room when Baba came back from his walk. He had been standing on a stool so he could reach the ceiling with the broom, and in his haste to vacate the room he forgot to put the stool back in the corner. When the first brother on the list entered the room for PC, the stool was still there in front of Baba's cot. When this brother got up from sastaunga pranam, Baba asked him to put the stool in the corner and sit properly. But instead of putting the stool in the corner and coming back to sit in front of Baba's cot, this brother put the stool in the corner and sat on it.

"What are you doing!" Baba said. "I told you to put the stool in the corner and then come back here and sit down. You are not a minister in your office that you will sit on a stool. Come here and sit on the floor!"

Baba scolded him but he was laughing when he told us the story once the PCs were over.

I will tell one more such story. This happened in Jamalpur. Once a Marwari gentleman came for PC. He was a corpulent man with a large belly. When he entered Baba's room he did sastaunga pranam as instructed but due to his protruding stomach he was unable to keep both his head and his legs on the ground. When he touched his head to the ground his legs came up and when he touched his legs to the ground his head came up. Baba started scolding him. "Don't you know how to do sastaunga pranam? It seems that you will have to be taught." Baba called a dada into the room and told him to put this brother's head on the ground. He did so but the legs came up. Then Baba asked him to put his legs on the ground but his head came up. "Okay," Baba said. "It seems that it is not his mistake. You can go now." Actually, Baba had been joking with this Marwari brother. The brother sat up and Baba continued the PC.

1971

I Become PA

*A*PART FROM THE years that I was Baba's PA, most of my life was spent in relief activities. In 1965 Baba made me Relief-In-Charge 1, 2, and 3. R2 is the department that attends to natural disasters and man-made calamities. I started working for that department in 1965 and I am still working in that department today. A few days after the May 1971 DMC in Ranchi, we had a clash with local thugs and it was decided to shift Baba to Patna. After the shift I went to Bengal to begin relief activities for the refugees that were flooding into Bengal from East Pakistan, soon to become Bangladesh. I began opening up refugee centres, twenty-one in all, and I became so busy with this work that I did not have a chance to go and see Baba for more than three months. During that time, I had little or no idea what was going on in the organization: the fact that Madhavananda had been caught by the Central Bureau of Investigation (CBI) and had turned government approver; the ongoing defections; the impending split in the organization—thankfully, Baba kept me away from all those things. I was totally engrossed in my work.

I remember there was one German margi who was on tour in India. He became so enamoured with my efforts that he and his traveling companion joined me for more than two months. He had a van and he became my driver. We used to carry supplies in his van. You may be surprised to know that the Indian government gave us more than thirty million rupees for supplies and materials. When it came time to wind up our operations, I returned 86,000 rupees to the district magistrate. He was very surprised. "Swamiji," he said, "why are you returning this money. Other NGOs are asking us for more money and you are returning money?"

"It is the government's money," I told him. "Here are our accounts. We did our work and this was left over."

Once I returned the money, I called Patna and spoke to Vishokananda, who was Baba's PA at the time. I told him that I had wound up our operations and I wanted to go to Patna to see Baba and show him my reports. "Of course you can come," he said. "No need to ask Baba. But if you want me to ask him I will. He is in the office now. Wait on the line." He came back to the phone a couple of minutes later with a message from Baba that there was no need for me to come to Patna. He was coming to Calcutta to hold a DMC. I should wait for him there and make arrangements for his stay.

The DMC was scheduled for September 30. I picked up Baba at the airport in a hired car and he sat in the back seat along with Mother and Laltu—Baba's son Gotam's nickname in the family was Laltu. I remember that Laltu asked many questions—Baba, what is this? What is that?—while Mother remained silent. Laltu also called him Baba, which means "father" in Bengali. At first there was some confusion as to where Baba would stay. Then Baba asked me where I was staying. I replied that I was staying in the office I had rented as our relief headquarters: 25A South End Park. It was not very big but Baba decided that he would prefer to stay there rather than in some hotel. So I gave directions to the driver and brought Baba to South End Park.

The South End Park apartment had two bedrooms, a kitchen, and a sitting room with a veranda. Baba took one room, Mother and Laltu the other, and I stayed in the sitting room. Vishokananda arrived shortly afterward—he had been taking care of some organizational matters—and he also stayed there. I remember that when he arrived he had a terrible headache. Baba was out on field walk so Vishokananda lay down in the sitting room. When Baba came back from his walk, someone told him about Vishokananda's headache. He came and placed his hand on Vishokananda's forehead and told him that it would be okay in a few minutes. After a few minutes the pain dissipated and he was able to get up and attend to his regular duties.

Though I had been out of the organizational flow for the previous few months, I quickly realized that there was something very strange afoot. Vishokananda and Mother were holding surreptitious meetings in front of Mother's door with certain other workers, such as Siddhananda, Prakashananda, and Chirananda, talking in low voices so they would not be overheard. They didn't include me in these conversations, and I remember wondering what kind of conspiracy they were hatching. Over the next couple of days, Mother made repeated trips to Baba's door, pressurizing him and threatening to leave. I never believed I could see such a thing—I had always held Mother in such high regard—but it was happening in front of my very eyes. Baba was sick at the time—he had dysentery and he was suffering from piles, so he had to make frequent trips to the bathroom—and it seemed as if they were taking advantage of his illness. The situation became quite tense. Finally Mother told Baba that she had made up her mind: she was leaving and she wanted his permission.

"How can I say that it is okay for you to leave?" Baba told her. "It is your choice. If you insist on leaving then I cannot stop you, but if you are asking for my permission then I cannot give you permission to leave this house. You should not go. This is not part of our culture."

I did not want to hear all these things but I could not help it. She was standing outside Baba's door, talking to him. Vishokananda was standing a few feet away. He had called a taxi for them and the taxi was waiting downstairs. I remember asking her when she started for the door, "Mother, are you really leaving?"

"Yes," she said. "Laltu and I are leaving, but you should not worry. Once everything is okay again, I will come back."

She took Laltu by the hand and went down to the taxi with Vishokananda, leaving me alone in the apartment with Baba. I was in a state of shock. I had no idea what to do. But when Baba came out of his room, he was totally calm and serene, his normal self. "Ramananda," he said, "you will have to be my personal assistant and secretary now." With tears in my eyes, I told Baba that I had neither the experience nor the capacity to do such a job, but Baba was very gracious. "I know you are worried," he said, "but you shouldn't be. I will teach you everything you need to know. If Vishokananda comes to hand over the charge, well and good, but if not, then I will guide you." Baba's words helped greatly to calm my apprehensions. He showed me a few things right away, such as how to respond to his calling bell, but I took it as a challenge to discover on my own how best to serve him. He assured me that I would be able to do the job and that made me feel strong. Vishokananda, of course, did not return to hand over the charge, but he did send the house keys and the keys to the almirah through Uma Sarkar's brother.

After she left the DMC took place as planned with myself acting as Baba's PA, but not all the workers attended—Mother held a parallel program at the same time and many workers attended her program instead. The organization was thrown into a state of confusion and I remember wondering in what direction it was going. All in all, thirty-seven workers defected with her, both avadhutas and avadhutikas. I remember that Satyananda became very reacted. After the DMC, Mother went to the *dharmasala* where the workers were staying and addressed them, criticizing Baba and trying to convince them to leave with her. Satyananda came running to inform Baba of what was going on. "I cannot tolerate this," he said. "These people are attacking you in public." But Baba was not perturbed at all. He pacified him by telling him that there was nothing to worry about. "Be calm, be silent," he said. "In time everything will become clear."

A few days later I left Calcutta with Baba and we embarked on a three-month DMC tour to different parts of India. Eventually we learned that Uma Sarkar had gone to Puri, where she was being sheltered by the CBI. She attempted to set up her own organization with those workers that had defected but it was short-lived and many of them soon came back to Baba. Vishokananda, however, became a government approver. But that is another story.

September 1971

Baba's Mother

*D*URING LEISURE PERIODS, Baba would sometimes tell me stories about his childhood and other subjects, just to make me feel relaxed. He would say, "Ramananda, you are always so busy with your work, you don't get any scope to talk. Now you should talk. Tell me freely anything that is on your mind." There was never anything I wanted to say so I would tell Baba that I didn't want to ask anything or say anything, I only wanted him. Then he would tell me stories to make me feel comfortable. During the day he would often scold me when I did something wrong. It was his duty to scold me—otherwise I wouldn't have learned—but later he would take the trouble to make me feel comfortable.

Once he told me a story about his mother. She was fond of worshipping Shiva and Krishna in the morning and used to keep their pictures on an altar in her room. After taking her bath she would put fresh flowers on the altar and begin her worship. Sometimes she would go into the garden and collect the flowers herself, but usually Baba would bring them for her. Then one day she saw the images of Shiva and Krishna disappear and in their place she saw Baba sitting there. When this happened several days in a row, she complained to Baba. "Bubu, why are you coming and disturbing my worship?" She always called Baba by his family nickname, Bubu. "Every time I sit down to worship Krishna I see you sitting there instead. You shouldn't do this!" Then Baba said, "Mother, it's because you love me so much. If you love a person that much then you will surely see his image wherever you look. That's all. It's because you love me that you see me instead of Krishna."

He also told me how she grew apprehensive when Ananda Marga started to occupy more and more of his time. Baba made a system that whenever he had to leave Jamalpur to give DMC in some other city, the PA had to go to his mother and request permission. She would give her permission but not before verifying what arrangements they were making for her son. She was especially concerned about his food. "Make doubly sure that they don't contaminate Bubu's food with onions or garlic," she would say. "He is very sensitive. He has not been able to take such foods since his very childhood."

I used to love to sit and listen to Baba telling these stories.

1971

Sarvajit

*I*N ANOTHER OF these leisure periods, shortly after I became PA, Baba asked me if I knew Sarvajit of Lucknow. I didn't and Baba told me the following story, which took place in 1968 or 69:

Sarvajit was the only son of a wealthy margi family from Lucknow and he had married the only daughter of the equally wealthy Sahani family from Delhi—the Sahanis were the owners of a string of cinema houses in both Delhi and Lucknow. Neither Sarvajit nor his bride were initiated at the time but they both took initiation after their marriage due to the influence of their parents. One day, while the parents of the bride were in Lucknow visiting the newlyweds, Sarvajit suddenly fell ill and despite the best efforts of the doctors he breathed his last on the following morning. Both sets of parents were extremely distraught but there was nothing more they could do, other than to lay him on a stretcher with a garland around his neck and take him to the burial ground for cremation, as per the Indian tradition. But then it flashed in Mrs. Sahani's mind that Baba's flight would be passing through Lucknow that morning on its way to Delhi. It was scheduled for a thirty-minute stopover, and as usual the local margis would be congregating at the airport to have Baba's darshan before he continued on his journey.

Feverish with hope, she asked her husband and her in-laws to delay the procession to the burial ground until she got back. Then she grabbed the garland that was lying on Sarvajit's inert body and rushed to get a taxi. She ordered the driver to drive to the airport as fast as he could and when she got there Baba was still in the VIP lounge, chatting with the margis and waiting for the announcement to re-board the plane. Mrs. Sahani rushed up to Baba with the garland in her hands and tearfully informed him of the tragedy. "Baba, please save him," she begged. "You are our only hope."

Baba accepted the garland and closed his eyes for a few moments. Then he handed the garland back to her and said, "Mother, take this garland and place it around your son-in-law's neck. And don't delay, not even for a single moment. Go as quickly as you can."

She gave Baba her namaskar and rushed back to the taxi. When she arrived at the house, the family was still gathered around Sarvajit's body, waiting mournfully for her return. She rushed up to her son-in-law, placed the garland around his neck, and started crying loudly, "Baba, Baba, Baba." The others joined her in her supplications and after a few minutes Sarvajit started breathing again. He opened his eyes and slowly began to move his arms. "Where am I?" he asked. "How did I get here?"

They took him from the stretcher and brought him back into the bedroom where they began massaging him, trying to bring the circulation back into his limbs. Gradually he recovered his sensation and by the evening he was feeling more or less normal.

Years later, after Baba's mahaprayana, I got to know Sarvajit, and he confirmed this story. "Dada, it was a new world I opened my eyes to," he told me. By then, he had shifted his business to the municipal market in Delhi, in Connaught Place. He was a tall man, of fair complexion, and entirely devoted to Baba. Whenever any dada would go there he would give them some contribution. "It all belongs to Baba," he would say, "since it was Baba who gave me back my life." The last time I saw him was a couple of years ago when I went there with Rameshvarananda, whom he continues to support. His family members are all margis and they all know this story very well.

1971

Subhash's Secretary Meets Baba

*U*TTAMCHAND MALHOTRA HAD been Netaji Subhash Chandra Bose's secretary before Independence and later he had profited from his position. After the plane crash in which it was reported that Subhash had died, many people believed that the news had been deliberately falsified. No body had been found and rumours that Subhash was alive continued to swirl. When Uttamchand heard about Baba he thought that Netaji might be masquerading as Anandamurti, so he came to Delhi in 1971, took initiation, and put his name on the list for PC.

While he was waiting in line, he heard the sounds of Baba beating the devotees. He became hesitant—I think by then he had realized that Baba wasn't Subhash—but he went in anyway. After he prostrated in front of Baba, Baba started to scold him. "Your intention in coming here is deceitful. You came to discover if I was Netaji or not. Is it not so?"

"Yes, Baba."

"I am not Netaji; I am the creator of Netaji. And I can see that you have committed a great crime. You have collected a great deal of money in Netaji's name and you have mismanaged that money. Now you will get what you deserve."

Baba beat him so hard that he broke his stick. Malhotra's back became beet red. Then Baba grabbed him by his ears and scolded him mercilessly until he promised that he would never commit such a mistake again. The scolding was so loud we could hear everything from outside. Finally Baba softened his tone. "Do you realize what you have to do from now on? Do you promise to be a good man, an ideal man?"

Malhotra was an aged man but it didn't matter. He promised and Baba patted him on the back and gave him his blessings. Then Baba asked him how he felt. Malhotra replied that he didn't feel any more pain.

17 October 1971

Fresh Lemon Water

*I*N OCTOBER OF 1971 we took a flight from Calcutta to Patna, where a
DMC was scheduled. Our flight was at 7 a.m. so we had to leave very
early for the airport. Whenever we travelled I would carry two flasks
with me for Baba, one for water and the other for juice or lemon water,
depending on the time of day. Since it was an early flight, I prepared
some sweet lemon juice at five o'clock, just before we were to leave for
the airport. The flight had a scheduled stopover in Ranchi, which is in
Bihar, where Baba grew up and where he began Ananda Marga. For that
reason there are more margis in Bihar than in other parts of India and
more acharyas as well. After an hour's flight the plane landed in Ranchi,
where we were to have half an hour layover while the Ranchi-bound
passengers deplaned and other passengers got on. As we were rolling to a
stop on the tarmac, Baba asked me to go to the door to see if there were
margis waiting for him outside—whenever Baba travelled, the margis
would be advised of his travel arrangements, and wherever there was a
stopover, whether by plane or by train, the local margis would gather
to have Baba's darshan—but as soon as the door of the plane opened
we heard a loud cry, *Parama Pita Baba Ki, Jai!* "No need to see if the
margis have come," Baba said. "Just go and show yourself at the door
so they know that we have come." Some five or six margis had gotten
permission to meet Baba on the tarmac and they were waiting for him
with garlands in their hands. Once the other passengers got down, we
also got down, and as soon as Baba's feet touched the ground the margis
put their garlands around his neck. They escorted us into the transit
lounge, where the rest of the margis were waiting. We remained there
for about half an hour and Baba was given VIP treatment by the airline,
courtesy of some influential margis.

While we were returning to the plane, Dr. Ramesh was walking
alongside Baba—he was a well-known doctor in Ranchi, president of the

Child Welfare Society of India. He asked Baba to please take some water before he boarded the plane but Baba declined. "I am thirsty," he said, "but I cannot drink while walking. I will take something on the plane."

Once the flight took off, Baba asked me if he could have a glass of fresh-squeezed lemon water. "Yes Baba," I said. "I have a thermos of sweet lemon juice right here."

"Is it fresh?" he asked.

"I prepared it this morning, Baba, just before we left."

"Then how can you call it fresh? Fresh is when you prepare it and give it to me. That is fresh. If it is prepared two or three hours earlier then it is stale. I didn't ask for stale lemon water. I asked for fresh lemon water."

Baba's tone of voice was rather stern but I was used to that. I looked upon him as my father and he would scold me just like a father whenever I made some mistake. I felt chagrin for not being able to serve him properly but at the same time I thought that if he is asking for fresh lemon juice then there must be a reason. I thought that perhaps there might be some on the plane, so I went and asked the stewardess, but she said that they only had canned juice; they didn't prepare any fresh juice on the plane.

When I came back to my seat and told Baba, he told me to leave it. "Ramananda," he said, "I think you must have asked the stewardess how long it will be before we land in Patna?"

"Yes, Baba. She said that we will be landing in ten to fifteen minutes."

"Then you shouldn't worry. Two people are preparing sweet lemon juice for me as we speak, fresh juice. When we arrive in the airport they will both approach you. You should accept the juice from the person on your right, not the one on your left."

Many margis were waiting to receive us in the airport. They had set up a chair in an open area for Baba to sit on while he waited for me to get his luggage and prepare the car. Just as Baba had predicted, two people came up to me with fresh lemon juice for Baba. On my right the mother of Braj Bihari approached me with a towel and a glass—she must have been about sixty-five at the time. The person on my left was Shashi Rainjan, who was a member of parliament and a staunch devotee. He was a very respected margi, but I had my instructions, so I allowed her to offer Baba the towel and then the juice. Shashi was disappointed but I explained to him that Baba could not take two glasses at one time. "I will keep your juice," I told him, "and I will give it to Baba when he arrives at Patliputra," which is where Baba stayed when he came to Patna. In the meantime, Baba drank the entire glass that the old lady had given him—usually he doesn't finish the whole glass—and she became very happy. Her face was shining. Later I learned that this had been her desire for the past six or seven years, to personally offer Baba a glass of juice, and because of her strong devotion she had been confident that Baba would take her juice and no one else's.

But later on, when we arrived at our quarters in Patliputra, I began to wonder if I had not mixed up Baba's instructions. It seemed to me that Shashi Rainjan was the much stronger devotee—certainly he was a much more well-known and well-respected margi. And he had brought his juice in a silver glass to show his love and affection, while the old lady had brought hers in an ordinary glass. Normally I would never make such a mistake. Whatever Baba told me to do, whether at home or while traveling, would become instantly recorded in my mind so that I would never forget it. And I was certain that I had heard him tell me to accept the juice from the right-hand person. But the more I thought about it, the more I wondered if I might not have made a mistake. It made more sense that he would want to take the juice from Shashi Rainjan.

At that moment Baba was in his room, getting ready to go into the bathroom. I was sitting outside his room with several important margis of Patna: Raj Mohan, Braj Bihari, and three or four others. Suddenly the door opened and Baba was standing there in his lungi and an T-shirt. He called us into his room and said, "All of you, listen. Ramananda has some confusion in his mind and I want to clear it up in front of you before I take my bath. Before we landed I told Ramananda that two people would come to offer me juice and that he should accept the juice from the person on his right, but now he is worried that he might have made a mistake, that he might have misheard and should have accepted the juice from the person on his left. But what he did was correct. I wanted to take the juice from the lady to my right because she didn't put any conditions in her mind before offering the juice. The person on my left had so many conditions in his mind: that he should be prosperous, that he should be given a grandson, so many desires. He is very good to me and I love him very much, but first I see the devotion and the purity of the person, and in this case the lady to my right was superior in her devotion and her purity.

Afterward I sent Shashi Rainjan on field walk with Baba. Baba talked with him for some time while they were walking and Shashi was very happy.

October 1971

Indian Airlines Loses Baba's Luggage

*F*ROM DELHI WE flew to Bombay with a nearly two-hour stopover in Jaipur, during which Baba gave darshan to the Jaipur margis. When we landed in Bombay, Baba's suitcase did not come out with the rest of our luggage. Normally I book two pieces of luggage: Baba's suitcase and my bag, in which I kept a spare set of clothes for Baba and two sticks for PC—if one stick got broken then the replacement was ready. When we couldn't locate the suitcase we went to the Indian Airlines staff to report it missing. By then the margis were quite upset so they started agitating inside the airport. At that time the intelligence people were watching Baba's movements very carefully and everyone suspected that this was some piece of mischief engineered by the CBI. The airline staff, on the other hand, always treated Baba very nicely. They were apologetic and took the matter very seriously. "This is Anandamurti's bag," they said. "Rest assured that we will get his bag to him as fast as is humanly possible." When I told Baba that his luggage hadn't come, he confirmed that the CBI was behind it. "They want to harass me and see what I have in my luggage," he said.

From the airport we took Baba to C. D. Muncy's house in Altamount Road, where Baba was to stay while he was in Bombay. Muncy is a devoted margi. At the time he was secretary of the Proutist Bloc of India—Shashi Rainjan was the president. I don't know if they have kept that room or not. I heard that they sold the building and it was made into a guest house or some such thing, but I am not sure. Anyhow, L. C. Ananda went to the tailors straightaway to get a new set of clothes made for Baba, and I reminded Baba that I had a spare set of clothes in my bag, but Baba was not interested in the clothes. "I want my suitcase back as early as possible," he said, and he was quite adamant about it.

When the margis heard that Baba was demanding that his suitcase be returned to him, they became furious. They rushed to the Indian

Airlines office in downtown Bombay and surrounded it, announcing that no one would be able to get in or out of the office until Baba got his suitcase back. This is a typical form of protest in India, called *gerau.* Shankarananda and some other workers led the *gerau,* and this state of affairs continued for several hours. In the meantime, the airlines found Baba's luggage and had it brought from Jaipur by a special flight. They asked the original pilot of the flight to bring it personally to Baba along with two other airline staff. When they gave the bag to Baba, they asked him to please not be angry with them, it was not their mistake. "Yes, I know," Baba told them. "It was not your fault. Certain people are scared of me, particularly the CBI; they have done it." Then the pilot asked Baba to check his suitcase and make sure that nothing was missing.

"No need," Baba said. "You people have brought me my suitcase, so there is nothing more to worry about." He gave the suitcase to me and I sent a message to the margis downtown to stop the *gerau.*

All in all, it was a peculiar incident and rather amusing.

18 October 1971

Savita Didi

SAVITA WAS THE daughter of Didi Ananda Bharati. She was married to the inspector general of police in Jaipur. She was a very respected, very loving, very sentient lady who was in charge of Baba's kitchen whenever he went to Jaipur. As the wife of the IG she had many contacts in the government and she was able to attract many ladies to Ananda Marga. They all thought that her guru must be a very great guru indeed if he was able to attract such a disciple as Savita Didi.

One morning in Jaipur, Savita arrived late due to some problem in the family—this was the fall 1971 tour, a very hectic time. When Baba came out for breakfast he was surprised not to see her. A newly initiated lady who had met Ananda Marga through Savita brought his breakfast to the table and I could see right away that he was not happy about it. He left his breakfast untouched and started scolding me and whoever else was in earshot. "You people don't take care. I won't eat. I'm going straight for field walk."

Just then Savita arrived. Parimal, Baba's bodyguard, was also there. I stood in front of Baba and pleaded with him. "No, Baba, please. You shouldn't leave without eating your breakfast. Savita has come now. Let her serve you."

"No, now I won't take. She should have come earlier."

Savita was also pleading with him but Baba went to the car where Major Daulat Singh was waiting to take him on field walk. Baba took his seat in the back and Parimal also got in. But then Baba turned to Parimal and said, "Parimal, they are weeping, especially Savita-di. The lady who was serving is unknown to me. For that reason I could not take my breakfast, but I cannot let Savita cry. It is my duty to go back and eat breakfast."

Actually, that lady was very new and did not have much devotion. That was the real reason. Baba came back and Savita apologized for her tardiness. "Baba, please forgive me," she said. "It was my fault that I allowed myself to get delayed. I will not let it happen again. This sister is new; don't blame her. I should have been here."

"Yes," Baba said. "I left because I didn't see you. Do you see now how much I love you?"

1971

N. R. K. Raju

*B*EFORE THE DMC in Vishakapatnam in October, Baba became upset with the failure of the local margis and workers to meet the conditions for DMC, such as a healthy school, a functioning press, master unit, and so on. In this case, if I remember correctly, there was no press and Baba became angry because they had told him that the conditions had been met. After morning darshan on the first day, he announced from the dais that he was cancelling the next day's DMC and leaving immediately for Calcutta. Both margis and workers became frantic. When Baba left the dais, they surrounded him and pleaded with him not to go, but Baba would not relent. It was a peculiar scene. They asked me to intercede but I was in a bind. I had to support Baba, despite my sympathy for their condition. This was when N. R. K. Raju came into the picture.

Raju was an old margi and very devoted. He was a lower court advocate who lived an exceedingly simple life. He earned enough to support his family—they are all margis—and whenever any didi or dada would go to Vishakapatnam he would not let them leave without accepting some food and a small contribution. He was also the Andhra Samaj secretary and was respected by all for his saintly nature. Tadbhavananda and the local RS had the bright idea of asking Rajuji to request Baba to stay. They brought him and placed him in Baba's path; thus Baba had no choice but to halt while Raju pleaded with him to stay. "Baba, if you leave now we will be nowhere," he said. "You know how much trouble and sacrifice we have undergone to arrange this DMC. If you cancel it, you know how pitiful our condition will be."

Baba turned to Tadbhavananda and said, "Why have you brought him? It is not his mistake. You people have made the mistake. You have not met the conditions. That is why I am cancelling the DMC. Why did you send Raju? He is a good boy, an excellent boy. He is doing good work. I cannot say the word 'no' to him." Raju continued to plead with Baba for mercy. Baba fumed and scolded the dadas for their artifice but their strategy worked. Raju was such a saintly man that Baba could not say no. In the end he yielded and the DMC program went forward. Of course, the margis promised Baba that they would buy a press immediately after the DMC and they fulfilled their promise. Gopal Shastri played an important role in purchasing the press.

After the DMC, when we were getting ready to leave for Bhuvaneshvar, Baba called the margis to his room and apologized for giving them so much trouble. He was laughing and asking them if everything was okay now. "Yes, Baba," they said. "We know that you scold us for our own good. It is your style. We don't mind."

This was a testament to Raju's purity and devotion. If not for him, there would have been no DMC.

24 October 1971

Baba Reveals a Secret

ONE OF THE things Baba taught me after I became PA was how to get a continuous tape recording of his discourses. In those days we had a cassette tape recorder. He instructed me to offer him a glass of water when I saw the tape getting to the end—I would always sit beside Baba and keep a flask of water and a glass for him in case he got thirsty. While he was sipping the water, I would get the time I needed to change the tape.

Baba revealed this secret to the public on two occasions during that first tour: in Bhopal and in Tatanagar. On both occasions, when the first tape was about to run out, I offered him a glass of water as per his instructions. He took a sip and then told the margis in the audience, "Do you know why I am sipping this water? It is because the tape is about to run out and Ramananda needs time to change it. So while he is busy changing the tape I will sip this water, and I will only give the glass back to him when his work is done." He turned and looked at me. "Is it or is it not a fact, Ramananda?"

"Yes, Baba, it is a fact."

Baba turned back to the crowd and said, "So, have you all understood now? Of course, I was a little thirsty, but that is not why Ramananda gave me a glass of water. He gave it to me to buy time so he could continue his recording." The margis all started laughing.

Actually, Baba gave me all kinds of detailed instructions concerning the day-to-day handling of his tours: how to see to his personal needs, how to take care of the tour arrangements, how to handle his interactions with the margis and the public and government officials, and so on.

1971

Bhulananda

*T*HERE WAS ONE margi advocate from Saharsa, I believe it was, who came to the DMC in Purnea in November 1971. He was a good margi and he had gone on field walk several times but he had yet to have PC. This was a very busy DMC and there were many people for PC, so I told him to come back the next day. He agreed but he asked me to put his name first since he had been waiting a long time. There were only five people on the list for the next day, so I put his name at the top of the list and he came early the next morning, but when I took the list to Baba he told me to modify it. "You can keep everything the same," he said, "but put the first name last. He has already met me several times, so what is the need for PC?"

"But Baba, he hasn't had PC."

"Then you put his name last, as I told you. If he asks, tell him that I will give him special attention. Now don't waste any more of my time. Send in the first person."

When I told this brother that he was now last on the list, he objected. "But Dada, you promised that I would be first, and I was the first one here this morning. Why are you putting me last?"

"I didn't put you last. Baba did. He told me to tell you that he will give you special attention."

"Really? Oh, then it is okay."

The first three brothers on the list went in and each of them received heavy punishment. He could hear the sounds from inside the room and he saw the tears in their eyes when they came out. When the brother in front of him was called he started getting scared. "Dada," he said, "Now that I think about it, I can wait until tomorrow. I will come back then." But I said no. I knew Baba would scold me if I let him get away, so I alerted the VSS to prevent him from escaping. When his turn came he didn't want to go in. We had to push him in and close the door from the outside.

When he entered Baba's room he did sastaunga pranam, but instead of sitting in front of Baba he crawled under Baba's cot and hid. When Baba didn't see anyone he rang the call bell. I opened the door and Baba asked me where he was. Then we heard a voice from underneath the cot. "I am here, Baba."

"Okay. Ramananda, close the door."

I closed the door and Baba asked him to come out from under the cot and sit in front of him.

"Baba, I won't come out until you promise that you won't punish me. I want your word; otherwise I will stay here."

"First you come out. Then we will talk."

"No, Baba. First promise that you won't punish me."

"You are giving *me* orders! Come out of there!"

"No, Baba," he repeated, still very scared.

"Okay, okay. I won't punish you. Are you happy now? Come out and sit properly. If you don't come out then I will go down there and get you."

"I am coming, Baba."

He came out and sat in front of Baba. Baba asked him about his family, the name of his acharya, when he got initiation, how many lessons he had—all the usual questions. But he had forgotten the name of his acharya. "That is not good," Baba said. "You should remember the name of your acharya. Think."

"Baba, I can't remember. Please remind me."

"If I remind you, will you remember?'

"Yes, Baba, I will remember."

"Okay, I will remind you, but if you forget again then I will punish you."

"Okay, Baba."

"His name is Hariharananda Avadhuta." Then Baba started talking about various things, his children's education and so on.

"Yes, Baba, by your grace my children are fine. We are taking good care of them."

"Very good, very good. Now tell me, what is the name of your acharya?"

He thought for a moment but again his mind went blank. "Baba," he said sheepishly, "I'm sorry but I forgot. Please remind me."

"You forgot! You are an advocate. How can you try cases in the court if you have no memory?"

"Baba, when I am in the courtroom pleading a case I remember, but when I enter your room I forget. Please remind me."

"Okay, I will tell you one more time, but if you forget again I will punish you. His name is Hariharananda."

"Yes, Baba, I won't forget. Hariharananda."

Again Baba started conversing on different subjects. He asked him about his profession, whether he was able to earn sufficient money to support his family, about the agricultural land he possessed in his native village, and so on. After a few minutes in this vein, Baba asked him again to tell him the name of his acharya, but again he forgot. "This is the third time you have forgotten," Baba told him. "If you forget again I will break all your bones. You asked me to help you, I reminded you three times, and each time you forgot. You see this cane. If it happens again I won't spare you."

Baba reminded him and this time, instead of listening to Baba, he kept repeating to himself, 'Hariharananda, Hariharananda, Hariharananda.' He was so intent on remembering his acharya's name that he didn't hear a word Baba said.

Finally Baba had to raise his voice to get his attention. "Listen to what I am telling you! Are you listening to me now?"

"Yes, Baba."

"Okay. Now tell me the name of your acharya."

"Bhulananda," he shouted.

Bhula means "to forget"; thus Bhulananda means "he who gets bliss from forgetting."

Baba started laughing very loudly. He was so amused that he didn't even punish him.

November 1971

Acharya Devakinandan

DEVAKINANDAN WAS A police inspector in Ara District when he came to know about Baba through one of his colleagues, Acharya Shyam Lal of Lahiriya Sarai. At that time he indulged in most of the vices that police officers generally indulged in—drinking, bribe-taking, and so on—but he left them all from the moment of his initiation and became totally devoted to Baba and the mission. Once Baba asked him if he was ready to take on some responsibility. "Baba, I am ready to jump in a well if you ask," he replied. Baba then made him an acharya and after some time his wife, Janaki Devi, also became an acharya. They had six children and all were married in the Ananda Marga system.

In the early days of the mission Devakinandan did a lot of prachar. He had a lot of difficulty in the police department after his initiation, due to the change in his habits and the fact that he could no longer be corrupted, but he faced all these trials with Baba's help and gradually rose through the ranks to the post of deputy superintendent of police (DSP). But one day—it was soon after I became PA—he came to Baba in Patna and told him that he knew he was not long for this earth. Baba told him not to worry about his death but to go on doing his work; everything was prearranged. And he promised to take care of his family when that day came.

One morning—it was *ekadashi*, fasting day—he sat for meditation and left his body in full consciousness. This is a very rare occurrence in spiritual life. The family came to Baba's house in Patna to inform him of Devakinandan's passing and Baba renewed his promise that he would take care of the family. His wife, Janaki Devi, is still there in Patna, and his family now has five generations of margis.

1971

Acharya Mathur

*A*CHARYA PREM BAHADUR Mathur of Patna was easy to spot even from a great distance due to his tall figure. Anyone who did not know him would automatically guess that he was a high-ranking officer from his imposing figure and dignified bearing. Those last couple of months before Baba's arrest were difficult times and we had not seen him for a little while. The CBI was harassing the margis and many of them were reluctant to frequent the organization due to fear of CBI reprisal. Mathurji had to be circumspect because of his position, so when he did come to see Baba he would come at night. One evening he came to me and requested permission to talk to Baba privately about a personal matter. "Baba knows my difficulty," he told me, "but he is the only one I can talk to about it." At that moment Baba was getting ready for his evening walk. When he asked who was available to accompany him, I told him that Acharya Mathur had come. "Very good," Baba said. "It has been some days since I have seen him. Send him."

After Baba came back from field walk, he asked me to send Mathurji to his room. It was very rare that Baba would ask to see someone who had just accompanied him on his walk but it happened in Acharya Mathur's case. Since I could tell that it was a private talk, I closed Baba's door so they could have complete privacy, but afterward Mathurji told me about his conversation.

When he entered the room, he said, "Baba, I have received a very great setback in my life. My wife has been diagnosed with cancer. For the past six months I have been trying to get her the best treatment possible but it has all been to no avail. It seems that she is beyond cure. You are my father and I thought that I should tell you first before I tell anyone else. I know that her illness is part of the natural course of things, and that it is your blessing, no matter how difficult it is for us."

Then Baba called me into the room and said, "Ramananda, are there any flowers in my garden? Good. Then please go and pick one flower and bring it to me, any flower."

I went outside and picked a hibiscus and brought it to Baba. He closed his eyes and muttered some incantation that I could not make out. Then he gave the flower to Mathurji and said, "Take this flower and keep it by your wife's bed. Let her know that Baba has sent this flower. No medication is required. Now go and see her. I think she will be all right."

Mathur was overcome with joy. Still weeping, he thanked Baba and rushed to see his wife, who was a very devoted margi. They kept the flower in her bedroom, even after it dried up, and his wife recovered. After the emergency, they came to see Baba and his wife was still in good health. They did not have any children so they decided they wanted to adopt a son, and one day Mathurji came to ask Baba's permission. "You do not need my permission," Baba told him. "It is your personal choice. Do what you feel is right." Mathur and his wife adopted an older boy who came and met Baba. He later became a computer engineer. Five years after his adoption Mathurji left his body.

1971

Baba's Arrest

THE MONTHS LEADING up to Baba's arrest were difficult times for the Marga. The CBI was making a concerted effort to infiltrate the organization, and through their covert operations and the external pressure they applied they managed to cause a split in Ananda Marga under the banner of Uma Sarkar, who tried to set up a separate organization with their help. At the same time, they conducted a malicious campaign in the media, making slanderous accusations against Baba in an effort to create a favourable climate for his arrest. Due to their constant harassment, many margis were scared to come around. Despite these trials and tribulations, Baba went on a three-month all-India DMC tour that proved to be tremendously inspiring. I saw with my own eyes how much hardship he underwent during this time, how he never paid any attention to his own comforts or convenience. He gladly accepted these ordeals in order to establish the organization.

In late December, we were staying in our rented house in Patliputra Colony when we got information from margis in the intelligence wing of the government that the CBI was laying plans to arrest Baba. After careful deliberations, certain important margis brought a proposal to Baba to bring him to Nepal, where it would be difficult for the Indian government to lay their hands on him, but Baba rejected their proposal. "I will not go into seclusion," he said. "I will remain with my sons and daughters and continue to work openly for my mission. How can I even think to leave them?"

During the last two weeks of that month the CBI stepped up their surveillance. We were followed wherever we went and there were conspicuous signs of police presence in the vicinity of the house at all hours. On the night of the twenty-ninth, Baba came out from his room and told me that I should be prepared. "Some people with bad intentions will be entering the property during the night," he said. "I may be arrested before daybreak. If they come for me, don't be alarmed. There is nothing to worry about. Just tell them to wait for four or five minutes. Inform me of their presence and keep them occupied. Five minutes will be all I need to get ready. Now we should prepare my suitcase."

Whenever Baba travelled I would help to pack his suitcase. He would sit on his cot and I would sit on the floor with the suitcase open in front of me. He would tell me where to put his t-shirts, where to put the toothbrush, where to put the towel. He would direct me and I would place everything according to his instructions. That way he would be able to find anything at any time, even in the dark, since he knew exactly where it would be. In fact, Baba used to get angry if anyone moved something from where he had put it. He did not like anyone to disturb his system. So I packed the suitcase and went out of the room so that Baba could take rest.

In the pre-dawn hours I started hearing the sounds of boots moving on the lawn and unfamiliar voices conversing close by. Several vans of police and CBI officers had surrounded the house and they had taken up positions inside the compound, creating a situation unlike any I had ever experienced. About two-thirty in the morning, the two top CBI officials—Mr. Hingurani, the director of the CBI, and Mr. Ahuja, the CBI superintendent of police—came to the door and said they wanted to speak to Baba.

"He has been expecting you," I told them, "but now is not the appropriate time. It is two-thirty in the morning. Please come back after a couple of hours. Baba will talk to you then."

They kept insisting, but when I asked them what they wanted to talk to Baba about, they would only say that they wanted to do namaskar, nothing more. When it became clear that they would not go away, I let them in. They would not even take off their shoes. I requested them politely, pointing out that it was against our spiritual culture to wear shoes in the house, but Hingurani and Ahuja paid me no mind, though a few of their assistants did. In an effort to delay them I asked our cook to make some tea. They accepted the tea but they quickly grew impatient. By now it was after three, so I went to Baba's room and informed him that the CBI director and SP had come.

"Ask them what they want."

"Baba, I asked them several times. All they said was that they have come to meet you. They wouldn't say anything else."

"That is out of the question. They are not margis; they are police. Ask them if they have a warrant."

I went and asked them if they had an arrest warrant. Hingurani said that he did not require a warrant, but after a few moments he produced one. He also claimed that there were two magistrates waiting outside in case there were any legal complications.

I went back and told Baba about the warrant. He told me he would be ready in a few minutes, so I did my best to delay them, but they told me they could not wait any longer. It would be light soon and their instructions were to take Baba before it got light. Baba came out and they asked him to come with them for questioning. I tried to convince them to allow me to take Baba in our car to wherever they wanted him to go but they would not permit it. While they escorted Baba out, I made a couple of hurried phone calls, informing our margis of the situation and asking them to post people at the courthouse and other likely places. Then I took Baba's suitcase to our car and tried to follow them as best I could, but with so many turnings I soon lost them—it was obviously their intention to confuse us so we would lose the trail.

I spent the rest of the morning contacting various margis, trying to locate Baba and get information about the CBI's intentions. Afterward I found out that Baba spent all of that day and most of the night in their car, moving from place to place while they awaited further instructions—they were afraid to bring him openly to the Patna courthouse for fear of public disturbance. Baba was fasting that day—the next day was ekadashi, the official fasting day, but Baba refused to accept even a drop of water from the perpetrators of this injustice. We had our people posted at the various jails, the courthouse, and other likely venues, and from them we occasionally got some snippets of information. Eventually, after getting a magistrate to remand him into CBI custody and continuing this odyssey around the city until nearly midnight, they decided to take Baba to Buxar Jail, a two-hundred-kilometer journey over the worst of roads—roads so bad you felt like giving up long before you arrived. Baba reached there between three and four in the morning, and I got there with his luggage about an hour and a half later.

In total, Baba spent a full twenty-four hours in the CBI car on a fasting day, being ferried from place to place under trying conditions. But this was just the beginning of the tortures that he was to undergo.

29 December 1971

The Superintendent's Wife Dreams of Baba

Now it so happened that while Baba was being brought to Buxar Jail, Mrs. Pandey, the wife of the jail superintendent, dreamed that a great saint would be brought to her husband's jail and that he would be fasting. In her dream she saw rays of divine effulgence emanating from the saint's body. When she awoke, she told her husband about her dream and urged him to go straight to the jail to see if it were true, and if it was, to ask this saint what she could prepare for him so that he could break his fast. It was barely five o'clock; dawn had not yet broken. Mr. Pandey normally went to the jail at ten but he heeded his wife's pleadings and left immediately.

When he arrived at the jail, the superintendent saw me and several other margis standing outside the gate with Baba's bedding and other belongings. He came to talk to me and I told him what had happened and who Baba was. He was sure then that Baba was the man his wife had dreamed about. He brought me inside and went to talk to the jailer, who told him that they had washed an empty cell for the prisoner and given him blankets that he had refused to use—it was the dead of winter and quite cold, but Baba was adamant, and our lawyers, who had arrived just before I did, were trying to convince the jailer to allow Baba to use his own blankets and other articles. Mr. Pandey then hurried to Baba's cell. As soon as he entered the cell, he told Baba about his wife's dream.

"Are you really fasting?" he asked.

"Yes, I have been fasting." Baba said.

"Then please tell me, what can I offer you? What can I bring for you to break your fast?"

"First of all, I do not want to use anything from the jail. If you wish to help, you can allow my belongings to be brought inside. I have my own bedding, my own glass, everything I need. My personal assistant will provide you with them. Today is the prescribed fasting day, ekadashi, but I fasted yesterday since I was in CBI custody and I did not want to give them an easy opportunity to get rid of me by slipping poison into my food. Our rules prescribe that one may fast either one day before or one day after ekadashi. As far as breaking my fast goes, my people will assist me with that."

"My wife and I are just ordinary people," Mr. Pandey said. "We have committed so many errors in our life. But I can see that my wife was right about you. I will do as you ask and whatever else I can do to make you comfortable while you are here."

When the superintendent came out from Baba's cell, he gave permission for Baba's articles to be brought to him. Shortly afterward, Rama Shankar and his family arrived with lemon water for Baba to break his fast—Rama Shankar is an important margi of Buxar. Later that day I discovered that his wife and the jail superintendent's wife were related.

Baba remained in Buxar Jail for two months before being transferred to Patna Medical College Hospital for health reasons. During this time, Mr. Pandey was very helpful to us. He went out of his way to make sure that Baba was comfortable and that he had everything he needed; unfortunately, the CBI blocked him at every step. On that first day, our advocates moved to have Baba classified as an A-class prisoner, but the CBI succeeded in having him classified as an ordinary prisoner. In this way they tried to block every effort we made to provide facilities for Baba. I remained in Patna during these two months but I would go to Buxar once or twice a week to carry information and see to Baba's needs. Rama Shankar came every morning to the jail to bring Baba his breakfast, and with the help of Mr. Pandey, who gave him permission to bring Baba food and other items, he was able to take care of Baba's daily necessities. We also made sure that somebody was allowed to meet with Baba in the jail every day: myself one day, the next day our lawyers, on another day Rama Shankar or some other margi.

30 December 1971

Bankipur Jail

*A*FTER SPENDING MORE than a month in Patna Medical College Hospital, Baba was transferred to Bankipur Central Jail on April 3 and kept in cell number thirteen, which had been a cell for condemned prisoners during British times, those who were awaiting hanging. It was a cramped concrete cell with no ventilation—never did we think that they would keep Baba in such inhuman, unhygienic conditions, and it made me both sad and angry. Those margis who were able to get permission to enter the prison became very sentimentalized when they saw Baba. The hot season was beginning, and without any ventilation Baba's cell was like an oven. Raghuvir Prasad, Collector of Customs and Central Excise, was one of the first to gain permission. He was so shocked by what he saw that he immediately went to Ram Tanook to begin preparing a legal motion to get permission for Baba to have a fan. The CBI tried to block it tooth and nail but eventually we secured permission from the court. Even then they managed to delay its installation. They also tried to prevent us from bringing in any of Baba's personal items, such as his clothes. There was one advantage, however, in being in Bankipur Jail: the other four accused—Sarveshvarananda, Satyananda, Pavitra, and Barun—were also there. Though they remained in a different cell block, they were able to spend time with Baba during the day and thus were able to look after his needs.

April 1972

Baba's Mother's Death

*A*FTER BABA'S ARREST, his mother started asking his brothers Himanshu and Manas why he hadn't visited. "I haven't seen Bubu for a long time," she would say. "Where has he gone?" They didn't want her to know that he was in prison—she was very old by then and her health was failing—so they told her that he was busy traveling, holding DMCs and so forth, and thus he had been unable to come and see her. She died without knowing that Baba had been arrested. That was in July 1972. When I got the news I conveyed the message to Baba. In India it is the eldest son's responsibility to put fire in the mouth of the corpse, as per Hindu law, in order to initiate the cremation rites, so Baba's lawyers, Ram Tanook and Nageshvar Prasad, both excellent advocates, submitted a motion to give Baba a two-day furlough in order to attend his mother's funeral. This is considered a very important responsibility in Hindu culture and under normal circumstances he would have been granted the furlough, but the CBI pressured the court to turn down Baba's request. At that time the CBI had a stranglehold over the judicial system as well as the political system. When I conveyed the news to Baba that they had turned down his petition, he said:

"See how they deal with me. If they do this to me, just imagine the fate of ordinary people who fall into their hands. I will tell you why they did this: it is because they are scared of me. They are scared because I think for the welfare of the entire human race. They fear my philosophy and for that reason I have to undergo these ordeals. What would be the harm if they gave me a two-day furlough to attend my mother's funeral? But they are too scared. Do you know, yesterday the government issued a secret order to put a net over the prison to prevent my escape. They believe that some overseas margis have made arrangements to fly a helicopter into the prison and take me out of India. If they are that scared of me, how could they ever think of allowing me to go to Jamalpur?"

A few days later the entire prison was netted, just as Baba had said it would be.

July 1972

Baba Scolds the IG Prisons

O NE DAY IN mid-November the Inspector General of Prisons, Mr. R.
K. Srivastava, came to inspect Bankipur Jail. The previous evening,
the jail superintendent and the jailer came to Baba's cell to inform him
of the IG's visit—it is tradition in India for political and government
figures to seek the blessings of a saint. I was sitting with Baba at the
time along with my four imprisoned brothers. As soon as the superintendent appeared in the doorway, Baba started scolding him and his
staff officers. "I don't want to see the faces of you immoral people!" They
turned and fled without saying anything, like a dog with its tail between
its legs. After they left, Baba started telling us how several days earlier a
truck had pulled up to the jail at midnight. The jail officers loaded the
truck with the food stores that were intended for the prisoners and later
divided up the spoils among themselves. "How dare they come to me to
seek my blessings after engaging in such corrupt acts!" Baba said. "Did
you see how they ran? They know that I am in their hands. They can
do anything to me they like but you see how weak they are. That is the
nature of immoral people."

The next day the IG Prisons was received at the jail with great pomp
and circumstance. He came with his team, perhaps fifty or sixty persons
in all, including the superintendent and other jail staff. When he came
to Baba's cell to get his blessings, Baba was lying down with his back to
him. That was insulting enough but then Baba sat up and started scolding
him in the severest of terms. The IG became completely flustered. He
tried to make some threatening remarks but Baba shouted at him to get
out and he left. He didn't have the force to face Baba's ire.

November 1972

Poisoned!

THROUGHOUT BABA'S STAY in Buxar, great pressure was put on the superintendent by the CBI. Why was he giving Baba so many facilities against their direct orders? For this reason, he was forced to keep a low profile and in time Baba developed some health problems. This enabled us to file for a medical transfer and at the end of February Baba was transferred to Patna Medical College Hospital. He remained there for a little over a month and then was shifted to Bankipur Central Jail.

The jail doctor at that time was Dr. Rahamatullah. He was not allowed to prescribe medicine for Baba on his own, however: it had to be prescribed by a board of doctors headed by the Patna Civil Surgeon. This provision was made because Baba was in special CBI custody. Baba began suffering from headaches due to the poor conditions in the jail, and in early February 1973 he requested some medicine for the pain. Rahamatullah communicated this to the civil surgeon, who in turn met with him and the other doctors on the board. They gave Rahamatullah some capsules and promised a promotion if he would give them to Baba in the evening.

Baba took the so-called medicine on 12 February at about eight-thirty or nine at night. Within minutes his eyes started watering profusely and he began feeling excruciating pain in his head and body. Shortly thereafter he went into a kind of coma, but before he lost consciousness he was able to communicate his condition to a warder who was checking the cells, asking him to get information to his people in Patliputra.

I got the message about seven in the morning. The warder had been waiting for someone to whom he could pass the message—I used to keep people at the gate to get periodic reports about Baba, but no one reached there until early morning. I immediately rushed to the jail and demanded to see Baba. By this time the prisoners themselves were agitating. I could hear them when I went to the gate. They were demanding that the jail authorities do something to help Baba and the superintendent was in a panic—he and the other jail officials were scared that they would be blamed for what had happened. I was the first visitor to see Baba and I was shocked by what I saw. His eyes were completely red and he could barely speak. He had tremors in his arms and legs and he was obviously in tremendous pain. "My nervous system has been damaged," he told me, his voice choked and barely audible. "My brain is not able to function. Let this message be conveyed to all margis and workers that I have been poisoned."

I was terrified—never could I have imagined that such a thing could happen—but I had to put my fear behind me and act. Reporters had already begun to gather outside along with margis and workers—they had been informed by the dadas—so when I left Baba after doing sastaunga pranam I fought back my tears and went out and told them that Baba had been poisoned and was in dire condition. How Baba survived, only he knows. But in the next days he was somehow able to begin writing letters to different officials, such as the governor, the chief minister, the president of India, and so on, with details of his poisoning and torture at the hands of the CBI in an attempt to liquidate him. Some letters were released with the consent of the jail authorities and others we managed to smuggle out without their knowledge through our channels. The CBI was especially hostile to us in the aftermath of the poisoning and they did their best to prevent us from meeting Baba.

Once Baba's condition was more or less stabilized, I went outside India to call attention to the assassination attempt. Baba wanted the news broadcast throughout the world so I went to Europe and South and North America. In New York I met with Amnesty International and similar organizations. I also went to the UN along with Dada Yatishvarananda, Didi Ananda Mitra, and Pramil. There we were able to meet the general secretary and plead our case. This visit was publicized in the Indian newspapers. In the meantime Baba continued writing letters. He demanded a judicial inquiry headed by a supreme court judge and let it be known that he would begin a protest fast if the inquiry was not opened by April 1. There was no inquiry and Baba began his fast on that date, a fast that would last until the day he was released from prison: five years, four months, and two days later.

Dr. Rahamatullah got his promotion shortly thereafter, as promised, but within a few years he contracted leprosy and was forced to retire. Subsequently he left Patna for his hometown of Muzaffarpur. After

Baba's release, he approached some members of the Ananda Marga community in Muzaffarpur. "I know that Baba is a good man," he told them. "I was not willing to administer the poison but my hand was forced. Please go to him and beg his pardon on my behalf so that my disease might be cured."

He accompanied the Muzaffarpur margis to Patliputra. Though he was not allowed inside the gate, they approached Baba and communicated his plea.

"I wish him all the best," Baba said. "I look upon all beings with equanimity. But it is out of my hands. Nature has punished him for his actions. There is nothing I can do at this point."

February 1973

Self-immolation

DADA DIVYANANDA WAS so shocked by Baba's poisoning and his continued torture that he decided to go on a protest fast. First he left food; then he stopped drinking water, vowing to the press that he would not drink another drop until his guru's torture ended. But still the terrible conditions under which Baba was being kept continued unabated. Finally, Divyananda told the press that if the government did not stop the torture he was going to commit self-immolation. At the time he was staying in our Patliputra office. We had three buildings then, all close to each other: the jagriti, Baba's quarters, and the office, which was just in front of Baba's quarters. It was a very sentimental time for us. The government had tried to assassinate our guru and now our brother was threatening to commit self-immolation in protest. We were not sure whether or not he would be able to go through with it, but the idea that he might left us deeply moved. Then it happened. We don't know how he arranged it, but without alerting anyone, he went to the parliament building in Patna early in the morning on the fifth of April, less than two months after Baba's poisoning, and set himself on fire. The news appeared on the front page of the papers and it was from the papers that Baba learned of the tragedy.

I and several other dadas were arrested in connection with the immolation. We were kept for a few days in Phulwari Sharif Jail and then released. When I went to the jail to see Baba—he had begun his fast four days before the immolation—he did not make any comment but I could see that he was affected. Later he told me, "He should not have died like this, but when he saw that his Ista was being tortured on false grounds he felt that he had no other alternative. He felt that he had to do something to stop my torture. In fact, it is the government's responsibility. They killed him."

The immolations did not end with Divyananda. Dineshvarananda committed self-immolation several weeks later in Lal Quila in Delhi. Then in December 1974, Atulananda immolated himself in Bankipur Central Jail. Prior to that, Atulananda had been acting as Baba's PA in the jail. He used to communicate Baba's messages to us. But when he heard that Baba's gold ring had been stolen he couldn't take the continued harassment of his guru any longer. He was able to get some gasoline—in the prison anything is available; wine, hashish, you name it, the prison mafia will get it for you as long as you can pay. He got some gasoline and immolated himself in his cell, generating a great public stir. Baba did not approve but he repeated that his sons and daughters could not tolerate what the government was doing to their guru.

Later there were more immolations, nine in all. They only stopped when Baba was honourably acquitted.

24 April 1973

Dr. Kalawar Quarrels with his Wife

*A*FTER THE DOCTOR who poisoned Baba was transferred, Dr. Kalawar took over his duties and the difference was like night and day. He was not a margi at that time but his wife was, and he grew to love Baba very much. Soon he began doing whatever Baba asked of him. His wife was always insisting that he follow the true path and later, after Baba's release, I initiated him. But even at this time, while Baba was in the jail, he used to help us very much. He used to pass us Baba's messages—Ananda Vaniis, organizational directives, whatever communication Baba needed to reach us. I used to meet him at the airport or the railway station or at other predetermined places, places where we would not be observed—at that time the CBI was closely monitoring the jail environment. So how did he become so good, so helpful to the mission? Well, there were many things, but one incident in particular had a great impact on his mind. This happened shortly after he came to work at the jail, not long after Baba's poisoning.

He and his wife had been quarrelling for some time and they had been unable to resolve their differences. Each blamed the other, convinced that the other was at fault. Finally they agreed to take their case to Baba and let him settle the matter. Whoever he said was at fault, the other would accept his judgment. Being the jail doctor, Kalawar had the authority to enter the jail at any hour of the day or night. It was a law that the jail doctor had to live within a certain distance of the jail so that he could reach there without any delay if there was a medical emergency with one of the inmates. They went to the jail about 9:30 in the evening, when the prisoners were locked up for the night, and made their way to Baba's cell, but when they entered the cell they saw no sign of Baba. Instead they found the room filled with a brilliant but soothing light. It was so intoxicating that neither wanted to leave. They remained there for at least ten to fifteen minutes, absorbed in their contemplation of that divine effulgence, a sight that most sadhakas rarely, if ever, see.

When they returned home they told each other that the purpose of their quarrel was so that Baba could show them that light, and they agreed never to quarrel again.

1973

Testing the Buttermilk

*A*FTER BABA BEGAN his fast, the CBI threatened to force-feed him, so after three months of these threats he began taking two cups daily of what we call "buttermilk," just to avoid the force-feeding. You prepare it like this: First you churn the milk to remove the butter. Then you make yoghurt from what is left—the milk minus the cream. Then you mix the yoghurt with water: three parts water and one part yoghurt. These were Baba's instructions. There was very little substance in it—it was mostly water—but it kept him from being force-fed.

For many months after the poisoning, the CBI made it difficult for us to see Baba. I had to secure permission either from the high court or from the IG Prisons before I could enter. One day a directive came down from Delhi that they had to test the buttermilk before they could allow it to pass. At the time they were claiming to the media that we had poisoned Baba, but they knew they would be crucified in the press if anything else of that sort happened, so they took certain precautions. They stepped up their security at the jail. At least five or six CBI officers were posted there to vet Baba's visitors—earlier there had been only one or two. Among them were several high-ranking officers, including a DSP and an ASP. Margis became afraid to get permission to see Baba in the jail because the CBI was adding them to their lists and thereafter harassing and threatening them. They questioned everyone who came to see Baba and took notes on them.

That morning I arrived at the jail about eight-thirty to make sure that Baba got his buttermilk on time. Baba was very particular about his timing. His fixed times for taking the buttermilk were ten in the morning and four in the afternoon. I would bring a thermos in the morning with two cups of buttermilk—Baba gave strict instructions that the thermos should contain exactly two cups, not a drop more. Baba would take one cup at ten and save the second cup for the afternoon. If the buttermilk didn't arrive in time then he wouldn't take it at all. He knew that if it didn't come by ten o'clock it was due to CBI harassment so he would send word that he wouldn't take anything. The CBI knew this so they used to invent excuses to delay letting the yoghurt water pass. For this reason I started going to the jail early, just to give myself enough time to complete the formalities and get through their petty harassments. But this was different. They didn't show up until 9:30, and when they arrived they told me that they had orders from Delhi that they either had to taste the buttermilk themselves or else send it for testing before they could allow it inside the jail. I tried to argue with them. "You don't trust me? Every day I have been bringing Baba his buttermilk and there has never been any problem. You people are the ones who poisoned him. This is harassment on your part, nothing more." We were in the office, between the outer gate and the inner gate. After going back and forth like this for some time, they told me that if I would not allow them to test the buttermilk, then they could only permit it inside the jail on one condition: one of the jail authorities would have to sign a document assuming full responsibility for the life of Mr. P. R. Sarkar. The jail superintendent was there and three or four jailers but they were scared of the CBI and none of them was willing to give such an undertaking. In the meantime Baba's *paniya*—the inmate who took care of his personal needs—was at the inner gate, calling for the thermos. "Ramanandaji, Baba sent me to see if you had come. Baba is waiting for his thermos." On a normal day, before these special security measures were instituted, I would go inside the jail and bring Baba his buttermilk. If I was early and Baba was engaged in other works, then I would sit outside his cell and wait until the paniya told him I was there and he called me in. But now I was in a fix. I told the paniya what was going on, about the conditions the CBI had put. He went and informed Baba and then brought back a message that if any third party so much as touched the thermos he would not drink it. It was getting very late by then, 10:30 at least, and Baba still hadn't gotten his buttermilk.

It was then that Dr. Kalawar arrived. Normally I would meet him twice a day, once in the morning before I went to the jail, and once in the evening. We would fix some predetermined place where we would not be observed and he would pass me information from Baba. In the morning it would most often be on the road or near the entrance to the prison. We would pass each other just as any two strangers would; he would whisper to me and then move on. But that morning he hadn't been there. I found out later that the superintendent had sent him to the court to represent the jail in a negligence case that some prisoners had lodged. The case had been lodged against a previous doctor but someone had to represent the jail—these cases are common and they often go on for years. Usually, when he had to go to court, he would inform Baba that he would not be there the next day for that reason, but on this morning he had been sent to the court without having been forewarned. Ordinarily he would have remained at the court for much longer, but as it so happened, goaded by some sudden impulse, he requested the jail advocate to postpone the hearing. When the postponement was approved he hurried to the jail. When he saw me he was surprised. "Ramananda, are you still waiting? Has Baba not gotten his buttermilk yet?" When I told him about the problems the CBI was creating, he became angry. He turned to the CBI officers and told them to let me in with the buttermilk. When they told him that they could not allow it unless some member of the jail staff took written responsibility, he said, "Give me the jail register. If anything happens with the life of Mr. P. R. Sarkar, I, Dr. Kalawar, will take full responsibility." He wrote as much in the jail register and the CBI finally let us pass. As I was going in, I heard them say to each other that he must have been bribed by some margi.

The doctor and I then went straight to Baba's cell. Baba was angry over the delay so the doctor told him that it was not my fault.

"Yes, I know," Baba said. "He comes very early. My paniya informed me that he was fighting with the CBI. It is the fault of those people. They are hell bent on harassing me. From now on I will not take any buttermilk. You can take it away. I will survive on light and air only. I can live for many years on sunlight and air."

Dr. Kalawar folded his hands and pleaded with Baba. "Baba, today I was called away to court unexpectedly. Had I been here, your buttermilk would not have been delayed. They have made new security arrangements that I was not aware of—they have orders that the buttermilk must be tasted by them before they can let it pass, but I have signed an undertaking accepting full responsibility for your safety. From now on it will arrive on time, I promise. Please take it. This will not happen again."

Baba kept mum for a few moments. Then he said, "My boy, you realize that the CBI will be after you for having done this? They will push to have you transferred. In spite of knowing this, you have signed such an undertaking?"

"Let them try, Baba. They cannot do anything to me unless you will it so. If you want me to remain here, then I will remain, and if you want me to be transferred, then I'll be transferred." Dr. Kalawar started relating how he and his wife had come to the jail the previous night to ask Baba to settle their dispute and had seen the room filled with light.

Baba was smiling now. "I was not in my cell last night, you say? But I was here, I was very much here."

Actually we were all smiling, all three of us.

1973

Four MPs Request Baba to Break His Fast

*I*N MARCH 1974 four prominent members of parliament met with Baba in order to request him to break his fast: Atal Vajpayee from the Jana Sangh, who later went on to become prime minister; Professor Samar Guha from the Socialist Party; Prasana Bhai Mehta from the Congress Party; and Shyam Lal Yadav from the Bhartiya Kranti Dal. Baba's fast had been discussed on the floor of parliament—it was a very sensitive issue, a protest fast by a famous religious figure—and it was their opinion that if Baba died in jail from his fast it would have serious repercussions for the government.

When they entered Baba's cell, Atal Vajpayee, who was famed for his oratory skills, acted as the spokesman for the group. "It hurts our conscience," he said, "to see a spiritual teacher such as yourself fasting in this great land of India due to the persecution of our government. Thus we have decided to come here personally and beg you to break your fast. We are convinced that you are innocent, and we give you our solemn promise that we will fight tooth and nail in parliament for your release. Please, break your fast and we will do our level best to secure your release."

But Baba was adamant. Though they promised Baba that they would pressure the government to accede to his demands, especially his demand for a judicial inquiry into his poisoning, Baba would not change his course of action. "I am not a politician," he said. "I am the head of a spiritual organization. I am fasting for an ideal, the ideal of dharma and morality."

"But what if you die from your fast?" one of them asked. "How can you serve your ideal then? If you break your fast and live then you can serve dharma better."

"My ideas are more important than my life," Baba replied. "The government tried to kill me because they are afraid of my ideas."

Then Atal Vajpayee said, "But if you continue fasting and you die it will only help the government."

"Even if I die, I die for an ideal," Baba said, "and that ideal will triumph, no matter what happens to me."

Baba further told them that democracy cannot survive without morality, and morality had become a victim of the Indira Gandhi regime.

There was little they could say or do to convince Baba. They left Baba's cell in silence, after promising that they would fight for him. Afterward they addressed the public in a huge open-air gathering. That same day they issued a joint statement to the press, cautioning the government and calling for it to stop its persecution of Ananda Marga. They then met with the governor and later in Delhi with the prime minister and the home minister.

The last of the MPs to leave Baba's cell was Samar Guha. Samar Guha had a great interest in Netaji Subhash Chandra Bose—he had searched for evidence that Netaji might still be alive—and when the other three left the cell he took advantage of the opportunity and asked Baba in a whisper if Netaji was still alive. When Baba said yes, he was alive, Samar Guha was beside himself with joy. Later he began to help Ananda Marga with its activities.

March 1974

The Plot to Assassinate Baba

THOUGH THE POISONING attempt failed, the CBI was not finished with their efforts to do away with Baba. Once the publicity died down, they thought they could assassinate him and make it look as if he had died from the prolonged effects of his fast. With this in mind, they brought two convicted murderers from Daltonganj Jail to Bankipur Jail and promised them easy access to Baba's cell and a reduction in their sentence in return for their services. The would-be assassins made two attempts but each time something inexplicable happened that caused them to turn back. The first time, they reached Baba's cell at the appointed hour but they saw Baba walking in the air inside his cell. They were so frightened by what they saw that they turned and fled. Under pressure from the jail authorities, they made a second attempt but this time they found Baba's cell empty. While they were looking around, wondering what to do, they heard a loud voice reverberating inside the empty cell: "Who is there!" Again they fled the scene. This time they were so unnerved by their experience that when the authorities pressured them to go back and do the deed they refused. "He is no ordinary human being," they told them. "There is no way we would ever dare try to kill him."

We learned about these attempts directly from the SP of central intelligence himself, Mr. Ahuja. At that time, Kunj Bihari was DSP of state intelligence for the government of Bihar, and he was their liaison with Ahuja on matters concerning Baba. Kunj Bihari was a strong margi—he was the elder brother of Braj Bihari—but he used to keep away from the organization so that he would not be in trouble with his bosses. Ahuja told Kunj Bihari about the plot and what the assassins had said, and together they came to see Baba in the jail. I was also there. Ahuja told Baba openly everything that had happened and asked for his grace so that he and his family would remain safe. "I have come here," he said, "because I want to confess what I have done and ask for your forgiveness.

I respect you and honour you, Baba, but I was under pressure from my bosses to kill you. I should not have succumbed to their pressure but I did. I have since told my boss, Mr. Hingurani, that I won't be a party to any more such attempts. He also knows what happened when the assassins came to your cell. They have become very scared, these two men."

Baba made a drama, as he often did. "But I was sitting right here," he said. "How can they say they didn't see me? If they want to do away with me, it is not very difficult. They know where to find me."

But Ahuja continued to beg Baba's forgiveness and after some time Baba gave him his blessings. He is still alive to this day, but Hingurani is no more. The murderers remained in the prison for some days more but after this warning we were very much on the alert and they were soon transferred out. We also heard from the other prisoners that they had known right from the beginning that there was something fishy about those two characters.

1974

Baba Gives his Statement

*T*HOUGH BABA WAS very weak from the effects of the poisoning and his subsequent protest fast, he still had to go to the court to give his statement—he had to be carried on a stretcher from the car to the courtroom. The courtroom was packed that day. Everyone wanted to hear what Baba would say—the lawyers, the media, and those members of the general public who were able to gain admittance to the courtroom. When the magistrate said, "Mr. Sarkar, we are now ready to record your statement; in which language would you prefer to speak?" Baba replied, "I know more than 250 languages of this world. In which language would you prefer me to give my statement?"

The magistrate didn't answer; he was too startled. In fact, there was a hush throughout the courtroom. Everyone was looking at Baba expectantly, waiting to hear what he would say next. Finally Baba said, "For your convenience and for the convenience of the court I shall speak in the Queen's English."

It seemed to me that day that everyone present in the courtroom, in one way or another, was reflecting on the obvious fact that Baba was no ordinary person but an intellectual giant with infinite capacity.

1975

Going Underground

IN DECEMBER 1974, Madhavananda was slated to testify in court against Baba. He was paid by the CBI to be the main approver in the case. One dada whose name I won't mention got hold of a revolver from a margi in U.P. and smuggled it into the courtroom. He tried to shoot Madhavananda when they brought him in but the gun misfired, so he ran from the courtroom and jumped into the river and was able to escape. I was in the court when this happened so I witnessed everything. He left the country after that and the CBI started claiming that I was the mastermind in the plot. In January, Baba told me that they were planning to implicate me in the case. "You will have to go underground for some time," he said. "At least for three or four months. Your name will be changed to Lakshmanananda Avadhuta. First you will go to Cairo for a few weeks and act as the sectorial secretary there under this name. They do not have an SS in Nairobi Sector at the moment, since Atmananda is not there, so from Cairo you can go to Nairobi and work there. Someone will send word when the situation normalizes and it is safe to come back."

I left India under the name of Lakshmanananda Avadhuta as Baba instructed. First I went to Manila, then to Cairo, then to Nairobi. Ananda Marga wasn't registered in Kenya yet so I got it registered and started bringing out one magazine in which I exposed the crimes perpetrated by the Indian government. It was not a big magazine, maybe sixteen pages, but it was full of facts about Baba's torture, the suppression of the Marga, and so on. The Indian ambassador became incensed when it was brought to his attention and he had me investigated. Jomo Kenyatta was president at the time and he had a good relationship with India. There was a bad drought in Kitui District so I collected relief materials and we were able to do a lot of good work—I was getting financial support from various professors and was getting good notices in the press—but the Indian ambassador found out who I was and started conducting a defamation campaign against me and against Ananda Marga in Kenya. Finally in June the Kenyan government deported me back to India, in response to pressure from the Indian government. Later I learned from the margis that the news came on the radio in India that my name had been changed to Lakshmanananda and that I was being deported.

I arrived in Bombay and passed through immigration wearing my avadhuta uniform. When I went up to the Indian airlines counter to buy a domestic ticket, the lady at the counter saw my dress and started talking to me. I told her that I belonged to Ananda Marga and that I had been deported—why, I didn't know. She became concerned and advised me not to tell anyone who I was or that I belonged to Ananda Marga, since the Indira Gandhi government had just declared a state of emergency and they were arresting known Ananda Margis. On her advice I bought a ticket to Madras. She told me that the Tamil Nadu government wasn't cooperating with the central government with regard to the emergency so she thought I would be safe there. But when I landed in Madras I found some twenty CBI officers and twenty or thirty policemen waiting to arrest me. The CBI kept me without trial for three days, interrogating me and beating me over the head with the butts of their revolvers, which led to clotting in the brain. Most of their questions were useless: for example, how much money have you sent for the underground movement of Ananda Marga? They promised to release me if I agreed to leave Ananda Marga but I refused to dignify them with an answer. Then they sent me to Madras Central Jail. When I was examined by the doctors there they said I had some clotting in the brain but that it would dissolve in time. That didn't prove to be the case, however.

1975

Handaji's Arrest

*H*ANDAJI WAS A devoted margi of Calcutta and a very robust man who was fond of taking rich foods—it was part of his family tradition. During the emergency he was taken prisoner for a short time. Since he was unaccustomed to being without his usual foods, he found it very difficult. In order to secure his release, the non-margi members of his family organized a Hanuman *puja*. When they visited him in the jail he told them to forget about the Hanuman *puja* or any other orthodox ritual. "If you really want to expedite my release," he told them, "you should organize an akhanda kirtan. Just do Baba Nam Kevalam kirtan, and I will be out of here in no time." So they organized a three-hour akhanda kirtan and the very next day he was released.

After Baba's release, Handaji would often come to Tiljala to see Baba. Sometimes he would come with Rathiji, who was just as fat and healthy as he was. One time, when Baba was getting ready to go for field walk, he stopped in front of them and asked, "Who will come with me on field walk today?" I replied, "Baba, two people can fit in the car if they are of normal weight but in their case only one can go." Baba started laughing and said, "But I love them both. Okay, let them decide among themselves who will come with me now." So they decided that Rathi would go then and Handaji in the evening. Baba often made us laugh like this.

1975

Ramchandra Seth

RAMCHANDRA SETH OF Coimbatore in Tamil Nadu was a successful Sindhi businessman and a great devotee of Baba. Throughout the time that I was Baba's PA, and up until his death, he used to send us a regular monthly donation for Baba's maintenance. He was a generous person who would always help whatever worker came to his house. First he would do dhyana and then he would put the money in an envelope and hand it to the worker, saying, "Baba has instructed me to give you this amount." If the worker would ask for more, he would say, "I'm sorry. I am Baba's treasurer and he has specifically instructed me to give you this amount. Please don't ask for more. It is not my money; it is his money."

When the emergency was declared, one worker came to his house and tried to convince him to go into hiding. Well-known margis were being put behind bars along with the workers and he was known throughout Coimbatore as a staunch margi. "If you stay here, you will surely be arrested," the worker told him, but he wouldn't heed his warning. "Who can possibly arrest me when Baba is always with me?" he said, and saying this he refused to budge. The CBI made a concerted effort to catch him. They went to his house on several occasions looking for him but they never found him, even though he was there in the house all along.

1975

Baba's Sentence

*A*FTER THE GUILTY verdict was given, the CBI spread the rumour that Baba would be sentenced to hang and that this would be the end of Ananda Marga. This rumour was everywhere. Before the sentencing, the CBI met with the magistrate and insisted that he give Baba the death penalty. Despite their pressure, however, the magistrate refused to sign such an order. Instead he gave a sentence of life imprisonment. In Indian jurisprudence there is a tradition that whenever a magistrate signs an order for the death penalty or life imprisonment he will immediately break the pen with which he has signed that order. He broke the pen and a few days later the hand with which he signed the order became paralyzed. Then he realized that he had sentenced an innocent man.

29 November 1976

A Special Mantra

*W*HEN THE EMERGENCY was lifted and I was released from Madras Central Jail, Baba sent a message that I should rush to Patna. In 1973 I had started doing Vishesh Yoga and once I made it to Patna, Baba started revising my Vishesh lessons. But he knew that it would be difficult for me to do them properly as long as I was PA. Often when I would be doing sadhana, both before and after Baba's release, he would ring the call bell and I would have to rush to his room to serve him. I would be doing pranayama and the call bell would ring so I would have to break my pranayama. Then, when I would sit again, I would begin pranayama again, and again I would have to break it to attend to Baba. This happened quite frequently, so while he was in the jail Baba gave me a mantra that I could use when I didn't get time to do my lessons properly. He told me that this mantra was the essence of Vishesh Yoga.

August 1977

Abdullah Bukhari

ABDULLAH BUKHARI WAS the chief Imam of Delhi and the leader of India's 250 million Muslims. He was a tall, dignified man and very outspoken. He met our delegation in India and became convinced that we were not criminals but spiritual people who were propagating universalism. Thus he decided to go to Patna along with other prominent Muslim leaders and request permission to see Baba in the jail, though in the end only he and several co-workers were allowed in due to want of space.

When he saw Baba he was very moved. He told Baba that he was convinced of his innocence and begged him to break his fast on behalf of all of India's Muslims. Baba replied to him much as he had to the parliamentarians who had come to plead with him several years earlier, and Bukhari left his cell greatly impressed with Baba's magnetic personality and iron determination.

This was in the morning. In the afternoon he held a large outdoor rally in the city. In the rally he proclaimed openly that Baba was innocent and that he was an object of government persecution. The government's allegations against him, he said, were an attack on the entire Muslim community in India. Bukhari was a powerful orator. He laid bare before the crowd the government's injustice, including Baba's torture and the persecution of Ananda Marga. Then he called for the entire Muslim community to rally behind his call for Baba's immediate release and an end to the persecution. It was very moving and was widely reported in the Indian press. This helped to stir sentiment for Baba's release.

Now it so happened that some French margis had visited Baba some days earlier and they had brought some special French perfume for him, which he had kept in his cell without the knowledge of the authorities. Muslims are fond of perfume—such fragrances are an important part of their culture—and Bukhari was especially fond of them. As he was leaving Baba's cell, Baba called him back and presented him with a nicely wrapped package. When Bukhari opened it that evening, he was surprised to find that it contained a particular perfume that he had tried unsuccessfully to obtain for the past several years.

1977

Shraddhananda's Visit

*B*ABA WAS VERY happy whenever anybody came to visit him in the
jail. This is the nature of prison life: when you are separated from
the world, you are happy if anyone is able to come and talk to you. So
as much as we could, we tried to send people to Baba, both margis and
workers. But from the organizational point of view, we usually had one
meeting a week, generally Mondays, that was devoted to organizational
matters. The acting general secretary—before the emergency it was
Keshavananda—would collect all the necessary reports and go to the jail
to discuss them with Baba: what to do with this worker or that project,
posting orders, and so on. Many decisions could not be made without
Baba's knowledge and instructions. I would take Keshavananda to Baba's
cell and remain there for the duration of the meeting, which would
usually last between forty-five minutes and an hour, depending on how
much leeway we got from the CBI and other intelligence people. In the
beginning they did what they could to block these meetings—often I
had to go to the high court to force them to allow us to meet with Baba,
and sometimes I was the only one who was allowed to go in; on those
occasions I had to do the work of the general secretary—but as time
went on they became more relaxed.

Whenever we had such meetings, the intelligence officers would sit
near the doorway and try to listen in on our conversations, but Baba
would not talk if they were sitting too close. He would scold them until
they moved far enough away that they could not hear what we were
saying. "These are my private talks," he would tell them. "He is my
secretary. You see that line. Don't cross that line." Taking my cue from
Baba, I would also scold them in the same way.

This also happened sometimes during ordinary visits. Once Dada
Shraddhananda told me that he wanted to see Baba. He had printed
one magazine, *Ananda Yuga*, and he wanted to personally give Baba a

copy. I brought him to Baba's cell but the two intelligence officers who were there on that day positioned themselves just outside the doorway, something Baba would not accept. At first Baba didn't say anything but his mood was grave. Then he started upbraiding them in a ferocious tone of voice. When Shraddhananda saw this he became worried. He had come for devotional purposes and suddenly the atmosphere had become very tense. But I was used to it. Strengthened by Baba's example, I also started scolding them. "How dare you sit there and try to listen in on our private conversation." The officers were taken aback by our forceful words. One of them tried to make an excuse. "We are just following instructions," he said. "Our boss has told us that we are to listen to your conversation." I threatened him that if they didn't move away we would leave and go directly to the press to complain about their harassment." This undermined their confidence and after a few minutes they moved far enough away that we could talk softly without being overheard.

As soon as they moved away, Baba's mood completely changed. One minute his scowl could have darkened the sun and the next minute he was smiling and laughing. "So Shraddhanandaji," he said, "what did you have for breakfast today?" As if nothing had happened, no difficulty at all. Shraddhananda used to take germinated gram and mung beans in the morning, and he told this to Baba. But he was still a little unsettled, so Baba said, "You see, Shraddhananda, if you are even a little lax with these people then before you know it they will be sitting on your head. But if you are strict with them and hold your ground then you will be okay. Sometimes you have to fight. Now tell me, why have you come?"

Shraddhananda told Baba about *Ananda Yuga* and presented him with a copy. Baba asked him to read some of the articles for him and praised him for his work.

The CBI had tried to harass us but Baba, as he so often did, turned the situation around and put us completely at ease.

1977

Baba Saves Moraji Desai

*B*Y COURT ORDER I was the only person allowed to bring Baba's but-termilk to him in the jail, his only nourishment during the five years, four months, and two days of his prolonged fast. One day in November 1977, after I had brought Baba his buttermilk, I was returning to our place in Patliputra Colony along with Mahendraji in a three-wheeler when we were struck by a speeding car that subsequently fled the scene. Mahendra and the driver of the three-wheeler were flung onto the road and I was thrown into a ditch where I lost consciousness. Fortunately, Mahendraji and the driver were not badly hurt, and they were able to bring me back to Baba's quarters in Patliputra Colony, though I was not aware of this at the time. I was only aware of the presence of an unseen force taking care of me. I could not understand who that entity was but I could feel that he was very caring and loving, and I trusted that I was in good hands. When I came to my senses that night I found that he was massaging me. I tried to speak to him but at that moment he disappeared.

The next morning, despite the pain, I felt well enough to take Baba his buttermilk, so I left once again with Mahendraji for the jail. Moments after I entered Baba's cell and did sastaunga pranam, the jail doctor, Dr. Kalawar, also entered. Baba was full of concern. "Ramananda, how are you after your accident?" I told Baba I was fine. Then I was shocked to hear him say, "Do you know, you were supposed to die in that accident. But you were saved, and it is by your grace alone that Moraji Desai was also saved from certain death."

I didn't know what to say. Baba then asked Dr. Kalawar if he had seen the morning papers.

"Yes, Baba. There is front-page news about Moraji Desai. His plane crashed yesterday in Jorhat and he had a miraculous escape."

"Yes," Baba said. "At the very moment when Ramanandaji's auto-rick-shaw was hit by the speeding car, the Prime Minister's plane was crashing in Jorhat. Instantaneous death was unavoidable for both of them. It was my duty to save Ramanandaji, but had I saved him and not the Prime Minister then I would have been accused of partiality. That is why I told you, Ramananda, that the Prime Minister was saved by your grace alone."

I was stunned. Then Baba asked Dr. Kalawar to bring him the basil sprigs that he had given him the day before. The doctor brought some basil leaves and Baba gave them to me and asked me to accept them as *prasad*.

It was only afterward that I heard the rest of the story from Dr. Kalawar. After I'd left the jail the previous morning, Baba called his peon, the prisoner who was deputed to assist him in the jail, and asked him to call Dr. Kalawar. When Dr. Kalawar came, Baba asked him if he could bring two or three sprigs of basil from the jail compound. He brought some basil and Baba held the leaves in his hands, shut his eyes, and recited some mantras. Then he uttered the word "saved", apparently with a sigh of relief. After that, he handed the doctor the basil and asked him to keep it safe until he asked for it. One margi who had gotten permission to see Baba that morning was also in the cell and he asked Baba what had happened.

"Just now two important men of our country were about to meet with instantaneous death, but due to divine grace, both of them have had a narrow escape."

It was at that moment that I was suffering my accident, the very same moment that Moraji Desai's plane was crashing in Jorhat. According to the details that came out in the paper, the plane had experienced engine trouble while approaching Jorhat and had been forced to make a crash landing. The pilot, flight attendant, and five passengers had died on the spot, but the prime minister and the chief minister of Arunachal Pradesh, Mr. P. K. Thungon, had escaped with minor injuries. When asked about his miraculous escape, Moraji Desai told reporters that a gentleman dressed in a white dhoti and kurta and wearing heavy black glasses had guided him to safety. "God sent this man," the prime minister said. "He led me to safety and then left without a word."

November 1977

A Letter to Baba

THERE IS ONE American sister from Oregon whose son was suffering from cancer, so she wrote a letter to Baba with photographs of her son. She met me in Patna and asked me if I could pass it on to Baba. Baba was still in jail at the time but I used to forward his letters to him through my secret channels. He would go through them and ask me to convey his comments to whomever had written the letter. I could not forward all the letters I received, so I would practice a kind of censorship. I would give preference to those letters that came from overseas and those from Indian margis whom I knew to be very devoted. Any frivolous letters I would filter out. So I brought the letter to Baba and he added his comments. By then she had already returned to her country but I sent her the letter along with a note from me explaining that it was Baba himself who had made the comments. A few years ago I met her when I made a trip to the US. I didn't remember about the letter but she reminded me.

"Don't you remember, Dada? You promised me that if Baba had a chance to go through the letter then you would let me know what he said. I received the letter back from you with Baba's comments and after that my son was cured."

1977

Baba's Release

*A*FTER BABA'S ACQUITTAL, there was still the matter of an earlier case to be cleared up, a minor matter for which a request for bail had to be submitted. The bail for this case was granted on July 30 and a couple of more days were needed to complete the necessary formalities. Earlier Baba had told me that it would be nice if his sister could be there when he was released—Baba always spoke in the most respectful tones about his sister, Hiraprabha Bose—so I called her and requested her to come to Patna. Acharya Svarupananda brought her the next day, the day before Baba's release.

On the morning of August 2, I drove Baba's old DeSoto inside the jail gate. All Patna knew that Baba would be released that day and the roofs and windows of the nearby buildings were filled with people who wanted to witness the historic event. Margis had poured in from all over India and the police had blocked off traffic in front of the jail to accommodate the crowd, which was in excess of fifty thousand. When all was ready, one dada—I believe it was Mangalananda—and Baba's attendant in the jail carried him to the car. Once Baba sat down, he folded his hands to his chest in the traditional greeting and kept them in that position throughout the slow drive out the gate and through the crowd. Everyone was throwing flowers on his car and shouting: *Parama Pita Baba Ki! Ananda Marga Amar He!* It is impossible to describe how joyous and exalted the mood was on that day.

Even though Baba had been honourably acquitted, he was adamant that he would not break his fast as long as he was in jail. Though there were many who wanted the privilege of preparing his first meal in nearly five and a half years, all agreed to accept the precedence of his elder sister, Hiraprabha. It was well known how much she loved her brother and how much he loved and respected her. The whole family was there at Baba's house in Patliputra Colony when we arrived, Baba's brothers

and their wives and children, but it was Hiraprabha who received Baba
at his house and prepared the food with which he broke his fast: a glass
of coconut water followed by *kitchuri*. She remained there for four or
five days more, taking care of the kitchen and cooking Baba's meals
with the help of Kalyani-di and Manju-di. Then she left him in the care
of his brothers but not before extracting a promise from Baba to visit
her in Chinsurah.

2 August 1978

An Unknown Disciple

ONE MORNING, WHILE Baba was recuperating from his seven-year ordeal in the prison, an unknown person came to the gate at Patliputra and asked to see him. When the security people asked him his name and his business he wouldn't say. He would only say that Baba had asked him to come and meet him. Security was very strict in those days—I think it was Vishnudeva who talked to him—and since he couldn't satisfy their queries the security people refused him entrance. Only known people, initiates and relatives, were allowed to see Baba. Even government ministers were refused entrance. Nevertheless he wouldn't leave. After a couple of hours Braj Bihari, I believe it was, asked the volunteers about this unknown figure who was loitering outside the boundary wall. He then went up to talk to him. The man told him the same thing he had told the security people, but Braj Bihari was impressed by his calm demeanour and his smiling face. He came and got me and I went down to the gate to talk to him.

"I cannot tell you who I am," the man told me, "because I am under strict orders from Baba. I know you don't know me, but I can assure you that Baba has called me here and that I cannot leave without seeing him. Please tell him that I have been waiting here for two hours to meet him and that these people are not allowing me to enter."

I went to Baba and described the visitor—a handsome, well-behaved gentleman of forty-five or fifty whom I took right away to be a spiritualist. At that moment Baba was getting ready for field walk. The car was waiting downstairs and the volunteers had been put on alert. But as soon as I mentioned the visitor, Baba told me to put the field walk on hold and bring the man to his room.

That day Baba didn't go on field walk. He remained closeted with that unknown person for more than an hour. The margis became curious and several of them asked me who the man was that I had taken to Baba's room. But there was nothing I could tell them. Finally Baba rang the call bell. When I opened his door he asked me to escort the gentleman outside and not to allow any of the margis to talk to him.

After I had seen him off, Baba called me and said, "Ramananda, there are some people who are doing my work whom none of the margis know. Even you don't know these people. I have given them some special duty and for that reason it is better that they don't have any contact with my margi disciples. I know that the security was only doing their job but he was detained at the gate for more than two hours. His time is too valuable to be wasted like that. In the future, if any such person comes to the gate asking for me I want you to attend to him personally. Come and inform me that such a person has come and I will let you know what to do."

1978

Baba Blesses Arun and Maya with a Child

EVAKINANDAN AND JANAKI Devi's other daughter is Maya. She married Arun of Daltonganj, a devoted margi, and for the first sixteen years of their marriage they were unable to have a child. They went to many doctors but none were able to help and they grew very sad. Soon after Baba came out of prison, he called them to his house in Patliputra. He counselled Arun to do a lot of tandava, which releases the male hormones, and gave them his blessing to have a child. Shantivrata was born less than a year later. He is a dentist now, living in Bangalore. After that Arun would dance tandava in front of Baba whenever there was a DMC program.

1978

Seeing Baba in Meditation

ONE DAY, SHORTLY after Baba's release, I thought I heard him calling me but in fact he hadn't called. I pushed the door open and saw Baba sitting in meditation. He was in *padmasana*, lotus posture. I cannot explain the atmosphere in the room at that moment, how blissful and otherworldly it was. My only thought was that Baba had graced me with this divine sight. Without opening his eyes, Baba said, "*Ke?*" Who? I closed the door and came out and sat for meditation. Later he told me that it was not my fault. "You are always thinking of me," he said. "That is why you thought you heard me calling you. But in the future when I call you I will also press the call bell. Then you will have your confirmation." After that Baba started bolting the door from the inside, though it sometimes happened that he forgot or that the bolt didn't go in the proper hole.

The second time I saw Baba sitting in meditation was a few years later in Lake Gardens. On this occasion he called me but he was still sitting in meditation when I entered. This time he was sitting in *siddhasana*, perfect posture.

1978

Kranti

O N SEVERAL OCCASIONS while Baba was in prison he told me about one sister from Jamalpur, Kranti, the niece of Ram Khilavan. She was a college professor whose husband had died in an accident, and Baba had fond memories of her devotion and love. I didn't know her but I was impressed when Baba told me how much she loved him, how she was always thinking about him, and about the sacrifices she and her family had made for him. One day, shortly after Baba came out of jail, he told me that he wanted to see Kranti. "Send someone to Jamalpur with a message that I want to see her," he said. "She may be afraid of the CBI, but when she hears that I am calling her she will forget everything and come running."

Soon after she got the message, Kranti came to Patna to see Baba. Her uncle, Ram Khilavan, accompanied her along with other members of her family. I got a chance then to see first-hand how much Baba loved that family and why. As soon as she arrived in Patna she started crying, and she continued to cry and make spiritual expressions throughout her visit, going in and out of trance and calling out Baba's name. When Baba saw her he said, "I knew you had not forgotten me, just as I had not forgotten you. You can ask Ramananda how many times I asked about you. So don't weep anymore. I know you are passing through some difficulties but I am here now."

Baba called the entire family into his room and they remained with him for nearly an hour. He inquired by name about those members of the family who were not there, especially her sisters and their families, and after they left he told me, "It is my duty to take care of Kranti and her family. They are just like my own family to me."

1978

Gifts

*I*T WAS MY job to keep track of the gifts that the devotees brought for Baba. I would store them in the room where I slept, in one of the large cabinets that we kept there for that purpose. Each morning after breakfast, or sometimes after field walk, Baba would inquire if any gifts had come. Mostly the people would give the gifts to me and ask me to give them to Baba. He would look them over and then give me instructions what to do with them. No matter what the gift was, he would ask me to tell the donor that he had used it or sampled it and that he was very grateful for the gift. If it was something edible he would taste it and then ask that the rest be distributed as prasad. If it was a watch, he would put it on and then ask me to put it in the cabinet. If it was a set of clothes, he would look the clothes over and then ask me to store them, though whenever possible he would wear them at some event where the donor was present. If it was a pen he would use it for some time and then put it away with the others. I remember that one dada once brought a very nice pen for Baba, a Cross pen, I believe it was. He had a strong desire to see his pen in Baba's pocket. That morning, when I showed Baba the pen, he said, "Oh, that is a very nice pen. Let me use it today." He put it in his pocket and when he went out in the morning that dada saw his pen in Baba's pocket and became very happy. Baba even made a little drama with him. "Oh, are you the one who gave me this pen? It's a wonderful pen, just what I wanted." The next day he asked me to put the pen in the cabinet with the others.

1978

Laldhari and the Divine Flute

WHEN BABA WAS released from prison many margis sent him gifts, especially clothes: shirts, dhotis, shawls, and so on. There were so many such gifts that they soon took up almost all our available cabinet space. One day Baba asked me for my opinion. "Ramananda, there are too many clothes to keep here. What should we do about it?" I kept mum. Then Baba said, "Why don't we give them to deserving margis who want to keep my clothes in their house as sanctified objects?"

"That is a very good idea, Baba," I replied. "Every year we receive at least ten or fifteen new sets of clothes, so we will continue to accumulate them."

But then the question arose, how to select the people? I suggested a couple of names and Baba gave the rest. He dictated the names and I wrote them down, just as I did when he selected the people for *microvita* sadhana.

The two names I suggested were Ram Rup and Laldhari, both of whom worked in Baba's house in Patliputra Colony. Both had been of great service during the years that Baba was in prison. Laldhari took care of the cows that we kept in the compound to provide the milk for Baba's yoghurt. He would feed them, milk them, and prepare the yoghurt each night. Early in the morning, Ram Rup would prepare the buttermilk from the yoghurt—he was very expert in this. Then he would accompany me to the jail to give it to Baba. He was also in charge of cleaning and ironing Baba's clothes. In both cases I never had anything to worry about; they were both good devotees and excellent workers. After their years of service, it was only fitting that they receive this special grace from Baba.

One day, just after Baba decided to hold the clothes distribution, Laldhari came to me in a state of distress. This by itself was unusual. Laldhari was as quiet, as serene, and as unassuming a person as I had ever met. He was an unlettered person from a small village near Ara who could not write his own name or even speak Hindi—he only knew his mother tongue, Bhojpuri. He had been taking care of Baba's cows since the Ranchi days and never had I seen him even the slightest bit agitated. He was a man who rarely opened his mouth; he simply went about his work peacefully and contentedly and then went home at the end of the day. But what was even more unusual was the cause of his distress. "Dada," he told me, "I am completely miserable. I haven't heard the flute sound now for nearly three weeks. I can't live without hearing that sound."

For a moment or two I was confused. "The flute sound?" I said.

"Yes, Dada. For years now, since Ranchi, I've been hearing a beautiful flute sound throughout the day. It was so nice, so pleasant. I would listen to it all day long while I worked and now it is gone and I can't bear it. Please tell Baba about my problem. Ask him to save me. If he doesn't save me, I don't know what I will do."

Finally I realized that he must have been talking about the om sound that elevated yogis hear when their kundalini rises to a certain level. In some of his discourses Baba talks about how a yogi in deep meditation will hear a beautiful flute sound coming from a far distance, which is actually the sound of the cosmic nucleus, the *omkara*. Could it be, I thought? Could this simple illiterate villager who had been taking care of our cows for so many years really have been hearing that divine sound while he worked? It seemed improbable, but the more I thought about it, the more it made sense. It would explain the calm and quiet aura that surrounded him, something I hadn't really paid much attention to before. So I asked him if anything unusual had happened to him recently. That's when he told me about his problems with his sons. He had three or four sons and none of them had been able to find a job. They had been pressuring him to help them, so for the last few weeks he had been going around to different politicians and government officers, asking them if they could find a position for his sons. He had even been absent from his work on several occasions, putting someone else in his place, while he went around to the offices of these politicians, hoping that one of them would help. Despite all his efforts, however, he had been unable to find jobs for his sons and it was clear that this was weighing on his mind.

After our discussion I told him that there was no need for me to talk to Baba about his problem: I would arrange for him to talk to Baba himself. I told him about the clothes distribution and counselled him to put his request to Baba directly when he went to receive the clothes. "Baba surely knows your problem," I told him, "so he will understand why you are there, but you should tell him and request his help."

The distribution began a few days later. I prepared the packets, some fifteen or twenty daily, and called the people. This went on for a number of days. They would stand in line outside Baba's room, and after explaining how they should behave when they went in and how they should treat the clothes as sanctified objects, I would escort them into Baba's room and Baba would give them their package with his own hands. When it came Laldhari's turn, he did sastaunga pranam and remained lying on the floor, trembling. Baba asked him to sit up and he sat with folded hands, but he was still trembling visibly. "*Kab hoyi?*" Baba asked him in Bhojpuri. "What's the matter?" But Laldhari had his eyes closed and couldn't speak. Baba had the package in his hand to hand to him, but Laldhari was sitting at a little distance so I asked him to move closer and take the package. When he took the package, still trembling with emotion, Baba looked at me, as if to inquire what was going on. I told Baba that he was unhappy because for some time he had been unable to hear the flute sound.

"How long has he been in this condition?" Baba asked.

"Some three weeks now, Baba."

"And where has he gone during these three weeks?"

"Baba, he has been visiting different ministers, trying to secure employment for his sons."

"That's why he is no longer able to hear that sound." Baba turned back to Laldhari and said, "Laldhari, listen. Stay away from these politicians and you will be fine. That is no environment for you. You have my blessing. From now on you will hear that sound. But don't visit these politicians anymore. Stay here, do your work, and enjoy that sound."

Laldhari jumped up, beaming with delight. "I got it, I got it!" he kept saying. "I can hear the flute again!" Baba was smiling and laughing. So was Laldhari. After that he kept the clothes in a locked box in his house and never again went to the politicians to ask for favours. I think one or two of his sons found employment shortly thereafter, but they did it on their own, without Laldhari's help.

1978

A Non-margi Touches Baba's Feet

SOON AFTER BABA'S release from prison, the margis decided to hold DMC in the four cosmopolitan cities: Calcutta, Delhi, Bombay, and Madras. Baba had been in jail for seven years, and for many of the margis this was their first chance to see him since his arrest; thus sentiments ran high and great numbers of margis attended the programs. During the flight to Calcutta it was announced that Baba would be given VIP treatment, and for some time thereafter, whenever Baba travelled, the government made this provision.

The atmosphere in Delhi was surcharged with spiritual energy. Baba stayed there for six days and gave many PCs. After the DMC, we went to the airport to catch our flight for Bombay and hundreds of margis came to see Baba off. It was a wonderful scene. The margis were sitting near Baba, enjoying his darshan and doing kirtan. Many were weeping, overcome by the spiritual vibrations. Among them was Raghuvir Prasad, Collector of Customs and Central Excise. It was well known in government circles that he never took a bribe—no one could influence him to compromise his ideals. Whenever Baba came to Delhi he used to pay for our tickets. Though it was ordinarily not allowed, Prasadji got permission from the airport authorities to accompany Baba onto the tarmac from where we were to board the plane. The margis came with him and many of them brought flowers and garlands. It was my duty to collect the garlands. There were so many of them I didn't know what to do. I ended up gathering together as many as I could hold for Baba to bless, then giving them to someone so I could take some more. This happened at least five or six times and each time more people arrived with garlands. Finally, when everyone had given their garlands, we did namaskar and boarded the plane.

It was Baba's custom to sit by the window. I would take the seat next to him, or if there were three seats and any margis were accompanying us, then I would sit on the aisle and give some margi the middle seat. This plane had only two seats on each side. After we boarded, the margis gathered outside Baba's window and Baba himself gave instructions that no airport staff should block the margis' view. The shouts of *Parama Pita Baba Ki* went on until the airline staff cleared the area so the flight could depart.

While all this was going on, one non-margi gentleman was watching the entire sequence. He was a managing director of Kirloskar, a renowned generator company; he was also a spiritually minded person. While he was walking in the airport he observed our gathering and it seemed to him that even though he was the president of several religious organizations—being a rich man and the director of such an important company, he was invited to serve on the board of many organizations—never in his life had he witnessed a gathering with such a strong spiritual vibration. He also boarded the flight to Bombay, and when he reached our row he stopped in front of Baba with folded hands and said, "Maharajji, if you would be so kind as to permit me, I would like to ask you one question." Baba motioned to me and said, "He is my secretary. He will be happy to answer any questions you might have." I told him I would be glad to talk to him but at that moment it was difficult since the other passengers were trying to get to their seats and the crew was asking people to move along. Before I could think of a solution, Baba suggested that if I wished, I could get up later and go talk to him. So I asked him to wait for me near the bathroom once the plane reached its cruising altitude and we were free to move about the cabin.

After we were airborne I saw that he was waiting for me, so I got up and went to talk to him. Without introducing himself he said, "Swamiji, I was watching what was happening at the airport and it aroused a great curiosity in my mind. Or rather, I should say a great desire to touch Maharajji's feet." Maharajji is a common form of respectful address in India for spiritual persons or highly respected persons. "Never in my life have I ever touched the feet of any spiritual leader or guru. Though I have been around many gurus, I never felt the desire to touch their feet, but this time I felt a force compelling me from inside—'why don't you touch his feet, why don't you go and touch his feet.' I felt that if I didn't touch his feet I would regret it for the rest of my life. But let me introduce myself. I am the managing director of Kirloskar. I am also the president of several organizations." Here he counted off the organizations by name. "I came to Delhi for a board meeting—all the directors were called—but I was forced to leave the meeting suddenly due to a family emergency. My wife called me today to tell me that my only son is very sick. He has been admitted to the hospital. As soon as she called I rushed to the airport to catch the first plane back to Bombay. But please don't tell this to Maharajji. I would not like him to think that I have an ulterior motive for wanting to touch his feet. I would never do such a thing."

At this moment they announced that everyone had to take their seats, so I told him that I would see what I could do and went back to sit beside Baba. By then the plane was passing through Rajasthan and Baba started talking about the history of Rajasthan, about the people, their dress, their habits, their cuisine, their language and religion. As the plane passed over Gujarat he did the same. But all this time I was thinking about this gentleman, though I knew I couldn't bring up the subject unless Baba asked. Then came the announcement that we were starting our final descent and would be on the ground in ten minutes. It was then that Baba asked me what the gentleman had been talking about.

"He wants to touch your feet, Baba, and do pranam. That was all he said."

Baba was silent for a few moments. Then he said, "He is a good man, a spiritual man. He has a strong desire, it is true. Whether or not he is allowed to touch my feet is for you to decide. You think it over. But that was not the question. Did he say anything else? Did he have any question?"

"No, Baba, he didn't say anything else."

"Nothing, nothing at all?"

"No, Baba."

"I think your memory is weak. Touch my big toe and you may be able to remember something more."

I was about to touch Baba's toe when Baba said, "Was he telling you about some family problem?"

"Yes, Baba, but he told me not to tell you."

"Even if you don't tell me, I already know, so you might as well go ahead and tell me."

So I told Baba that his wife had called him while he was in the middle of a meeting to tell him that his only son had been rushed to the hospital. I kept silent after this.

Baba nodded and said, "You should tell him that he has no need to worry. His son is fine now. Both he and his wife will come to meet him in the airport. They will be arriving within ten minutes. As far as touching my feet goes, you know the rules. But as I have told you, he is a good person with a spiritual bent of mind."

The plane landed, and as the passengers were deplaning I had a chance to exchange a few words with that gentleman. "I can arrange for you to touch Baba's feet after we get off the plane," I told him. "And don't worry about your son. Baba told me about him without my mentioning anything. He said that your son is fine and both he and your wife are waiting for you in the airport. Once Baba and I get down from the plane, I will signal you when it is okay to touch his feet. You should be ready. The scene will be much the same as you saw in Delhi. You will see many people doing sastaunga pranam in front of Baba. You should also do sastaunga pranam and then look to me for an indication that you can touch his feet."

When we came out of the plane many margis were waiting on the tarmac to receive Baba. They were crying and holding their garlands and singing kirtan. The devotional wave was even more palpable than it had been in Delhi. Baba was still physically week at this time. His weight was sixty-four kilos instead of the seventy-five it had been before his arrest, so the margis had gotten permission for his car to meet him at the plane. As soon as they saw Baba at the top of the steps they starting shouting *Parama Pita Baba Ki*, over and over again. Once his feet touched the ground they started crowding round him and doing sastaunga pranam. This man was also waiting there and he was so carried away by the spiritual wave that he couldn't control himself. Instead of waiting for my signal, he caught hold of Baba's feet with his hands and touched them with his forehead. He was sobbing like a baby, though he was approaching middle age. I told him to stop, that he should not touch Baba's feet. This way Baba could not scold me for neglecting my duty, for of course it was the rule that no margi could touch Baba's feet without his permission, what to speak of a non-margi. My duty was to tell him that he could not touch Baba's feet and I did my duty. But Baba said, "No, it is okay. You can allow him." After a few moments Baba said, "Get up, my boy, get up. Your wish has been fulfilled. Get up now." Baba tapped him on the shoulder but he was so overcome by his emotions that he was having trouble getting up. So Baba asked a couple of margis to help him up. He was weeping profusely and it took him a little while to become normal once they helped him to his feet.

After that we headed toward the terminal to get Baba's luggage. Many more margis were waiting inside the airport to see Baba, those who hadn't been allowed onto the tarmac. Before we went inside I told the man that he should go and meet his wife and son now; they were waiting for him inside. Baba told me to tell him where we would be staying and asked me to invite him to the program along with his family. So I gave him the address and he went inside to meet his wife and son, who were having him paged over the intercom. When he found them he told them that he had not been worried because he had met a saint on the plane who had told him that his son was okay. He asked them to wait for him and then he joined us once again to see Baba off. By this time we were packing Baba's luggage into the car. Shashi Rainjan, the president of Prout, had made the arrangements, and he accompanied us in the car to Altamount Road, where Baba was to stay.

The next day the man came with his wife and his son. He took initiation and he attended the DMC a few days later, on November 26. In the meantime he got another chance to meet Baba and he thanked him for having given him the chance to recognize him and for having thus changed his life. When we were departing from Bombay he brought a bag full of money to Baba and said, "Maharajji, I want to give you this as my *guru dakshina*." In India there is a tradition that after initiation the disciple will give an offering to the guru. However Baba told him, "Your acharya failed to tell you that this is not the system in Ananda Marga. You have already given yourself during your initiation, body, mind, and spirit. That is the real guru dakshina. But if you wish, you can give this to the regional secretary of this area for the social service projects he is managing. It will be of great service to the poor but it is not guru dakshina."

21 November 1978

Rajdeva Falls Asleep in Baba's Room

ONCE IN PATLIPUTRA Colony I sent Rajdeva into Baba's room to give Baba a massage before he retired for the night. That was Baba's usual habit. Around midnight or so he would ask me if there was someone I could send for massage. Baba would generally fall asleep while he was being massaged, and it was his standing instruction that the person should leave quietly once he was asleep. But this time, unaccountably, Rajdeva fell asleep himself. When Baba woke up at 3:15—that was his usual time to wake up and begin his practices; he used to keep a watch on the night table that would say "get up" in English, though he usually got up before the alarm sounded—he found Rajdeva asleep on the floor in front of his cot. Baba got up without disturbing him and came to me—I would always sleep in front of his door and I would wake up whenever I heard any sound inside the room. "Rajdeva is taking rest inside my room," Baba said quietly. "It is time for my meditation now. I am going to the bathroom. In the meantime, see that he has someplace comfortable to take rest." As soon as Baba went into the bathroom I woke him up. He was very repentant for having fallen asleep in Baba's room but I said, "No, Baba was not bothered at all." I arranged a place for him to sleep and then went back into Baba's room to spread his blanket for meditation. Normally I would spread his blanket if the door was not bolted and I heard him enter the bathroom in the early morning. Sometimes Baba would call me to spread the blanket. Afterward, Baba told me that Rajdeva was a very good person—and indeed he was a very staunch devotee—but in the future I should find someone for massage who would not fall asleep in his room. "If I am resting," he said, "they should do sastaunga and go out." Of course, nothing like that had ever happened before—or since.

1979

Baba Disciplines Shashi Rainjan

IN 1969 BABA asked Shashi Rainjan to resign from the central government to become the chairman of the Proutist Bloc of India. His
resignation was a blow to Indira Gandhi, and after that her attitude
toward Ananda Marga became increasingly hostile. Shashi took his
responsibilities very seriously, but in time, due to certain difficulties
in the family, he became less active than he had been. The dadas who
were working for Prout were aware of this and one of them complained
about him to Baba during a reporting session after Baba came out from
prison. This dada told Baba that he had not gone to Tripura when they
had asked him to, and that he was not supporting the work financially,
though he had the means to do so. Baba took the report very seriously.
We were in Delhi at the time and we had a flight to Calcutta the next
morning. That evening Baba told me to tell Shashi that he would not
be allowed to accompany him on the flight. It would give the workers
the wrong impression if he allowed him to travel with him after such a
bad report. Now it was Shashi Rainjan who generally made Baba's travel
arrangements—as a former MP he was able to arrange VIP seats even
when flights were fully booked—and most of the time he travelled with
us on the same flight. I knew this would come as a blow to him but I
wasn't prepared for how hard he would take it.

I called him to my room, which was just next to Baba's room, and
gave him the message, though I didn't say why Baba had made that
decision. He started weeping piteously and would not stop. Soon some
of the workers became so moved by his obvious anguish that they also
started weeping, and they began wondering aloud why Baba had given
him this punishment. Shashi spent most of the night in that condition,
though he knew why Baba had taken such an action. He told me that
he was having some difficulties in the family—several family members
were not margis—and he knew that he was not doing as much for the

organization as he could have been doing. Finally in the morning, before we were to leave for the airport, Baba asked me to tell Shashi that he could go with him. Shashi had been crying all night, but he had his ticket in his hand. Somehow he had been sure that Baba would not leave him behind.

When we got to the airport and sat in the VIP lounge with the margis, Shashi maintained his distance, still chastised by his punishment, but when he got on the plane I switched seats with him so that he could sit next to Baba. His eyes welling with tears, Shashi asked Baba never to give him such a terrible punishment again. "I never expected you could give me such a huge punishment, Baba," he said. "Never have I felt so much pain in my life. It was intolerable." By now he was crying openly. Baba patted him on the cheek and said, "I love you very much, Shashi, and I know how good you are, but there was something wrong in you that I had to remove. Now tell me, what do you have to do?"

"Baba, I don't know Bengali very well, but I am ready to go to Tripura. I can fly there tomorrow. And I promise that I will help the Prout department financially to the best of my capacity."

Then he bent down and kissed Baba's feet. Baba gave him his blessing and after that he was okay. It was a very peculiar scene, very surprising.

January 1979

Raghuvir Prasad

*D*URING THE EARLY days we did not have a place of our own in Delhi. The margis used to rent a guest house or a private house for Baba's visits, but when the CBI started ratcheting up the pressure against the organization it became increasingly difficult to find anyone willing to rent to us. Even if they said yes initially, the CBI would pressure them and threaten them until they became scared and cancelled the rental. For that reason the margis decided to book a room in the Ashoka Hotel for Baba's visit in January of 1979. But when we arrived at the entrance to the hotel, Baba became uncomfortable. "What is this place?" he asked. I said, "Baba, it is a hotel." By then, Prasadji, who was in the lead car, had gotten out and was standing beside Baba's window. "Baba," he said, "I have been trying to arrange a proper house for you but the CBI is making it nearly impossible for us to find a place. But I am still working on it. I hope to have a suitable place for you within a few hours. In the meantime, I have booked a room for you in this hotel so you won't be put to any inconvenience."

"Do you know, Raghuvir, that this hotel has the highest consumption of beef in all of India? I will not set foot within its doors."

Navin Joshi was also standing there. He is originally from Jaipur but he was living in Delhi and he had been helping Prasadji to find a place, running from one landlord to another in different respectable areas of the city. "Baba," he said, "My house is not very large but there are only three of us. We can move in with some friends and have it ready for you in one hour."

Baba was pleased with this arrangement, so we took him to Navin Joshi's house. In the meantime, Prasadji was moving heaven and earth to find a suitable place for Baba and the accompanying workers. He had found a landlord in Janakpuri who was willing to talk to him and after much discussion the landlord finally agreed. Initially he was as scared as all the other landlords but I saw with my own eyes how Prasadji infused him with courage. "My guru is being harassed by the CBI because he is against their exploitation and corruption," Prasadji told him. "He is a staunch moralist and they cannot abide this. But you should not worry. I am the Collector of Customs and Central Excise and I will make sure that no harm comes to you, no matter what happens. Neither I nor my guru will compromise with these immoral people, and if you have the courage to rent your house to us you will have his blessings and his grace. A great man will stay in your building and you and your family will be blessed for having helped him."

The man was so impressed, not only by Prasadji's words but by his courage and his confidence, that he agreed to rent to us. We shifted to that house in the morning, but later that day the CBI started pressurizing the landlord to cancel the agreement. Prasadji asked the landlord for the agents' names and immediately went to the court to file a complaint. After that the CBI stayed away and Baba's visit took place without any further complications.

When the emergency was declared, Prasadji was arrested by the CBI and was given slow poisoning. Even though his family was related to Indira Gandhi's, and his mother and Indira were close friends, he was not spared. He spent nearly two years behind bars. When the emergency was lifted and Gandhi was ousted from power, he was released from the prison but his health was severely compromised. Even then he continued his fight against injustice and corruption in the government. When Moraji Desai's son was caught smuggling gold into India, Desai, the then finance minister, and his government tried to pressure Prasadji into letting him off. They offered him a promotion and other perks and made some veiled threats should he not go along with them, but Prasadji defied them and put the finance minister's son behind bars. "I am an Ananda Margi," he told them. "Promote me or demote me, it doesn't matter. I will never compromise with an immoralist."

Prasadji left his body not long after this visit. Thereafter, whenever Baba came to Delhi, he would comment on how much he missed him. "You know," he would tell me, "whenever I come to Delhi I feel Raghuvir's absence." Baba always called him Raghuvir. "There is no one in Delhi who takes care of me the way he did. He did many things I cannot forget and he was fearless when it came to his principles. Even the government feared him."

January 1979

Putting Baba's Shoes on the Wrong Foot

EARLY IN 1979, we went to Meerut for three days, where we stayed in the house of Professor Tyagi. Meerut belongs to the state of U.P., and there is one community in U.P. called the Yat community. The Yats are a tall, strong people; they are strong-minded as well. Once they consider someone to be God no one can change their mind. One member from the Yat community had been initiated not long before our visit to Meerut. He had heard stories about Baba and had seen his picture, but he had yet to meet him, and he had conceived a strong desire to touch Baba's feet. During the three days that we were there he came every morning and evening to see Baba with this intention—to do pranam and touch his feet—but due to the throngs of devotees that always surrounded Baba he did not get the chance. Finally it was time for Baba to return to Delhi. I got everything ready, loaded the luggage into the car, and came to tell Baba that everything was ready for his departure.

"Are you sure?" he said. "Have you checked everything?"

"Yes, Baba, but if you want I can check again." So I checked the room and the bathroom again, and told Baba that everything was in order.

"Okay, if everything is ready then let us start."

I went outside and told the VSS to get ready. Whenever Baba left his room the atmosphere would instantly change. Everyone would be on alert. All eyes would be on Baba from the moment he appeared in the doorway to the moment he disappeared from sight. When he reached the outside door he asked if there was anyone there who could put on his shoes. This Yat fellow jumped forward like he had been shot out of a gun. He grabbed Baba's shoes before anyone else could react and started putting them on Baba's feet. But he was having some difficulty. The shoes were not fitting properly and he had to press Baba's feet to get them in the shoes. This ended up taking several minutes. When I saw the delay, I asked someone who he was and then told him that he was not permitted to be there. But just then he gave one last shove and the shoes went on. Then he did sastaunga pranam, stretching out on the ground in front of Baba. "Are you happy now, my boy?" Baba said. "Okay, now you can leave. Your desire has been satisfied."

We started moving toward the car through a corridor of margis who were chanting slogans and holding out garlands to put around Baba's neck. After eight or nine steps, Baba turned to me and said, "Ramananda, have you brought new shoes for me?"

"No, Baba," I said. "They are your old shoes. I checked them."

I looked down and saw that this man had put Baba's left shoe on the right foot and the right shoe on the left. In his devotional fervour to touch Baba's feet he had not realized what he was doing; that was why it had taken so much time. I called for a chair and when Baba sat down I put them on the correct feet.

February 1979

Puttuswami

*P*UTTUSWAMI WAS AN income tax commissioner in Bangalore. It was an important position but unfortunately rife with corruption. Before he became an Ananda Margi, Puttuswami, like most income tax commissioners, took advantage of his position in various ways, but once he took initiation he abandoned those unsavoury practices and began to adhere to the strict code of ethics that Baba taught. Soon he became a highly respected margi in his area and also the bhukti pradhan.

After Baba came out of prison he came to Calcutta along with Acharya Girijananda, who was then the local RS, to invite Baba to hold DMC in Bangalore. Baba agreed and we came to Bangalore in February and stayed in the house of H. B. Lal. Baba and I stayed on the first floor and the workers on the ground floor. Unfortunately, Puttuswami had been in a serious car accident a few days before the DMC. His leg was badly injured and for that reason he was unable to attend the program. When Baba asked for him, I told him what had happened.

"Do one thing, Ramananda," Baba said. "Since he can't come here, make arrangements so that I can visit him at his house. He is a good person. He organized my program here. I want to see him."

I arranged our schedule so that we could pay him a visit and then informed Puttuswami that we would be coming. When he heard this he started weeping. He could not believe that the Lord could be so gracious as to visit him at his home.

When we arrived at his house the front door was locked—his wife had locked it and forgotten where she had put the key. But someone went to the back door and was able to open the front door for Baba. When Puttuswami saw Baba enter the room in which he was convalescing, his joy was so great that he attempted to get up from the bed, though he was unable to do so. Baba came to his bedside and said, "When you could not come to the DMC I had no choice but to come here. How could I leave Bangalore without seeing you, knowing that you were weeping for me in this bed."

Baba sat in a chair beside the bed and Puttuswami's wife offered him a glass of coconut water. After drinking it he said, "This happened due to your samskara but you should not worry. In a short time the samskara will be finished and you will make a full recovery. You do not know the reason for your accident but you will come to know later on."

Puttuswami recovered soon afterward and thereafter he and his wife were regular visitors to Calcutta and Anandanagar, especially at the time of the biannual DMCs.

18 February 1979

Baba's Cousin Nanku

I HAD NOT MET Baba's cousin Nanku before Baba came out of jail but I had heard Baba mention his name once or twice. His full name was Ajit Vishvas but the family called him Nanku because he was born in 1921, the year of the non-cooperation movement. He was the assistant secretary of the Home and Political Wing for the Government of West Bengal. Not only was he Baba's cousin, the son of his maternal aunt, but he had also been Baba's close friend while they were growing up. They studied together in Calcutta when Baba went to Vidyasagar College, and after Baba returned to Jamalpur, Nanku used to visit him during his vacations. They would often go walking together in the hills.

When Baba came out of prison he expressed a desire to see Nanku, whom he hadn't seen for many years. At first we didn't have any luck tracking him down, but with Dr. Samar's help we were able to locate him in Calcutta and pass on Baba's message. Nanku sent a reply that he was very eager to see Baba but it would be difficult for him to get leave—at the time we were still in Patna. He said that he would come as soon as possible, but due to his job and other reasons he was unable to come.

Some months passed and on March 4, 1979, we moved to Calcutta, to a house that we purchased for Baba in a residential area called Lake Gardens. Once we were installed there, Baba again told me that he wanted to see Nanku. He was very emphatic this time. "I know the house," he said. "I have gone there many times. He lives in Rajarhat, on the first floor of a house on such-and-such street. Get your driver ready and I will guide him there."

One morning we got in the car and set out for Rajarhat. Baba guided the driver the entire way. "Now turn left at this street," he would tell him. "Now turn right." And so on. As it turned out, Nanku was still living in the same house that he had lived in when he and Baba were young. When we pulled up in front of the house, I sent someone to inquire if an Ajit Vishvas lived there. "Yes, he lives in this building, on the first floor," someone said, and this same person went up to see if he was in. When Nanku came downstairs and saw Baba, he let out an exclamation of surprise. "My word, is it really you?" They embraced and he took Baba up to his room, where they sat and chatted for a half an hour or an hour.

He was a fair complexioned man with a smiling nature. Though he was a year older than Baba, he was still a bachelor who led a very simple life. Baba invited him to Lake Gardens and thereafter he became a regular visitor.

1979

N. K. Mallik

D R. NARENDRA KUMAR Mallik and his wife were devoted margis who used to contribute regularly to various service projects, especially medical projects. They also donated some land in the Salt Lake area of Calcutta on which we built the RAWA recording studio— their son helps run the studio. They live in Bangao, a small town about one hundred kilometres from the Bangladesh border, in Twenty-four Paraganas District, about two hours by car from Calcutta. Dr. Narendra had his medical practice there, but he also kept a house in Calcutta. I used to consult him often on matters of Baba's health and he was always ready to rush to Calcutta on a moment's notice to attend to Baba. I remember Baba telling me that he was a very good devotee who loved him very much and that if there was ever any need to send him on field walk I should not hesitate.

Once he asked me to help him invite Baba to Bangao. He was not sure how best to approach Baba, so I told him that I would be on the lookout for the right opportunity. One morning, shortly thereafter, Baba came out of his room in Lake Gardens for breakfast but when he saw the food he started expressing his displeasure. "What is this? The same thing again? Doesn't this cook know that if you give someone the same food day after day he won't like it? Let us go for field walk. I won't take breakfast today."

Obviously, Baba was in a scolding mood. Sudhar, the cook, didn't dare say anything. I also scolded him for serving Baba the same thing every day but internally I was wondering if it were not in fact my mistake. I tried to appease Baba, telling him that I would get something new made, but he said there was no time for that and started heading down the stairs. He went first to the garden, as he usually did before going for morning field walk. He started his usual circuit, moving toward the Krishnaliila statue and asking about the condition of the different plants, whether they had been given manure, and so on, while I remained near the gate where the car was waiting to take him on walk. At this moment Narendra Kumar and his wife arrived by car with a hot pack of food that she had prepared for Baba's breakfast. When they saw me they told me that they had prepared a hot breakfast for Baba and asked if there was any chance that Baba might take it.

While I was talking to them somebody came to tell me that Baba was asking for me. By this time he had reached the lotus pond behind the house. I went to him and said, "Baba, your breakfast is ready."

"Really, so quickly?"

"Yes, Baba. Narendra Mallik's wife prepared it. She brought it in a hot pack for you. You should not go for your walk without eating something."

Baba smiled. "Yes, they were a little late in arriving; that is why I delayed my breakfast. She prepared it with so much love and affection, I couldn't disappoint her. Since I didn't want to waste even a single second of my time, I decided to come down and do my garden walk until they arrived."

Dr. Narendra and his wife were thrilled that Baba had agreed to take their food. When Baba finished his breakfast, he told me to tell them how tasty it was. Then he went into his room. I went to Narenda and told him to get ready. "Baba is in an excellent mood now," I said. "This is the perfect moment to invite him to Bangao." I sent him into Baba's room and Baba started inquiring about his family and other matters. He extended his invitation and Baba promised him that he would visit.

One week later, Baba told me that he wanted to go to Narendra's house. I telephoned him and asked him if he could be ready to receive Baba the next day. He assured me that everything would be ready and the next day we travelled by car to Bangao. Baba gave General Darshan for the margis and spent the night in Dr. Narendra's house. Nowadays he preserves the room Baba stayed in as a shrine, along with the things that Baba used while he was there.

1979

Mrs. Rathi Goes Abroad

ONCE BABA DECIDED that he would go abroad to visit the margis of other countries, he began to assemble a team to go with him. When Rathi's name was proposed, Baba readily approved it. Rathi used to take care of Baba's travel arrangements in Bengal and other parts of India, so it was only natural that he would accompany us overseas and help with the travel arrangements. It didn't occur to Rathi, however, to consider bringing his wife. When he told her that he had been approved to go, she became very sad. She didn't object or complain but she was clearly disappointed. She was also a devoted margi; while Rathi used to take care of Baba's travel arrangements and physical comforts, she would take care of Baba's food. But he was a businessman and didn't want to take on the extra expense of bringing his wife—businessmen are always thinking about how to save money. When we brought it to Baba's attention that Mrs. Rathi was unhappy because her husband was going so far away and she wasn't allowed to go, Baba mood turned serious. "It won't look good if he goes alone," he said. "Both are equally devoted. This is a spiritual journey. It will be better if both husband and wife go together. Call them. I want to talk to them." They came to see Baba and he told them that it would be better if they both went.

At first Mrs. Rathi was a little hesitant. "Baba, I don't know English," she said.

"That doesn't matter," Baba replied. "You understand the words yes and no, don't you?"

"Yes, Baba."

"If someone asks you—Do you want some food?—will you understand?"

"Yes, Baba."

"That's enough. You are going with a team; if you need to know anything else they will help you."

After that she became very happy. She began preparing Baba's favourite pickles and other items to take on the journey, and during the tour she took care of Baba's kitchen along with Didi Ananda Karuna.

April 1979

Baba in Holland

FROM GERMANY WE went to Holland, where we stayed for two days in the Rotterdam jagriti. One morning we went for field walk to a dyke—most of the city is below sea level and the dykes are necessary to hold back the sea. It was a scenic place, full of daffodils in bloom. There was a lawn on one side of the path where flamingos were walking, seemingly unafraid of us humans. They were walking in a group, some six or seven of them, as if they were also on field walk, while we were some twenty or twenty-five margis. At one point Baba stopped, which he rarely did on field walk, and asked us to be sure not to disturb the birds. "They are also walking," he said, "so let them walk. We will do our duty and we should let them do theirs."

While we were stopped, Baba asked the unit secretary to pick some daffodils. When he handed the flowers to Baba, Baba closed his eyes for a few moments and then handed them back. "Take these flowers and bring them to your mother," he said. "She is waiting for you. It is your choice but it is better if you go right away."

I learned afterward that his mother was in the hospital and that he hadn't had a chance to visit her that day because he was busy with Baba's program. When he arrived at his mother's room with the flowers he found that she was feeling much better, so much better that the doctors had decided to release her. He came to the jagriti in the evening and gave Baba the news.

23 May 1979

Baba in Spain

$\mathcal{A}$T THE END of May we travelled from Stockholm to Valencia. Karunananda had made arrangements for Baba to stay in an old Catholic monastery, a beautiful place in a small village outside the city. One of the priests who lived there was initiated and he had arranged everything—though he hadn't seen Baba yet, he was very sincere. The facilities were excellent but the other priests had an unfavourable reaction. They started whispering among themselves: "Who is this man? Why is he here?" At one point, one of them created a disturbance outside Baba's room. Karunananda explained the situation to me: though the other priests knew that Baba's visit had been arranged by one of their brothers, they were feeling uncomfortable, so he was working on arranging an alternate place for Baba to stay. By then Baba had already informed me that it was not a suitable place for him; he had sensed the problem as soon as we'd arrived. Karunananda made some calls and one local margi offered his house for Baba; other margis agreed to put up the rest of our team. Once everything was arranged, he informed me and I went into Baba's room and told him that we had found a better place to stay. Baba asked me to call the priest who had arranged the monastery for us.

When I ushered him into Baba's room, Baba was very gracious. "My boy," he said, "you have taken so much trouble for me. I cannot forget this, but for your convenience I would prefer to move to the house of someone who is willing to have me. Do you understand? If I stay here any longer it will only create further problems for you with your brother priests. But remember, whenever you find yourself in any difficulty, call me, whether in meditation or otherwise. I will always be with you."

When we were leaving the compound the priest came to Baba with folded hands and said, "Baba, I was so fortunate to have you at my place, even for such a short time. The other priests are opposing me but wherever I go I will work for your mission."

After we left the monastery, Karunananda took us on a tour of Valencia while the margis and workers were rushing to get the margi's house ready for Baba, buying new bedsheets and so on. We had a very nice program there and that priest attended. Later we heard from Divyalokeshananda that he is still involved with the mission. He was transferred to a church in some other city, and he still talks about Baba and cooperates with our workers.

29 May 1979

A Tale of Two PCs

*G*OPAL KRISHNANJI WAS a district court judge in Trichur who had been a devotee of Satya Sai Baba before coming in contact with Ananda Marga, After he met Baba, both he and his wife, Shanti Devi, became staunch margis. They used to attend all the DMCs in South India, as well as the annual DMCs in Anandanagar. When Gopal Krishnan had his PC, he asked Baba about the death penalty. "Baba, many cases come before me with overwhelming proof, and on some occasions I have been forced to give the death penalty, even though I didn't wish to. What is your opinion on this?"

"I am against the death penalty," Baba told him. "Even a diehard criminal should be given the scope to rectify himself."

"Then what should I do in such cases?"

"Before passing sentence, meditate for some time and take second lesson. Then contemplate the case and decide on a sentence. If you meditate and take your second lesson, then you will give the correct judgment. But you should never give capital punishment."

From then on, Gopal Krishnan followed Baba's advice. In certain cases he would give life imprisonment but never the death penalty.

It was after his PC that he and Shanti Didi came to Kolkata for the first time. I have seen him standing for hours outside of Baba's house, weeping while he waited for Baba to come out. He would always sit in the front for General Darshan and he would invariably be crying. Even when he accompanied Baba on field walk he would be weeping. It was astonishing to see, a district court judge weeping openly in front of all the margis. His wife was also of a similar mould.

When Baba came out of jail, Gopal Krishnan invited him to Trichur, and in July of 1979 we held a DMC program in Ernakulam, which is just nearby. We stayed in Gopal Krishnan's house and Shanti Didi took care of the arrangements for Baba's stay. That morning, when we arrived from field walk, Baba asked me if there was anyone waiting for PC. Three brothers were waiting. Of these, the third brother was a newly initiated margi, a simple man who knew neither English nor Hindi. He spoke only his mother tongue, Malayalam, the state language of Kerala. When Baba travelled in South India he would generally speak English with the people—not many people in South India were conversant in Hindi—and for this reason the local margis were concerned that this brother would not be able to understand Baba. With that in mind, they instructed him to do sastaunga pranam and then sit near Baba until he got a signal from Baba that he should leave the room.

The first two brothers' PCs were relatively short, though they knew English, and I assumed this brother's PC would be as well, since he would not be able to understand what Baba was saying. But his PC lasted for a full twenty minutes, much longer than the other PCs. Finally Baba pressed the call bell. I entered the room and found the man on the floor crying.

"He is a little abnormal just now," Baba said, "but he will be okay in a little while. Wait a few minutes and then have him taken out."

Once he was helped out, everyone wanted to know what had happened inside Baba's room. Had Baba beaten him? Had he understood anything Baba had said? When he told his story, everyone was flabbergasted. Baba had spent the entire twenty minutes talking to him in his mother tongue! First he had asked him to come and sit nearer. Then he had started telling him his whole family history, both his mother's and his father's sides. He narrated various disagreements between his father and his uncles, and described the various family problems that had become a cause of much suffering to him. Finally Baba narrated the mistakes he had committed and asked him if he were ready to take punishment. By this time, he was crying profusely. When he accepted his mistakes, Baba lifted his stick, as if he were going to deliver a huge blow, but he brought it down very softly and merely tapped his hands. This brother fell to the floor, overcome by feelings of ecstasy.

After he finished the story, he said, "He is more than my mother and my father. Never in my life have I felt so much affection as Baba has given me today. I will never forget it. He has promised me that from now on he will take care of all my problems. My only duty is to remember him."

15 July 1979

Baba Misses the Flight to Vishakapatnam

FROM ERNAKULAM WE flew to Madras—Chennai—where Baba held a DMC, and from there we were to go on to Vishakapatnam via Hyderabad. There was a small turnout in Chennai, maybe three or four hundred margis, unlike Bihar where thousands of margis would attend DMC, but the program was very intimate, very devotional. Some overseas margis attended and one of them drew Baba's praise when he participated in the tandava presentation. "Bravo, my boy," Baba told him. "You have done Rudra tandava." Then Baba explained about Rudra tandava, which is where the leg is lifted above the trikuti. It is very rarely seen and very good for a sadhaka's spiritual progress. Lord Shiva used to practice Rudra tandava, and his avadhutas as well. As far as I remember, that brother later became a dada.

Baba stayed in Shiva Bhagawan Goenka's house in Chennai, along with several workers, and it was his standing instruction during DMC tours that we should leave immediately after the conclusion of the program, so as not to task the local margis. The DMC talk was at night, as it usually was, and our flight was early the next morning at 6:30, so as per our normal routine we packed everything before going to bed.

That night, Baba asked me to knock on his door at four a.m., so that he would know it was time to get ready to leave for the airport. I put out the items he would need for his morning bath, packed the suitcases, and retired to take rest. At four in the morning I knocked three times on his door. I didn't hear any sound from inside the room so I thought that he must still be meditating. Not wanting to disturb him, I sent a couple of people to load the things in the car and then I knocked again after fifteen minutes. Again there was no reply. I was a little worried now about the time so I knocked again after another five or six minutes. This time Baba answered. "I heard you the first time," he said. "I will be ready at the right time." He didn't sound annoyed, just firm. So I sat to do some more meditation while I waited for Baba to come out.

When Baba finally came out it was already six o'clock. Even then he was not in a hurry. He chatted for a few minutes with the margis and made a couple of last-minute preparations. By then it was much too late to catch the plane, and I told him so.

"We must reach today," Baba said. "The margis have organized a program for me."

"Then we will have to travel by car, Baba. The plane has already left."

"Then don't delay. Arrange a car. The margis of Vishakapatnam are waiting for me."

I went to talk to Shiva Bhagawan. He arranged two cars for us and we got them ready as quickly as possible. By road it takes at least nine to ten hours to reach Vishakapatnam. Some of the roads are good but some are not. Shiva Bhagawan did not want to trust Baba to his driver so he decided to drive Baba's car himself. I was in the back with Baba; Bharat Goenka and Shiva Bhagawan were in the front.

In our hurry to leave, Shiva Bhagawan forgot to fill up the tank. Before we had gone fifty miles, the gas gauge had reached empty and unfortunately there were only diesel pumps on the road between Chennai and Vijaywara, a distance of some three hundred kilometres. When the gas gauge reached empty Shiva Bhagawan started panicking. He kept turning around to look at me—he avoided looking at Baba—whispering that we were going to run out of gas at any moment. Finally he stopped at one station but they only had diesel. Baba got impatient. "Why are you wasting our time stopping here?" he asked. Shiva Bhagawan, with tears in his eyes, admitted to Baba that we were about to run out of petrol. "I'm sorry, Baba, but we won't be able to take you all the way."

"Just drive," Baba ordered. "Don't waste time stopping at any more pumps. We have to reach as quickly as possible."

So we started driving again with the gas gauge on empty, and we didn't stop until we reached Cardoon, the first place on that route that had a petrol pump. It was over two hundred kilometres away and we made it there on an empty tank.

From there we continued on to Vijaywara, where we were hoping to catch the same flight, since the plane was to stop in Hyderabad for an extended layover before going on to Vijaywara and from there to Vizag—Vishakapatnam. But when we arrived at the airport in Vijaywara we got the news that the plane had not arrived—the flight had been cancelled.

Shortly thereafter, at Shiva Bhagawan's office in Vijaywara, we learned
that the plane had crashed in Hyderabad. The wing on the side where
we had our assigned seats had hit the ground while landing and that side
of the plane had suffered heavy damage. No passengers died but some
were injured and all had to stay over in Hyderabad until the next day.

From Vijaywara we telephoned Vishakapatnam and informed the
margis that Baba would be arriving by car. Baba asked me to convey a
message to them. "Tell them that I have given my word that I will arrive
today and I will keep my word. They should not be disheartened or think
that I won't come. I will be there as promised." I remember that on the
road from Vijaywara to Vishakapatnam Baba dozed off in the back seat
with his head resting on my shoulders. That would happen sometimes
on long road trips. His head would lean against me when he took rest
and sometimes my head would lean against him.

We lost our way near Vishakapatnam and got even further delayed
but we finally made it there about three a.m. The margis were still awake
and waiting for us. I brought Baba to his room and asked him what he
needed. "Nothing," he said. "First I want to meet my children. They
have been waiting for me all this time." Baba made a quick trip to the
bathroom and then went right to the dais to sit with the margis for a
few minutes. Later that morning he gave General Darshan and in the
evening, DMC.

17 July 1979

Ambareshvar Vanik

*B*HUVANESHVAR IS THE state capital of Orissa. The margis there are very devoted—fanatic, I should say—but they are also rather poor. For some time they had wanted to invite Baba to hold a DMC in their place but the local dadas were not very enthused because they knew they would ultimately be held responsible for raising the money for the program, a considerable expense. Nevertheless, Baba accepted their invitation and the margis were somehow able to raise the money; we went there in July, after the DMC in Vishakapatnam.

One margi of Bhuvaneshvar, Ambareshvar Vanik, had been the head-master of a high school but he had since retired and moved back to his native village, which was a long way from the city. In the early days he used to see Baba frequently and attend all the organizational programs but since retiring to his village he wasn't able to have such frequent con-tact with the organization. When he heard that Baba would be coming to Bhuvaneshvar for DMC, however, he was determined to attend the program at any cost. He made the long walk from his village to the nearest bus stand and then journeyed by bus to the capital. On the way it occurred to him that it was unlikely that anyone would think to give Baba *muri bhaja*, a simple snack of roasted puffed rice that was a specialty of that area. They would be serving him many fine foods, he thought, but he doubted they would think of serving him muri bhaja. Yet he knew that Baba liked muri bhaja very much and he was convinced that if he prepared it himself then Baba would be sure to take it.

Thus, on the morning after the DMC, he prepared a special batch of roasted muri and brought it to the house where Baba was staying. Baba was sitting for breakfast when he arrived. As soon as Baba sat at the table, he asked us if we had prepared any salty item for him. "I want to vary the taste," he said. "It would be nice to have something salty." But we had not prepared any salty item that morning and there was insufficient time to do so—it was time for him to go on field walk. But Ambareshvar Vanik had just arrived and he was asking if Baba needed anything. We told him that Baba was asking for some salty item but that there wasn't time to prepare anything for him. "Don't say no to Baba," he said. "I have brought some fresh muri bhaja for him."

We sent him into Baba's room and he served Baba the muri bhaja. After Baba had eaten some, he said, "You know, Ambareshvar, I couldn't leave Bhuvaneshvar without eating some of your special muri bhaja. It's so tasty. I don't think I have ever had such good muri. I was waiting especially for you, but not just because of the muri. It is your love and devotion that compelled me to wait." Baba patted him on the cheek and Ambareshvar was as happy as a man could be.

20 July 1979

Taiwan

*W*HEN WE WENT to the Philippines, Marcos was president. The Vatican pressured him not to allow our visit—the Philippines is a highly Christian country—and as a result we were deported from there. While we were being deported, Baba talked about Marcos and told us the secret reasons behind the deportation. He told us that Marcos did it under duress, but that would not save him from the negative consequences of his actions. He should have faced up to the Vatican, Baba said, rather than succumb to their pressure.

From there we went to Bangkok. The immigration authorities did not want to let us enter without a security deposit, so Dada Abhidevananda offered to use his gold card as security for myself and Baba, but Baba would not enter under those conditions. Either the entire entourage entered or none of us. After some negotiation they allowed our entire team to pass. We went to Shyam Bang's house, where we had stayed before the deportation. While we were there, a message came from Rameshananda, the sectorial secretary of Hong Kong Sector, that the Taiwanese government was ready to receive Baba as a special guest. When we got the news, Baba said, "Just see the contrast. One country is deporting me and the other is giving me VIP treatment."

Baba accepted the invitation and we soon left for Taiwan. When we arrived at the airport, several government officials met us with folded hands. "Mr. Sarkar," they said, "my government has given us the honour of welcoming you to Taiwan. You are our special guest. We hope that you will be quite comfortable here and that you will enjoy your stay in our country. We will try to provide as best we can for your comfort. We have reserved fourteen rooms in one of our best hotels for you, one for each member of your entourage."

While this was going on, Om Prakash, an Italian margi married to a Japanese sister, was standing nearby. He earned his living as the manager of a big international hotel, and when he heard about the government arrangements he started weeping—he had vacated some eight or nine rooms in his hotel for our entourage and he had prepared his own house for Baba and myself to stay. He told this to the officials and a discussion ensued. In the meantime, he was praying that Baba would stay in his house.

Finally Baba himself resolved the matter. He told the officials in a gracious manner, "I accept the hospitality and the honours bestowed upon me by the government of Taiwan, but I would prefer to stay with my small child Om Prakash."

After that Om Prakash was all smiles. The government cars took Baba to his house and Baba stayed there for nineteen days. All the PCs that Baba conducted in Taiwan took place in his house, more than seventy in all. All those who had PC had tears in their eyes when they came out of Baba's room. They would sit for sadhana afterward with the tears rolling down their cheeks and I assumed that Baba had punished them. But when the PCs were over, Baba specifically told me to ask those who had been given PC if he had beaten them or given them punishment. They came and Sanjay translated. "Please tell me why you were crying when you came out of Baba's room after personal contact," I asked. "Did Baba give you punishment?"

"No punishment," they said. "Baba showered us with love and affection and he spoke some words to us in Chinese. That is why we were crying."

Later Baba told me that he had sometimes used his stick to punish certain disciples in Europe and other places, but not in Taiwan. There was no need to, he said, because they were very pure and very devoted.

At that time Taiwan was a relatively poor country that had no diplomatic ties to India. After Baba's visit the country became wealthy.

August 1979

Moti's PC

*I*NDRAVASHISHTA WAS THE son of Didi Ananda Bharati. His daughter
Reshama was married to an Indian margi named Moti who was
living and working in Hong Kong. Reshama was a very strict margi,
very good in sadhana, but her husband had a number of bad habits. She
tried to get him to change and to some extent she was successful—he
had been a chain smoker and under her influence he gradually gave up
smoking—but he still had many defects. Finally, she thought that the
best solution was to have Baba punish him. Throughout her life she had
seen how Baba had rectified even the most inveterate sinners, and she
wanted Moti to experience the healing balm of Baba's stick. When she
heard that Baba would be coming to Taiwan she began insisting that
they attend the program.

"It will be a perfect opportunity for you to get PC," she told him.

"We can see Baba when we go to India," he countered.

"Taiwan is much more convenient," she said. "It is only a short flight
and whenever we go to India we have to spend so much time visiting
our relations that we rarely have a chance to see Baba."

After going back and forth for some time Moti finally gave in. When
they arrived in Taiwan, Reshama came to me and said, "I have brought
Moti here for PC and he has agreed, but I want to ask one favour of you.
Please tell Baba that he should be beaten very severely."

As you can imagine, I was quite surprised. "Whether Baba beats
someone or not is his choice," I told her. Moti was equally surprised—he
was standing close enough to overhear what his wife was saying. He was
already scared about getting PC—he had heard many stories about how
Baba would punish his disciples—and hearing his wife's request made
him all the more anxious. As a result he started avoiding the PC line.

On the second day Reshama brought him to me and said, "Dada, the
main reason we came here was for Moti to get PC. It will be good for

him, and he promised also, but he is trying to change his stand. Please talk to him."

So I told him what a precious opportunity it was and after that he agreed to put his name on the list.

When it came time for Moti's PC, I told Baba that Didi Ananda Bharati's granddaughter was here and that she had brought her husband for PC. I didn't mention anything about the beating, however, because I knew that Baba would have jumped on me. Then I ushered him into Baba's room and shut the door. Once he was inside he did sastaunga pranam and went and stood in one corner of the room, as far away from Baba as possible.

"My boy, why are you standing in the corner?" Baba said. "Come here and sit in front of me."

"Baba, I don't want to get beaten," Moti answered. "Please promise that you won't beat me."

"Whether I beat you are not is my concern. Now come and sit down."

After much persuasion, Baba convinced him to sit in front of his cot. He asked him about his acharya, his sadhana, how many lessons he had, and so on, and then started enumerating all his bad habits. Moti readily admitted that it was all true.

"You have committed so many mistakes," Baba said. "You deserve to be severely punished, but you have admitted your mistakes."

"Yes, Baba, I am guilty of everything you say, but please don't beat me. I don't think I can take it. Even my parents never beat me."

"I am more than your parents. It is my responsibility to see to it that you become a good person and an asset to the society, and for this to happen punishment is a necessity."

Moti started crying. Actually Baba had not given punishment to anyone in Taiwan but he didn't know this, since the sadhakas had not disclosed their experiences.

"Should I punish you?" Baba asked.

Moti gathered his courage and said, "Baba, it is your choice. I have accepted my mistakes and I will accept whatever punishment you decide to give me."

"Stand up."

Moti stood up and Baba pulled his stick from under the pillow. "Stretch out your hand."

Moti did as Baba asked and Baba tapped him on the hand with his stick. In a conspiratorial voice he said, "Okay, now you have been punished, but don't tell your wife that I only tapped you on the hand. Just tell her that Baba punished you. She brought you here because she wanted me to punish you, but it is only because she wants you to become a good husband and an ideal man. She is a good sadhaka and her intentions were good. You have some defects and she wanted me to remove those defects."

After his PC Moti was laughing. He told me what had happened but asked me not to tell his wife. After the last PC, Baba asked me what Moti had said. "Did he accept that I punished him?" he asked.

"Yes, Baba."

When Baba came out for field walk, Moti and Reshama were waiting near the car. Baba stopped just in front of them and said, "How are you, my boy?"

"Baba, your punishment has removed all my sins," Moti replied. When she heard this, Reshama became very happy.

August 1979

Haifa

WHEN BABA ARRIVED in Haifa, many students from Haifa university came out to protest his use of the swastika in our pratik. One margi brother, Arun, was also a well-known student. He explained to them the true origin of the swastika and why Baba used it in the pratik, and they were so impressed by his talk that some twenty students took initiation and ended up attending the DMC.

Arun had a great talent for poetic and musical composition; he also played guitar very well. He had composed some devotional songs for Baba and he was hoping to get a chance to sing one of them in Baba's presence but the opportunity never materialized. When we went to the airport on the day of our departure, we found that our flight to Copenhagen was delayed for one hour. About twenty-five margis had come with us to see Baba off and Arun had been given security duty. During the delay, Dada Dharmavedananda, who was in charge of security, told Baba what a good job Arun had done as a volunteer. He also mentioned that he had composed some songs for him. "Very good," Baba said. "Then let him sing one song. I think you have composed this song in Hebrew?"

"Yes, Baba."

"Good. I will only understand a little, but you will all understand."

The song was very beautiful and the atmosphere was so charged with spiritual vibrations that everyone started weeping. To everyone's amazement, Baba started translating the ideas of the song into English. Finally Baba said, "This boy has composed this song for my departure, but I am not departing, because I am always with you. How can I leave? My boy, I think you are happy now?"

"Yes, Baba."

15 September 1979

Istanbul

FROM HAIFA WE flew to Istanbul on Turkish Airlines. One of the margis in Istanbul was a Muslim lady by the name of Khatuna Banu Begum. She was from an upper-class family, a princely family, and was one of the people who had helped to arrange the program. She had a very fine garden and every day she would ask her gardener to prepare a bouquet of roses for Baba—they are very fond of roses in Turkey. Each day she would approach Didi Ananda Karuna and request permission to give her bouquet directly to Baba but Didi would not allow it. She told her that she could give her bouquet to the dadas and they would give it to Baba. On the last day she showed up with a beautiful garland as well as the bouquet of roses, but when Didi asked her to give them to the dadas she refused. She was adamant that she would give them directly to Baba and to no one else. That morning, when leaving the house, she had talked with Baba in her mind. If he truly knew her heart and mind, she told him, then he would accept those flowers directly from her.

We were leaving for the airport that morning, from where we were to take a flight to Iceland. I got the car ready, packed the luggage in the trunk, and accompanied Baba to the car. There were several other cars as well, with the dadas, the security people, and some margis. In the meantime, Khatuna was standing near the gate with her bouquet and her garland. She had her eyes closed and was praying to Baba to accept the flowers from her. I gave the signal and the cars started moving out the open gate, first Baba's car and then the others following close behind. Suddenly, when we had gone some ten to fifteen meters past the gate, Baba asked me to tell the driver to stop. At Baba's request I asked the driver to start backing up the car into the compound. I signalled to the cars behind us and they also started backing up. I was sure I hadn't left anything behind so I thought that perhaps Baba needed to use the bathroom, but when our car was right in front of Khatuna, Baba told me to stop the car and asked me to roll down his window. Baba was sitting on the right side and she was also on that same side. Baba called her up to the window and said, "Mother, I believe you wanted to give this garland and bouquet directly to me? I have come back to accept them from you." Baba took the flowers from her hand, blessed them, and then gave them back to her. "Take these and keep them in your room," he said. "Are you happy now? Very good. And from now on your name is not Khatuna Banu Begum. From now on your name is Liila." Baba gave her his namaskar and we started once again for the airport.

After we came back from the world tour I found a six page letter from Liila waiting for me. In it she narrated the whole story: how she had told Baba in her mind that morning that if he were really God he would accept the flowers directly from her; how after Baba left she had gone into trance for half an hour, with no idea of where she was.

September 1979

Jamaica

*T*HE INDIAN GOVERNMENT was not content with harassing us inside India. They also put pressure on Interpol to harass us when we went abroad. From Taipei we were supposed to fly to Hong Kong and from there to San Francisco, where the American margis were waiting to receive Baba. But when we boarded our connection in Hong Kong, on American Airlines, the immigration police entered the plane and started looking for a Dr. Sarkar. Dr. Pathak stood up and told them that there was no Dr. Sarkar on the flight but that he was Dr. Pathak. "They have mistaken P. R. Sarkar for Dr. Sarkar," Baba told him. "Go and find out what they want." Dr. Pathak went to talk to them and we learned that they had received a message from the States that Baba's visa had been denied; thus they were required to take us off the plane.

Before we left India, Baba had given me secret instructions to always keep two tickets to India in reserve during the tour in case we ran into any difficulty entering certain countries. So I had two extra tickets back to Delhi, one for me and one for Baba, and there was a flight leaving Hong Kong for Delhi in a few hours. The other members of our team were able to change their tickets and they flew with us on the same flight. Once we reached there, Baba ask us to consult with the sectorial secretaries of Cairo, New York, and Berlin sectors, to see if there was any possibility for us to visit their sectors, with the stipulation that we should first try to arrange a program for Cairo sector.

At that time Sudhiirananda was posted in Istanbul as the SS. We talked to him and also consulted Dada Abhidevananda and other workers, and we decided to add both Israel and Istanbul to the program. But our biggest problem was how to secure the visa for Israel. This was where Peshawari Lal came into the picture. At the time he was Collector of Customs and Excise in Bombay and a good friend of Israel's commercial mission in that city. He came to Delhi to see Baba and promised that he would get him a visa for Israel in a single day with the help of his connections. In the meantime we got word that Britain, Australia, and Canada, in addition to the U.S., Italy, and the Philippines, were not going to allow Baba to enter. When he heard the news, Baba said, "If any country does not want me to be their guest then I don't want to set foot on their soil. At the same time I don't want my children to be deprived of the opportunity of meeting me. We should find a way to hold DMC in New York Sector, just so long as I don't set foot in the U.S." Different possibilities were then bandied about and finally, after consulting with Dada Yatishvarananda, the SS of New York Sector, we settled on Jamaica. Our program then became Haifa, Istanbul, Frankfurt, Denmark, Sweden, Norway, Iceland, Jamaica, and finally Venezuela.

Among the margis who had gathered in San Francisco to receive Baba was a Jamaican margi by the name of Brigadesh, and his wife. He was a stout man of dark complexion and relatively well-off. Both he and his wife were good devotees, though neither of them had seen Baba yet, and like everyone else in New York Sector, they were sorely disappointed when they got the news that the US State Department had denied Baba permission to enter the country. When they got the news that Baba would be coming to Jamaica, however, they promptly offered their house for Baba's stay. Their children were grown and they were happy to move out of their house while Baba was there. We flew from Iceland to Jamaica, changing planes in London, and due to Brigadesh's contacts in the government everything went smoothly. Our stay there was very comfortable. He took care of our lodging, our food, and all other conveniences. "Whatever you need," he told us, "just tell me and I will arrange it for you." He was also Baba's driver while we were there. Each day he took us to see the various interesting sites of that place and during those field walks Baba told many stories about the history of Kingston and Jamaica, about its people, its flora and fauna, and so on. Most of the American margis came there to see Baba and there was no problem whatsoever for their stay.

Since there were so many margis, Baba did not have time to give PC to everyone. For that reason, he restricted PC to local fulltimers and wholetimer candidates. At least seven or eight brothers and sisters went to training after that, several from Jamaica itself. Just before we left, Baba met with Brigadesh and his wife and thanked them for their generosity. They gave Baba some gifts that are now in the museum, and

Baba inspired them to be an ideal couple and to do great work for the human society.

September 1979

From Jamaica to Caracas

F ROM JAMAICA WE took a chartered flight to Caracas. This was in late September. It was a small plane, maybe thirteen or fourteen seats, and the flight was full. Before the doors were closed Baba asked me if everyone had come. I told Baba that everyone was on the plane but he said, "No, I think someone is still outside. Go and check." So I checked and saw that Vishvamitra was outside. He had brought his belongings and was hoping to get on the plane but he was not on the list and there was no room. I told this to Baba but he said, "Can't we accommodate him? If the pilot agrees I think we should be able to fit one more person on the plane." Baba was talking to me but the pilot was standing nearby and he could hear what Baba was saying. Baba was talking so nicely that the pilot was charmed. Vishvamitra joined the conversation and after a few minutes the pilot agreed to find room for him. Vishvamitra brought his belongings and he had a joyous journey. In Caracas he was always with Baba and if there was some difference of opinion among the workers he would solve it. In fact, Baba told me that if any such difference of opinion arose I should take the help of Vishvamitra and Dr. Pathak to diffuse the situation.

24 September 1979

Baba Refuses to Eat

*T*HERE WAS A DMC in Nagpur in October 1979. Nagpur is a city in Maharashtra. At the time it was considered the second city in Maharashtra but it has since been supplanted by Pune. Bombay, of course, is the first city. The DMC discourse was a little longer than usual, and it was late when Baba exited the pandal for the guesthouse that had been arranged for his stay. Those margis who had been selected to cook for him were waiting there with his food, some sumptuous local dishes. Baba went into his room to change his dress, and when he opened the door one margi was holding a basin of lukewarm water and a towel for him to wash his hands, while a couple of margi sisters were setting the table and bringing his food. Suddenly Baba shocked everyone by saying that he wouldn't take food from this place. He went back into his room and shut the door. I was in the bathroom at that moment, taking half-bath, because when Baba takes his food I also take mine. When I came out of the bathroom everyone was crying. They asked me what they had done wrong. Why had Baba done this? So I went and knocked on Baba's door three times. After a few moments he opened the door and I requested him to take his meal.

"No, I won't eat now," Baba said. "It is too late. You are also responsible for this. You didn't advise me while I was on the dais that it was getting late." Baba turned around and went to his cot and repeated that he wouldn't eat. The door was still open. I was holding the door and the margis were able to see the whole drama through the open doorway.

"Baba, you have to eat," I said. "Tomorrow is fasting. It is ekadashi." Baba was very strict with fasting. He used to fast four times a month without water: both ekadashis, the new moon, and the full moon.

"No, it is too late now," he repeated. "You should have advised me that it was getting late."

"Yes, Baba, you are quite correct. It is my mistake. Give me any punishment you like, but I don't want you to go without food. Tomorrow is fasting. You should eat something."

"I said no. I won't eat."

Now it so happened that one margi doctor from Betiah, Khublalji, had come to Calcutta not long before and prescribed some homoeopathic medicine for Baba's piles. Baba had promised him that he would take the medicine every day after dinner. The doctor had given me the medicine and I would give it to Baba every evening after his meal. I knew this would give me some leverage so I reminded Baba that he had promised to take this medicine after dinner. Still Baba resisted. "Not today," he said. "Today I won't take it."

But I pressed my point. "Baba, you gave Khublalji your word that you would take it and you cannot take it on an empty stomach, so you will have to eat. I have accepted my mistake and asked for punishment, and in the future I promise that I will advise you if the program is running late. But now you need to eat so you can take your medicine."

This time Baba kept mum. When a person keeps mum it means that they accept your arguments, even if they don't say so. I went to the cot, put my hand under Baba's armpit and lifted him to his feet. He was very light then because he had lost more than ten kilos while he was in the prison. Baba didn't object. He was smiling when I brought him to the dining table. So were the margis who had watched the entire scene through the open doorway. I asked them to serve Baba his food and he ate very happily and chatted with them as they served him.

These are the dramas that Baba creates. Sometimes he behaves just like a child. Sometimes he will scold you and then he will shower you with affection the very next moment. He will laugh with you and at the same time he will get angry with somebody else who is there. But there is always a reason for everything Baba does. You have to be alert for the lesson. As Baba was eating he asked if everything was all right in the kitchen. I caught the hint and made some inquiries, and I found out that there had been a non-margi in the kitchen who had helped in the preparation of the food. This might have been the reason why Baba staged this particular drama, though I'm sure it was also to teach me to be more careful with his time.

16 October 1979

Jamalpur

*D*URING THE FALL 1979 DMC tour in India we travelled by chartered flight to some twelve or thirteen places, spending two or three days in each place. After the Anandanagar DMC in late October, we flew from Bokaro to Jamalpur, the first time Baba had been back to Jamalpur since the end of 1966. At first, we were not sure that we would be able to fly directly to Jamalpur itself because Jamalpur did not have an airport. There was a landing strip, however, left over from the British days, and eventually the pilot got confirmation that a four-seater would be able to land there. So we took off from Bokaro with Shashi Rainjan and the pilot in the front, and Baba and myself in the back. Once we were airborne Baba asked some questions about the flight—what route we were taking, how long the flight would take, and so on—but he didn't converse directly with the pilot. He asked Shashi Rainjan and Shashi asked the pilot for the information. Before we landed Baba gave me some special instructions:

"Ramananda, in Jamalpur you should not be so strict with the margis. In other places you have to be strict, as per the rules, but in Jamalpur you will have to break the rules. This is my childhood place. Many of the Jamalpur margis have been my friends since I was a young boy. So if they crowd round me don't restrain them. Tell the security people that they should do the same. Whoever comes to me should be allowed to come. If the crowd gets unruly you can try to pacify them but you must not be rough or harsh with them. The security people have to do their duty, I know, but you should make sure they understand that the margis of Jamalpur are allowed to come to me freely, with no unnecessary restrictions."

When we landed, a large crowd of margis, several hundred strong, was waiting for the plane. Some of them had brought a pot of pure cow's milk and as soon as Baba got down from the plane they started washing his feet with the milk. Ordinarily I wouldn't have allowed such a thing, certainly not without Baba's permission, but I remembered his instructions and didn't say anything. They were in such a devotional mood that they didn't even give Baba sufficient time to remove his shoes. The milk splashed on his shoes and splattered his shirt and dhoti. But Baba didn't seem to mind. He was all smiles and the margis were intoxicated by his presence. While they were washing his feet with the milk—they finally removed his shoes—he turned to me and said, "Ramananda, do you know why they are washing my feet with milk? In the purity of their hearts and minds they believe I am Shiva. In the villages of this area the people go to the temple and pour milk over the Shiva linga. They believe that by doing this their samskaras are burned and thus they are purified. It is a local tradition."

When they were done, Baba said to them, "Are you all happy now that I have come to meet you? I promised you I would come and I have kept my promise."

So long as we were in Jamalpur, the atmosphere was completely relaxed. There were many touching incidents that took place there. I don't recollect them very well but I will never forget how devoted the margis of Jamalpur were.

24 October 1979

Gadopur

SOMETIMES BABA WOULD ask us to consult the margis in a certain place to see if it would be feasible to hold DMC there, but mostly the margis would come to Baba and request him to visit. He would then refer them to the dharma prachar secretary, whose duty it was to see if such a program would be feasible or not. Occasionally, however, the margis from a particular place would directly approach the DPS and he would bring the request to Baba. The margis from Muzaffarpur took this approach. They went to the DPS and he brought the application to Baba, but Baba's reaction was anything but favourable. "There are fourteen acharyas living in Muzaffarpur," he said, "but they don't do any work. They are good people, I know, but organizationally speaking, they are good for nothing. They sit there all day long and chew betel and spit it out. So I reject this application."

We conveyed Baba's decision to them but they decided to play a different game. They asked Dada Chandranath to put their request to Baba, thinking that dada's close relationship with Baba would be enough to sway the decision in their favour. At the time we were in Patna, in Baba's house in Patliputra Colony, which was only an hour by car from Chandranath's farm in Gadopur. Dada came to Patna at the margi's request, but when he learned from the DPS that Baba had rejected the margi's application, he came to talk to me. It was nearly time for Baba's breakfast and as usual I was sitting outside Baba's room. After discussing the matter for a few minutes, I told him that though Baba had rejected the application in my presence I would arrange for him to discuss the matter personally with him. Just then Baba rang the call bell for breakfast. In those days in Patna, during Baba's recuperation period, I would keep three people nearby to help serve Baba his breakfast: Ram Rup, Raj Mohan, and Braj Bihari. One would bring Baba his breakfast, another a basin of water, and the third a towel. When I sent them into

Baba's room, Baba asked me if any other margis had come. "Yes, Baba," I said. "Chandranathji is here."

"Chandranathji? Why has he come?"

"Baba, first eat your breakfast. When you are finished I will send him in."

Once Baba finished eating, I sent Chandranathji to him. He did prostration and Baba patted him on the cheek and asked him how he was.

"Baba, I am fine, by your grace. But I have come with a request."

"I don't have much time now. Better you come with me on field walk. We can talk then."

As usual, Baba was busy with so many engagements—PCs, organizational meetings, and so on. So Chandranathji went in the car with Baba, and when they came back I started sending people into Baba's room for PC. While Baba was giving PC Chandranathji came to talk to me.

"Dada, I have discussed the matter with Baba. It took much persuasion but he has agreed to hold a DMC in Muzaffarpur, as long as I take full responsibility for the program. He made a point of saying that he is agreeing to my request, not to that of the Muzaffarpur acharyas. I hadn't known how unhappy he was with them. Anyhow, since Baba has agreed, I will go and talk to DPS."

After PC was over, Baba called myself and DPS into his room. "I have discussed the question of the Muzaffarpur DMC with Chandranath," he said, "and I have agreed to his request. This is a sentimental issue; he is very attached to me and I am also very attached to him, so I cannot say no to him. You can fix the dates and announce the program, but actually the DMC will not be in Muzaffarpur. Chandranathji has offered me his place in Gadopur for the DMC and I have agreed. Since Gadopur is part of Muzaffarpur District, it will count as the Muzaffarpur DMC but it won't be in Muzaffarpur city. Don't tell anyone this. I will disclose it at the appropriate time."

The appropriate time came about a week before the DMC, when Baba was passing through Muzaffarpur. He called those acharyas and started scolding them right and left. It was quite a drama. When he was done, he said, "In spite of your failings I will still go ahead and hold the DMC but it will not be in Muzaffarpur. It will be in Gadopur. Chandranathji, are you willing? Will you have enough time to make the preparations?"

"Yes, Baba. Don't worry, I will take care of everything."

Though it was very short notice, the arrangements in Gadopur were first class. I don't know if I ever attended such a well-arranged DMC in my entire life. Chandranathji had a simple house, but it was so neat and clean and well decorated. Baba's room was wonderful, as was mine. The kitchen was also tip-top and Dada's wife, Acharya Ram Pari Devi, oversaw the arrangements for Baba's food. Everybody in his family was involved in the preparations, especially his second son Ramananda, who is nearly as disciplined as his father. They erected a beautiful pandal in a mango orchard that belonged to Dada and the arrangements for the margis' stay and food were excellent. It was a wonderful program, very devotional. Gadopur is in Bihar, and whenever there was a DMC in Bihar you would always hear the margis crying and shouting and see them going into trance. For three continuous days it was like that, a continuous devotional flow.

When the program was over, Baba told me that he wanted to meet with Chandranathji's family members. They had been so busy working during the program that they hardly had any scope to see Baba. Before we left, they all crowded into Baba's room, the whole family—Chandranathji's four children with their wives and husbands and their children, even the youngest ones. Baba apologized for putting them to so much inconvenience and took the time to say something to everyone individually. Then they begged Baba's forgiveness for any mistakes they might have made or any inconvenience they might have caused him due to their ignorance and inexperience.

"How can you cause me any inconvenience?" Baba answered. "There was no inconvenience whatsoever and even if there had been, this is my house. When you return to your house do you feel any inconvenience? No. You are glad to be home. This is how I feel, like I have returned home."

After Baba left, the family kept Baba's room as a shrine, with all the things that he used while he was there, such as his plate and towels and so forth. Whenever they enter that room for meditation they feel Baba's presence. And those same acharyas that Baba scolded became re-energized. They raised a lot of money for the local Ananda Marga school and other projects and began working sincerely for the mission. So Baba created that pressure just to remove their shortcomings.

26 October 1979

Ramchandra Reddy

WHENEVER BABA WENT to Hyderabad he used to stay with Ramchandra Reddy. Ramchandra was Asimananda's initiate and he used to keep a room in his house exclusively for Dada's use. When Asimananda was murdered, he organized a large protest and from then on he would always commemorate that date, April 2.

When Baba first went to Hyderabad it was difficult to find a proper place for him to stay. A hotel was proposed and then a *dharmasala*, a pilgrim's inn, but Baba categorically refused to stay in either of those places. We sent word to Asimananda and the other workers of South India that Baba would only stay with a strict moralist, and after some deliberation they settled on Ramchandra Reddy. He was the head of a number of public institutions and he had a reputation in Hyderabad for being a man of impeccable character. He was quite well-off—his house was practically a mansion—but he had earned his money by honest means, as a chief engineer, and had never taken a bribe. They approached Ramchandra and he was all too happy to agree. "I am not a great spiritualist," he said, "but if Baba is willing to stay in my house then I will take care of the arrangements and vacate the house while he is here."

The first time I went to his house was in 1971 as Baba's PA. One day during that visit I was sitting outside Baba's room with Ramchandra, conversing. We were sitting on chairs, since he had some problem with his back. Suddenly Baba opened his door and called us inside. "Come, come, why are you sitting out there? Come inside." After a minute or two, Baba said, "You know, Ramananda, Ramchandra was a great sadhaka in his past life. That is why he will not put up with any immorality in this life. Otherwise, he would have made a great fortune from his position. That is why I prefer to stay with him whenever I come to Hyderabad." So Ramchandra may have not thought he was a great spiritualist but Baba did not agree.

When we went to Hyderabad in November 1979, our first visit since the emergency, several marriages were solemnized. While the preparations for the marriages were going on, Baba asked about the couples' mother tongues. They were all Marathi speakers but the marriage vows were going to be read in English. Baba then gave the instruction that the marriage vows should be translated from English into Marathi for the ceremony, and from then on the marriage vows were always translated into the local language wherever we went.

11 November 1979

Hissar

WHENEVER BABA WENT to North India he would always stop in Delhi, whether for a DMC or for a visit. On one of these occasions, Professor Mallik of Hissar Agricultural University in Harayana and a couple of other margi professors from the same university came to Baba's quarters in Gadaipur to invite him to visit their place. The next stop on Baba's tour program was Gwalior but since Hissar is only two hours from Delhi by car they hoped they could persuade him to come to Hissar for a day and give darshan to the margis there. They also invited him to visit the agricultural college.

At first the dadas told them that it would not be possible for Baba to change his itinerary on such short notice, but they persisted and the dadas sent them to me. I arranged for them to meet Baba, and when they began telling Baba about Hissar and how much the margis there were hoping that he could visit, Baba agreed to their proposal. Of course, they had to meet the conditions—school, master unit, Baba's quarters, and so forth. Or if not all the conditions, then at least some of them. It didn't seem possible, since Hissar didn't have any Ananda Marga project at the time, but they rose to the challenge. They got on the phone to Hissar and went to work. We told them that at the very least they had to purchase land for a master unit and give their word that they would develop the project, and by the following day they had raised the money and purchased the land. I conveyed this to Baba and the next morning we left for Hissar. Baba gave a DMC there in the evening and we spent the night in Professor Mallik's house.

The next morning, before we left for Delhi, Professor Mallik and his colleagues took us to Hissar Agricultural University for Baba's field walk. They also invited their non-margi boss, the director of the university. The director led the tour, pointing out to Baba the various rare and important plants that they had in their collection along with their botanical and popular names. But he was surprised when Baba started commenting about the plants. Baba began talking about their origin, how their leaves had come to have that shape, what kind of fertilizer gave the best results and why, and a myriad other interesting details that went well beyond the scope of the director's knowledge, spending at least seven or eight minutes for each plant. As you can imagine, the director was astounded. The tour took an hour and well before it was over he realized that Baba knew far more about his plants than he did. When the tour was finished, Professor Mallik told him that Baba was his guru. The director touched Baba's feet and asked for his blessing. When he expressed his surprise at Baba's knowledge, Baba said, "No, no, you are exaggerating. But was it correct, what I said?"

"Yes, Baba, it was all correct."

Afterward, Professor Mallik told me how the director had praised Baba after he left. He had gone on and on about how great he was.

20 November 1979

Pune

PARADESHI WAS THE bhukti pradhan of Pune when we went there for DMC in November 1979. He was a devoted margi and the principal organizer of the DMC. He was also successful in his personal life, holding a top government post in that district as the director of telecommunications. Paradeshi harboured a secret desire that Baba would stay in his house when he came to Pune, but since his parents were not margis a conflict arose in his mind and he decided that it would be better to accommodate Baba in the government circuit house, so that Baba would not feel any uneasiness at having to stay in a house with non-margis.

When his parents learned of his decision they were offended. "Do you think you are the only devotee in this family?" they told him. "We may not be initiated but we love Baba more than you do. Why shouldn't he stay here? You do what you feel is best, but we feel that Baba should come here. Not only that, we feel that he *will* come here." Paradeshi did his best to explain to them his reasons, but they were not convinced.

Thus Baba and I stayed in the government guest house. When Paradeshi welcomed Baba to the guest house on behalf of the local margis, Baba asked him if his parents would be attending the DMC. "No, Baba," he said. "My parents are not initiated."

"You know, your parents love me very much," Baba told him. "Tell them that if they come to the DMC pandal tomorrow they will be allowed to attend. Ramananda, inform security that the mother and father of the bhukti pradhan will be allowed to enter the pandal tomorrow without gate pass."

The next day his parents came to the pandal and attended the DMC. The following morning, when we were preparing to leave, Baba asked me if he had completed all his duties. "Has anything been left undone?" he asked.

"No, Baba," I answered. "There is nothing left to do. The DMC was very successful."

"No, I feel there is still one duty that I have left undone. I should visit Paradeshi's house. From there we can continue on to the airport. Is there anyone here who knows the way."

I made some inquiries and found that a local margi who was coming with us knew the way—Paradeshi was then at the DMC pandal, attending to some last-minute work; he was to go straight from the pandal to the airport to see us off. Baba then gave instructions that the other cars coming with us were to maintain some distance when we stopped. Only our car would stop at the house.

When we arrived at the house, Baba and I went up to the door and Baba himself rang the doorbell and asked the servant who answered the door to inform Paradeshi's parents that he had come. When we were led into the house we found that Paradeshi's parents had been waiting for Baba. When Baba entered their room and sat on their cot, they wept openly in front of him. "Baba, you heard our call," they said. "We told our son that he was not the only person who loved Baba in this family, that we love you even more than he does, but he didn't believe us. But you love us even more than we love you. You have fulfilled our wish. For the rest of our lives we will never forget that you have blessed us with your presence in our house."

"It was your desire that compelled me to come here," Baba told them. "Now I have to go to the airport. Do I have your permission? I cannot go without your permission." They were weeping unabashedly at this point. "Don't cry," Baba said. "Crying is not a solution. Just remember that I am always with you. Whenever you feel a strong desire to see me, you will find that I am there with you. Now, may I leave?"

"Yes, Baba, but before you leave we have one prayer. Please leave us with some lasting imprint of your presence so that we may never forget you."

Baba laughed softly. "You compelled me to come and now you are adding another condition? Okay, but I will also add some conditions: you will have to do some sadhana and do some service for the suffering humanity, whatever is within your capacity. Is it okay?"

"Yes, Baba."

Baba closed his eyes, and said, "*Shubhamastu*"—let it be according to your wishes. Then he did namaskar and we left for the airport.

When we reached Calcutta, Paradeshi called. He had heard the whole story from his parents. That is when I learned what his parents had said to him before the DMC, how they had been sure that Baba would come to their house, despite their son's arrangements. He told me that after Baba left his parents' room it was filled with the scent of sandalwood, and the scent was still there when he called. One month later he called again and the sandalwood scent was still in the room. It was Baba's lasting imprint.

Paradeshi's parents began meditating and doing service to the poor, whatever was within their capacity as a middle-class family.

27 November 1979

Am I a Tiger?

PROFESSOR NILAM'S BROTHERS and sisters were margis. After he took initiation they started pushing him to get PC but he was a little scared. He had heard many stories about the punishments Baba would mete out, the scolding and the beatings, how no one could hide their sins from him. But he had also heard how loving and beautiful Baba was, and gradually he became convinced that he should go for PC. He was from Gandhidham, so when Baba came to Bombay in November 1979 he attended the program and put his name on the list.

His PC was in the morning—usually Baba gave PC after morning field walk, before reporting, though occasionally he would give PC in the afternoon as well if there was no other work. I gave Professor Nilam his instructions and sent him into Baba's room. He did sastaunga pranam as instructed, but instead of sitting close to Baba's cot, he kept his distance. Baba laughed and said, "Don't be scared. I know you have done many bad things and that is why you are scared, but you shouldn't be. Come, sit closer." But instead, he backed even further away.

"What are you doing?" Baba said. "Am I a tiger that you are so afraid?"

"Baba, you are more than a tiger," he answered.

"No, no. For others I may be a tiger, but not for you. Sometimes I have to deal with bad elements. I have to be very strict with them; otherwise they will not learn their lesson. But that is not the case with you."

"Baba, I am scared."

"There is no need to be."

Gradually, through persuasion, Baba coaxed him to sit closer. Then Baba started narrating many of the bad things he had done in his life.

"Now," Baba said, "do you think you deserve punishment for your mistakes?"

"Yes, Baba."

"Good. Stretch out your hand."

He closed his eyes and stretched out his hand, sure that Baba would beat him very severely. "Don't close your eyes," Baba told him. When he opened them again, Baba took his stick and tapped him on the palm. "This is your punishment," he said. "Now forget everything that has happened in the past. Your past samskaras have been burned. You are a good boy and you are my son. From today you have been given a new life. I expect to hear good things of you in the future. " Baba then patted him on the cheek and blessed him.

He told me all this when he came out from his PC. He is living in Ranchi now, teaching philosophy in the university.

28 November 1979

S. M. Mathur

*T*HERE WERE A number of prominent margis who worked in the excise and customs departments, such as Peshawari Lal, Raghuvir Prasad, and so on. They were all highly respectable persons who embodied Ananda Marga ideology in their actions and thus became great assets to the mission. S. M. Mathur was another of these persons. He was instrumental in developing the Baba's quarters at Gadaipur in Delhi, which we purchased just after Baba came out of jail.

Mathurji was a customs collector. Since he wouldn't accept bribes, he was limited as to how much financial help he could give the organization. He was also very scrupulous about his dealings with the wealthy people he caught smuggling or otherwise trying to evade the law. He considered it a breach of ethics to ask them to support the organization. Prasadji was more liberal in this regard. He would tell the culprits that there was one charitable organization that was doing excellent work. "If you wish, you can contact them directly and donate to their cause," he would say. "I cannot accept anything on their behalf, but I will put you in contact with certain people and after that it is up to you." Prasadji helped the organization a great deal in this way. People would show up ready to donate hundreds of thousands of rupees due to their dealings with him. But Mathurji was not willing to ask for donations as long as he was a government servant.

When he retired, he began to work as a defence lawyer defending high-profile smugglers, the same people he had prosecuted when he worked for the customs department. He was also a trustee of the P. R. Sarkar Educational Trust in Delhi, and one day the dada in charge of the Gadaipur property approached him for a donation so that they could develop the Baba's quarters. This got him thinking. Now that the government could no longer accuse him of taking advantage of his position, he thought, why should he not approach his clients for donations?

They were rich people, for the most part; they could afford it. All he took from them was a modest fee, and that didn't leave him much with which to help the organization financially. But if he were to win their case, why should they not show their gratitude by contributing to a worthwhile service project? He began approaching his clients, but in a different way than Prasad. When he felt that his client might be open to his suggestion, he would tell him about the project. "Go there and see the project for yourself," he would say, "and then you decide. If you feel like helping, then you can talk to the swami in charge and he will let you know how you can help." Then he would say to the dada—at the time it was Arteshananda: "Tell him that you don't want money. If he wants to help, he should take direct responsibility for the work. Tell him that you don't know how much it will cost but you will trust him to get the best price and do a good job." For example, Dada told one of Mathur's clients that he needed a tube well. This client contracted a professional company and paid them to complete the well. So Mathurji had a different style than Prasad, but he was also a great asset to the organization.

1979

Baba's Love for Plants

*B*ABA TOOK A great interest in his garden from the moment we moved to the Lake Gardens house in Calcutta. Some margis were professional horticulturalists, such as Ram Lagan and his daughter. Baba called them to Calcutta and asked for their advice, and soon he started requesting the margis to bring him plants, especially rare plants from other parts of India and overseas that were hardly ever seen in Calcutta, even in the local botanical gardens. It quickly became compulsory for workers coming to Calcutta for reporting to bring plants; in some cases, Baba requested specific plants, especially from workers coming from distant lands who had access to plants that were unavailable locally. I remember that Baba once asked for a particular magnolia from Japan. Krishnabuddhyananda managed to bring it after crossing many hurdles—immigration and so forth—and this made Baba very happy. If I am not mistaken, Baba gave it the Sanskrit name *mayapushpa*.

Plants began arriving every day and Baba gave his personal attention to each and every one of them. As soon as Baba finished his breakfast, the garden-in-charge would show him whatever new plants had arrived. Previously this was Asimananda. Later it was Ananda Karuna, and then others started helping. First Baba would ask where the plant came from and who brought it. Then he would give the name, both the botanical name and the Sanskrit name, and someone would write the name down and tag the plant. Then he would describe the plant's characteristics and give instructions as to what type of care it needed: how often it should be watered, what type of soil or fertilizer it liked, and so on. Sometimes he would graft the plants. He would keep a pair of scissors nearby for this purpose. Finally he would assign it a home, either in a specific part of the garden or else in some other project like the MG quarters in Anandanagar. Baba knew the director of the botanical gardens in Calcutta and also the director of the zoological gardens.

When they learned that Baba was distributing plants, they also began requesting rare plants from Thailand and America and other countries, as well as from distant parts of India—they were especially interested in Himalayan orchids. Sometimes Baba used to send plants to them also. He also gave plants to other non-margis, such as his eye doctor, who on one occasion asked Baba if he could get him coconut palms from Port Blair and the Andaman and Nicobar islands. Baba said yes, he could get them, but only on the condition that he took proper care of them. The doctor promised and Baba asked some workers to bring those coconut palms for him.

When the distribution and tagging was complete, Baba would make a circuit of the garden to check on the condition and health of the plants before going on field walk. Baba was very strict with the workers and gardeners who took care of his garden. Every plant had to be cared for according to his exact instructions. He used to take care of his plants the way he took care of his disciples. If a plant died he would get angry; he would scold the responsible party and give him punishment. "How could you let this plant die?" he would say. "Did I not give you specific instructions how to take care of it? Why didn't you follow my instructions?" Then they would have to replace the plant within a stipulated number of hours, depending on how far away the plant came from and how long it would take for a replacement to arrive. Nor could they hide anything from Baba. He knew where every single plant in his garden was and what condition it was in. If he saw that a plant was looking dry from insufficient watering, he would scold the workers who were taking care of his garden, and he would ask for regular reports on the plant's condition until it was fully recovered.

Baba also introduced the first cold-climate greenhouse in the city. He had it constructed originally for the brahma kamal, the famous Himalayan lotus, which is only found in the Valley of the Gods in the high Himalayas, also known as the Valley of Flowers. When the summer sun finally melts the ice, it blooms and emits a very powerful, very beautiful fragrance. It is said that the Lord loves the brahma kamal above all other flowers, which is why that valley is called the Valley of the Gods, and certainly Baba loved its fragrance very much. He wanted it in his house, but for that he had to simulate the Himalayan climate. After the greenhouse was built, he was able to keep other cold-weather plants there, such as Italian roses.

In time, Baba's garden became one of the horticultural wonders of Calcutta; it gained a deserved reputation among horticulturalists throughout the city.

1979

R. Bhaktavatsalyam

*A*FTER MY ARREST in 1975 I was sent to Madras Central Jail, along with Shiveshvarananda and Bal Kishan Goenka, the father of Shiva Bhagawan Goenka, Shyam Sundar Goenka, Om Prakash Goenka, and Sushil Goenka. Bal Kishan had close ties to the state government—his family was very close to the family of Sanjiva Reddy, Andhra Pradesh's first chief minister and later president of India—thus he never imagined he could be arrested, and his family immediately began petitioning for his release. Shyam Sundar was imprisoned in Bombay but he was released after ten days and he joined his brothers in their efforts to free their father; after two months Bal Kishan was granted his release. In the meantime, Bhaktavatsalyam was also arrested, which brought our total to four. At first we were all in separate cell blocks, but then the jail superintendent put us all in the same place, which was a great comfort to us. We did regular Dharmachakra and the other inmates would ask us to give lectures, which Bhaktavatsalyam, who was an educated person, would translate into Tamil. Jail life was not easy, but the satsaunga made it bearable. For Bhaktavatsalyam, however, it was particularly difficult due to the great attachment he had for his wife and children. He was a well-to-do businessman, owner of the Sadhu Trading Company, and the secretary of the Tamil Samaj. All in all, he was a very established and highly respected margi, but he was also a very emotional man and he found it difficult to adjust to the absence of his family. He was also very fond of food—he was a stout man, dark complexioned, and the prison food was a trial for him. Soon he began weeping for his wife and children and doubts about Baba began to creep into his mind: "Why have they not come to see me? Are they all right? Baba, you are a god and I have never even thought ill of others. I have been busy maintaining my family and doing your work. Why are you so cruel to me? Why are you not allowing them to come see me?"

Actually, his family had tried to come and see him. They had not been allowed in, but he did not know this at the time. He was weeping continuously for many days, and I had to spend long hours trying to console him. Finally the family secured permission to visit. The warders called him to the office where his family was waiting for him with a hot pack full of idly and dosa and such things, all his favourite foods. They started weeping when they saw each other. "I don't know what I have done to deserve this," he told them. "I never expected that anything like this would ever happen to me. Let us see how Baba helps." When the visit was over, he brought the leftover food into the prison for us—there was a lot of it, all the rich, delicious foods that you will never get in prison. After that Bhaktavatsalyam was able to relax. His family started coming religiously, once or twice a month, and whenever they came they brought a feast for the four of us. They lived about 350 kilometres away but they had relatives in the city and they used to come and stay in their house.

Not long after Baba's release, Bhaktavatsalyam travelled to Calcutta to meet him, their first meeting since before the emergency—this was in Lake Gardens. When I went downstairs to see who might be available for field walk I didn't see him—he must have been in the bathroom. When Baba asked me if there was anyone to go with him to the field, I told him that there was no suitable person. Every once in a while this happened. But since this was our day to go to the nurseries to see if they had any new plants, it wasn't a problem, as I always went with him to the nurseries. I would bring the money and buy whatever plants Baba wanted. When we came downstairs and Baba sat in his car, however, he saw Bhaktavatsalyam through the window giving him namaskar. "Ramananda," Baba said, "you told me there was no one to go with me on field walk. Bhaktavatsalyam is here. If there is no one else, then why not let him come?"

"I'm sorry, Baba, I didn't see him when I came down to check."

Since he obviously met with Baba's approval, I opened the door and allowed Bhaktavatsalyam to sit in the back seat next to Baba, and then I took my seat in the front. The first thing Baba said when Bhaktavatsalyam got in was, "Bhaktavatsalyam, you should not be so sentimental. A sadhaka should not have attachment. I heard your cries when you were in the prison. I heard you crying for your family. Why did you doubt me? Did you think that I did not see them? Do you not know that I was taking care of them? That is my responsibility. You had nothing to worry about."

Bhaktavatsalyam started crying piteously. "Yes, Baba, you were there to take care." He became so emotional that he reached down and grabbed Baba's feet right there in the back seat, crying very loudly the whole time. I felt very uncomfortable—it was becoming an unpleasant scene—so I asked Baba if I should take him out of the car. By then workers and volunteers, seeing the commotion, had crowded round the car. Parimal, Baba's bodyguard, opened the door and said, "Dada, I want to take him out of the car." But as he was opening the door, Baba said, "Ramananda, let him be. It will be okay. Let him come with us on field walk."

Parimal backed off and Bhaktavatsalyam started gaining some control over his emotions. As the car eased out of the gate, Baba started talking to him again. "Bhaktavatsalyam, you should not be so sentimental. A sadhaka should not be like this."

"Yes, Baba, you are right. I have been very sentimental right from my childhood."

"I know that you have attachment but you should try to work on it. There was a reason you were separated from your family for that period of time. You may not know the reason now but later on you will know it. It was for your own good, and for theirs also. Now dry your tears."

The rest of the field walk was fine. Bhaktavatsalyam calmed down and Baba started discussing Tamil Samaj with him and giving him certain instructions. He asked him to continue his good work and to take care of the workers there. In the end, it turned out to be a very pleasant field walk.

1979

Amitananda

*A*MITANANDA WAS THE rector master of Anandanagar for many years, and he used to take excellent care of Baba whenever we visited. As RM he would come to Calcutta to formally invite Baba for the biannual DMC, and when it came time for Baba to travel to Anandanagar, he would return to Calcutta to accompany Baba. He would sit in the back seat with Baba while I would be in the front seat with the driver. When Baba started collecting fossils for his museum, Amitananda took it on himself to unearth fossils in Anandanagar and send them to Baba. On one of these occasions, Baba mentioned how the Jains used to guard the entrance to their temples with twin pillars, one carved with the image of a *yaksha* and the other with that of a *yakshinii*. They believed that this god and goddess protected their house of worship.

The next time that Baba came to Anandanagar, Amitananda had a surprise for him. He was in the car with us, giving instructions to the driver. We came via Pinjarajora and when we neared the gate to Baba's house we could see two pillars standing on either side of the gate, one with the image of a *yaksha* and the other with that of a *yakshinii*. Amitanandaji pointed them out to Baba, who got down from the car and began inspecting them and talking in great detail about their history and the customs of the Jains. "But how did you bring them?" Baba asked. "It must have been very difficult." And indeed, it must have been, for these were large stone pillars, exceedingly heavy. Dada recounted how he had begun searching for a pair of such pillars after hearing Baba talk about them, knowing that Baba would be happy with the gift. He eventually found such a pair lying half-buried in a field near an abandoned Jain temple. He organized a group of students and a bullock cart, and with their help he brought the pillars to Baba's house. When the local villagers found out what he was doing they became very angry, but he was not about to let anyone stop him from fulfilling Baba's desire.

A couple of years later Amitananda fell sick with a rare disease of the nervous system, and he died relatively young. After that, whenever Baba would come to Anandanagar he would tell me how much he felt Amitananda's absence. I felt the same. He was a great sadhaka and an extraordinary man who had no equal in both honesty and sincerity. Anandanagar has never been the same since.

December 1979

Hiraprabha

*W*HEN BABA CAME out of prison, he promised his sister Hiraprabha that he would visit her at her house in Chinsurah, a little over an hour from Calcutta by car. It took a couple of years but Baba fulfilled his promise. When we were getting ready to return to Calcutta after the biannual DMC in Anandanagar, Baba asked me to arrange for us to stop by Hiraprabha's house on the way back. I planned our arrival so that we could take lunch there, knowing that Hiraprabha would want to have an opportunity to cook for her brother. When we arrived, Baba presented his sister with a gold necklace. She was very surprised. "But Bubu, why are you giving me this?" she asked.

"Do you not remember the promise I made when you were getting married?" Baba replied. "Everyone was giving you ornaments as wedding gifts but I was too young, so I promised you that when I was bigger I would also give you such a present. Now I am grown up and the time has come for me to fulfil that promise. Please accept this necklace as your wedding gift."

It was a deeply sentimental moment for both of them. Hiraprabha started crying. "Forty-three years and you still remember!" She was very moved. I should also point out that Baba didn't buy the necklace with organizational funds. He bought it from the royalties he received from his books. He was always very scrupulous in such matters.

After this, the entire family came and chatted with Baba before sitting down for lunch. Hiraprabha had three or four sons and they were all there with their wives and children. One of them is an engineer, one is with the telephone company, and one, Samar, is a doctor. He is director of health services for the state of West Bengal. Baba gave him the name Shyamal, and after that his family members also started calling him Shyamal.

Throughout the visit, Hiraprabha was the perfect host, making sure that everyone was comfortable and had everything they needed, whether

her guests or her children and grandchildren. She was a very respectable lady with a commanding nature, very similar to Baba in this respect. I can still see her in front of my eyes, such an august personality. It was also evident how much love and mutual respect there was between her and Baba. When it was time for us to go, there were tears on all sides.

1980

Krishnagar

NOT LONG AFTER Baba came out of prison, Acharyas Manas and Sukhen came to Lake Gardens to invite him to hold DMC in Krishnagar. As usual, they brought some special sweets for Baba—Krishnagar sweets are quite famous in India—and I sent them on field walk so they could ask Baba in person. Baba's standing instruction was to only send people on field walk if he recommended them. Usually he would ask me whom I was sending and then give his consent. Sometimes, if I was very busy attending to Baba, I might only have one or two minutes to make my selection before he was ready to leave, but it usually worked out okay. The general rule, however, was that I would inform Baba ahead of time who had come and who had requested to go on field walk. While Baba was taking breakfast, I would make sure there was somebody to attend to him; then I would go downstairs and make a note of who was there. Sometimes people would come up to me when they saw me and ask to go on field walk. When I went back upstairs and was putting Baba's shoes on his feet, he would ask me if there was anyone who could go with him on field walk that day. I would tell him that so-and-so had come and he would tell me if it was okay for them to go. But there were certain persons that Baba liked me to send whenever they came. Acharyas Manas and Sukhen were among them. I would show Baba the sweets they had brought, put them in the fridge, and then send them on field walk, as long as there was space available in the car.

Baba accepted their invitation and about six weeks later he told me that he wanted us to make the arrangements for him to give DMC in Krishnagar. "As long as we are going to Krishnagar," he said, "we should include some other places in Bengal, such as Siliguri, Kishanganj, Barampur, and Shantiniketan; from there we can return to Calcutta. But only if they finalize the DMC in Krishnagar. Get in touch with Manas-da and Sukhen-da. See if they are ready to receive us."

So it turned into a tour—this was May 1980—and interestingly enough it was Baba who decided where we would go and by what route. I contacted Manas and Sukhen and the preparations got underway. Holding DMC involves a considerable expense and the margis of Krishnagar did not have much money, but when Manas and Sukhen told them that Baba had expressed his desire to go there, they were sure they would have his blessings. They all contributed to the cause and in a short time they raised the requisite sum.

Here I should say a few words about these two acharyas. During Baba's time they used to conduct mass initiations with regularity. Both of them were the acharyas of thousands of margis and of many avadhutas as well. In Bengal at that time there was a lot of anti-Ananda Marga propaganda due to the CPM government, but they never let this deter them. They would go to different neighbourhoods and the surrounding villages after office hours and on weekends and talk about the philosophy. In this way they became well-known and highly respected throughout that area. There was one other acharya in Krishnagar also, Haraprasad Haldar, but he was not very active at that time.

They arranged a house for Baba to stay in and a large school hall for the darshans and the DMC program. When it came time for the first darshan, there was a big rush by the public to attend Baba's talk. Since they held Sukhen and Manas in such high regard, they thought that they should make every effort to see their guru. It was the security volunteers' duty, however, to keep out anyone who did not have a gate pass, and gate passes were only allotted to initiated margis. The situation quickly grew unruly. The public began pushing and complaining that they were not being allowed to enter. Baba was already in the hall by then. When he saw the commotion he called Sukhen and Manas and asked them what was going on.

"Baba the local people are clamouring to see you and hear you speak, but the security people are not allowing them in, since they don't have a gate pass."

"Do you know these people?"

"Yes, Baba, we know them. They are good people, religious-minded people. They have heard that a great saint has come, and they feel that they should not miss the opportunity to see him."

"How do you recommend we handle the situation? I have come here because of your invitation and you know these people, so you should give me your opinion."

"Baba, they are good people. They will not cause any harm if we allow them to attend the darshan."

"Very well then. If you permit them, then let them come."

Sukhen and Manas gave orders to the volunteers to open the doors and windows and to set a couple of speakers outside the hall. Members of the public began crowding inside, and those who could not squeeze in were able to listen through the open doorway and windows. Baba gave a wonderful lecture and when he was finished he asked the people how they felt. Everyone was extremely happy. Afterward, they were remarking what a saintly person Baba was, how blessed they felt to have had the opportunity to see him. Many of them took initiation after that.

May 1980

Kishanganj

*F*ROM KRISHNAGAR WE went to Siliguri and from there to Kishanganj. Kishanganj is a small town—recently it has become the district headquarters. Geographically it is situated in Bihar, but it is just on the border between Bihar and Bengal, and in our samaj system it comes under Amra Bengali. While we were in Siliguri, Baba asked me where we would stay once we reached Kishanganj. Baba had been to the nearby towns of Purnea and Sahasar on various occasions, but this was his first visit to Kishanganj. All I knew was that Bhola-da, a leading margi of Kishanganj, was taking care of the arrangements.

Unbeknownst to me, Bhola was having a difficult time finding a suitable place for Baba. He was a popular figure in that area, a tall, robust man who had stood for election and made a good impression when he talked in public. He had many contacts and had lined up several good possibilities, but unfortunately none of them was available for both days. Finally he decided that he had no alternative but to put Baba up in his house. The problem was that he lived in a simple thatched house and he was afraid that Baba would be greatly inconvenienced by such humble accommodations. Nevertheless, he did all that he could to make it presentable. He had a new bed made for Baba and a new wardrobe with hangers for his clothes; he also bought new bedsheets and towels and so on.

When we arrived at the entrance to Kishanganj, a huge crowd of margis was waiting to receive us. They had made a gate and were waiting with garlands in their hands. We stopped the car and Bhola came up to the window to greet Baba. "Is there any place for me to stay?" Baba asked Bhola after he gave him his namaskar. "Yes, Baba," Bhola said. "I have fixed up my small hut for you. It is a very simple place but I have done the best I could to make it presentable."

Baba was all smiles. After he accepted the garlands we followed Bhola to his house. He showed Baba to his room and Baba was very happy. He sat on the cot and started praising the accommodations. "Oh, the bed is very nice. Is this where I will hang my clothes? Very nice, very nice. This is a very good place." After that, all of Bhola's hesitation vanished. I hung up Baba's clothes, and after Baba was settled in, Bhola showed me the rest of the house. "This is where Baba will take bath; this is where you will stay," and so on. He had arranged another thatched house just next door for the workers, and all in all, the accommodations were quite pleasant.

There are a number of Maethili-speaking acharyas in that part of Bihar who had done a lot of prachar there over the years and they were all in attendance, including Dipnarayana, Kshitij, and Natkat Kedar. In fact, the majority of the margis who attended the DMC were Maethili speaking, although Kishanganj is seventy-five percent Bengali. After the first darshan Baba called these three acharyas to his room and told them that he felt as if he were in Maethila, since the majority of the margis were from Maethila. Both Kshitij and Natkat Kedar were excellent singers, and in General Darshan Baba asked them to sing for him. Soon everyone was crying, especially the acharyas. Natkat Kedar sang one of his own compositions for Baba in Maethili—this was before Baba gave Prabhat Samgiita. Baba sat in silence, listening to the song, and a great devotional wave was created. It had been Natkat's secret desire to sing this song for Baba. His other secret desire was to have a chance to massage Baba, and in the evening Baba called him for massage. Natkat was an expert in massage and Baba stayed up late talking with him while he was being massaged.

Before Baba left that place he called the acharyas to his room. Bhola was also included. "Baba," he said, "I am so fortunate that you have sanctified my house by your presence, despite all the difficulties you have had to face. It is your special grace."

"There was no difficulty," Baba said, "and it is not my special grace. It is my duty. I am always most comfortable when I stay with my devotees. I am glad I had a chance to stay in your house."

Bhola still keeps that room as a shrine to Baba. The fact that Baba stayed in his thatched house should not be forgotten.

29 May 1980

Etwari

ONCE BHUVANESHVARI, THE unit secretary of Dhanbad, invited Baba to visit Dhanbad on his way back to Calcutta after the biannual DMC in Anandanagar. Baba's brother Himanshu lived in Dhanbad and he sent a letter with Bhuvaneshvari requesting Baba to come and stay with him—usually Baba would stay in Himanshu's railway quarters residence when he spent the night in Dhanbad. Baba agreed to the visit, but on one condition: they would have to agree to secure some land for a future school and Baba's quarters. Bhuvaneshvari agreed and we put the visit on our itinerary.

We stopped there for two days and Himanshu's wife, Kalyani, took care of Baba with her customary aplomb. She was an excellent cook who would usually prepare Baba's meals when she and her husband came to Calcutta. She was a very devoted sister whom Baba loved very much. There are many good cooks in Ananda Marga who used to cook for Baba, but I can say that I never saw anyone whose food Baba enjoyed more than Kalyani's. On the day we were leaving, however, the margis brought in a hired cook to prepare Baba's lunch. He was a simple man but an excellent cook who had prepared food for the governor and other dignitaries. They didn't tell Baba who had cooked—they only told him that they had arranged some special food for his parting meal: *alu dhum* and other tasty dishes. Baba ate together with Himanshu and his family, and during the meal he expressed how much he was enjoying the food:

"Today I am getting a special taste," he said. "You were not exaggerating when you said that you were arranging some special food for me. Kalyani's food is always special but this food is even more special. Who has prepared it?"

"Baba, his name is Etwari. He is a well-known chef of Dhanbad and we wanted you to have a chance to sample his cooking."

"Really? Call him. I want to meet him."

Himanshu brought Etwari from the kitchen and introduced him to Baba.

Baba was in a jolly mood. "Why did your parents give you this name Etwari?" he asked. "It must be because you were born on a Sunday."

"Yes, Baba. It is because I was born on a Sunday." Etwari means "Sunday" in Bhojpuri and he was a Bhojpuri speaker.

Baba continued chatting with him for several minutes and repeatedly praised his food. He spoke with him as if he were a favourite nephew and Etwari was thrilled to receive Baba's attention. In the years that followed he would always tell people how Baba had praised his food. I heard from Himanshu that he died a couple of months ago and right up until the end he would reminisce about how Baba had talked to him and praised his cooking.

The night before we left, Bhuvaneshvari and some of the local margis told Baba that they wanted to show him the piece of land they had purchased. Baba was happy to go. "Yes," he said, "I want to see my land." They took us there and Baba commended them for having fulfilled their promise and done some good work for the mission. "Oh, it is a very good place," he said. "How were you able to arrange such a good land in so short at time?" Bhuvaneshvari asked Baba to sanctify the place by touching it with his feet and Baba obliged him by getting down and walking around. Nowadays they have built a school on that land and it has become very popular in Dhanbad.

1980

Arguing Over a Bed Sheet

*I*N JULY OF 1980 Baba gave four DMCs in the space of ten days. The second of these was in Bhavnagar in Gujarat. In those days we used to do tandava in the airport wherever Baba went, complete with skulls and knives, although the authorities always objected and often arrested the dadas involved. Before the Bhavnagar DMC, Nigamananda contacted the police and he was able to secure official permission to dance tandava in front of Baba when he arrived in the airport.

This story is about two margis who attended that DMC: A. K. Saha of Ahmedabad, and P. C. Mehta of Bombay, both very devoted to Baba. It was not a large gathering, several hundred margis only, and Baba was staying in a private house. Both had brought a gift for Baba, and on the first day, while Baba was out on field walk, they each went to Baba's room to clean it—normally Baba's room is cleaned while he is out on field walk and they had both volunteered for the job. By coincidence, each a brought the same gift with them to the room: a beautifully woven bed sheet made by the people of the Kachi tribe—different colours and patterns but otherwise the identical gift. And they both had the same motive for requesting permission to clean Baba's room: to get the chance to spread their sheet on Baba's cot. When they saw that they had both come with the same motive they fell to arguing. This went on for at least twenty minutes: "Do you think Baba is only yours? He is just as much mine as yours, if not more!" And so on. In the meantime, Baba came back from field walk. I went to the room to make sure that everything was in order and found them in the midst of this heated discussion. When I asked them what was going on, they each showed me their bed sheets.

Baba was right behind me. When they saw him they suddenly became like children, each holding up his bed sheet and saying, "Baba, I brought this for you."

Baba was very diplomatic. "Both of you are my loving sons," he said. "Ramananda, spread both bed sheets on the cot. I will sleep on both of them tonight."

In an instant the quarrel was over. They spread their bed sheets, Baba sat on the cot, and they bent down to touch Baba's feet. "Now both of you sit together, side by side," Baba said. "I want to see you laugh."

It was a funny scene. Both were highly educated, highly dignified persons, but when it came to Baba they fell to quarrelling like little children fighting over a piece of candy. But in the end they were laughing together, just as Baba wanted.

23 July 1980

Nine-day Kirtan

ONE DAY THE secretary of the Maethili Samaj came to Lake Gardens along with two other margis from Darbhanga. They told me that they were planning on holding a nine-day kirtan in the village of Ganj Raghauli, about ten miles from Darbhanga, and they had come to invite Baba to attend. Baba was in his room taking rest after lunch, and I was sitting outside the room talking to them. Now it was Baba's standing instruction that if any urgent work arose while he was taking rest, I should enter his room, call his name, and touch him lightly on the arm. This would let him know that there was some urgent work that required his attention. Since their train was leaving in two hours' time, and traffic in Calcutta being what it was, I decided that this qualified as urgent. I asked them to wait while I went in to talk to Baba, so that they might have the opportunity to request him personally.

When I entered his room, Baba saw me so there was no need to touch his body. "Baba," I said, "Dhruvendra, the Maethili Samaj secretary, has come with two other margis who are well known to you, Ranadhiira and Sukhen Prasad. They have something they need to ask you."

"Oh yes, I know them. Should I sit up?"

"No, Baba. You can lie down. I'll just send them in."

"No, when somebody comes to visit it is better to receive them sitting up. Bring me my shirt."

Baba was then in his lungi and an T-shirt. He took a few minutes to get ready and then he asked me to call them. After they did sastaunga pranam, he asked them why they had come.

"Baba, we have decided to hold a nine-day kirtan in Ganj Raghauli, near Darbhanga, and your presence there is needed. We have brought you an invitation."

They handed Baba a beautifully lettered invitation. "Very good," Baba said. "I accept your invitation. Go ahead with your kirtan. It is a very worthwhile program. Ramananda, note down the dates of the program."

After they left, Baba told me to remind him about the kirtan program when it came time for it to be concluded. It was going to begin in two or three weeks so I noted it in my diary. Then, on the morning of the final day of the kirtan, I reminded Baba and told him the exact time that the kirtan would finish: one o'clock, just after Baba's lunch.

It was Baba's regular routine after lunch to walk up and down in his room one hundred steps. Baba used to say "one hundred steps" but actually he would specify a certain period of time, usually twenty minutes, and someone had to keep track of the time. Either I would do it or I would depute someone. When the twenty minutes were up you had to tell Baba. It could not be twenty-one minutes. If it was twenty-one minutes then Baba would scold me for not controlling the time properly. After walking he would go to the bathroom and then lie down on his cot. While he was resting I would send in someone to read him the newspaper headlines: *Ananda Bazaar*, *Yugantar*, *Statesman*, *Amrita Bazaar*, and *Notun Prithibi*, the five papers he used to keep on his bed. Before the emergency he would read them himself, but after his eyes were damaged by the poisoning he used to ask for someone to read them to him. Most of the time I would send Jagadishvarananda. If he was not there, then Mantreshvarananda. If Baba was still awake after the papers were read, he would ask me if there was anyone I could send in for massage. I always had somebody ready. That person would massage Baba for fifteen to twenty minutes and then the afternoon's work would begin. Or else, if I saw that Baba was asleep, I might postpone the work to allow him to get some extra rest. Once I saw that Baba had gotten up, however, I knew that he was ready for work.

Normally Baba would take lunch at twelve or twelve-thirty and the rest period would last for about an hour. But this day there was a change in the routine. After Baba finished his lunch he told me that he was going to take rest for the next half an hour and during that time no one should be allowed to enter his room. He told me that I should also not enter his room, even if there was some urgent work. This was precisely when the kirtan in Ganj Raghauli was concluding.

About a week after the kirtan the same three margis came to see Baba. When Baba came out for his field walk they were standing near the car and Baba stopped to speak to them.

"Baba," they said, "you were so kind to us. You appeared at the end of the kirtan."

Baba feigned a look of surprise. "How is it possible? I was here in Lake Gardens the whole time."

"Baba, everybody saw you. We all had the same experience."

Baba smiled. "Even if you had not invited me," he said, "it still would have been my duty to be there. Whenever there is any kirtan I am always present. But since you went to the trouble to invite me I had to do something special for you."

Later they told me that as soon as the kirtan ended, everybody saw Baba's physical body projected in the centre of the room. He was sitting on the *mandap*, and his image remained in full view throughout the gurupuja and the svadhyaya reading, a period of exactly half an hour.

1980

Sharmaji

SHARMAJI WAS BABA'S official photographer, right from the days of the early black-and-white photos. He worked in a photo lab in Park Street, and from his earnings he was able to maintain his family.

When we were getting ready to go abroad after Baba's release, we needed six photos for the passport application, so we called Sharmaji. He came to Lake Gardens and chose the Shivaliila room, adjacent to the reporting hall and just in front of Baba's room, as the best place to take the photos—at the time I was living in that room. We had informed Baba that he would be coming; nevertheless Baba acted surprised when he saw him. "Why is the photographer here?" he asked.

"Baba, he has come to take your passport photos," I replied.

Baba smiled and nodded his head. "Okay, but I don't want my time to be wasted; it has to be quick. I have to go for field walk and after that I have a lot of work to do."

Sharmaji also smiled. "Baba, it will take a little time to get a proper snapshot. We have to set up the proper lighting. I'll have to take several exposures."

Baba laughed and sat as Sharmaji directed him. Sharmaji asked two dadas to hold a pair of umbrellas at precise angles to shade Baba from the lights. He put them in the right position and then coached Baba on how to sit and when to smile: "Very good, Baba, very good, but it can be better. Can you turn your head a little to the right; okay, now a big smile …" Baba followed his instructions as if he were a small boy. It took a few minutes and several plates—it was one of those old-style cameras—but he got a good snap and delivered the prints the very next day.

One night, we got the news that Sharmaji had died, though he had not been sick or suffering from any known disease. When we informed Baba in the morning, he let out a sigh. "Ah, such a good soul he was. Let us go there and pay our respects." That morning on field walk we brought Baba to the crematorium in Kalighat where the body was being prepared for cremation. The margis were just beginning the shraddha ceremony when we arrived. Baba got out of the car and paid his respects to the departed soul. This was a very rare occurrence.

1980

Calcutta to Anandanagar Travel

*P*RIOR TO THE construction of the Vishnupur Baba's quarters in 1981 we had no place of our own where Baba could stop between Calcutta and Anandanagar or Ranchi. Sometimes we would make the journey in one go—it took six hours to Anandanagar under ideal conditions—but generally Baba found it more convenient to break our journey along the way. After the quarters in Vishnupur were finished, we used to stop there as part of our usual routine, but before then we used to depend on B. D. Rathi to find a place for us to stay. Rathi was a handsome, robust man with an attractive personality. He was a successful businessman who enjoyed telling stories about the various times that Baba saved him and his family. Whenever Baba would travel anywhere, inside or outside Bengal, he would take it upon himself to ensure that Baba would not face any inconvenience during his journey. Thus, in the days before the Vishnupur quarters were built, I would always ask him to make the arrangements for Baba's stay when we were preparing to travel from Calcutta to Anandanagar or Ranchi.

In those days the CPM government was very much against us; thus it was difficult for me to reserve a place for Baba in a government rest house. But Rathi was a very confident man. "Don't worry, Dada," he would tell me. "I will take care of it. I can get a place for Baba anytime, anywhere." And really, it was true. Generally Baba liked to stop about halfway on the journey—usually in Bankura, a three-and-a-half-hour drive. When he would ask me if it would be possible, I would say, "Baba, by your grace, I don't think we will have any difficulty. I am sending Rathi."

"Oh, if Rathi is there, then I think he can manage. Yes, then by all means, let us stop over."

Rathi would make the journey a few hours in advance. He would go to the guest house and ask to see the officer in charge of the bookings. Rathi was an imposing man—his way of presenting himself; the way he moved; his manner of talking, polite but full of confidence; his very physical bulk: the officers would invariably be impressed, thinking him to be a very important person. "We only have two rooms available," they would say. "Only two rooms are necessary," he would answer. "We will be leaving early in the morning so we will be no trouble to you. Will it be possible to get sentient food?" "Yes, certainly. My cook is there. He prepares only sentient food."

Rathi would continue chatting with the officers about different subjects, overwhelming them with his natural charm; then he would go out to the road and wait for us to arrive so he could escort us to our rooms. He always secured very nice rooms and excellent service. When we went overseas he came with us and took care of the passports and so many other arrangements. I also heard that he received some vishesh yoga lessons from Baba.

1981

Chitmu

OUR BIANNUAL DMCs in Anandanagar were very special. Margis from all over India would attend in great numbers and the vibration was always very powerful. There was one ritual in particular that was always observed before each of these DMCs, and that was the reception that the local margis gave Baba when he passed through the village of Chitmu, a few kilometres before central Anandanagar. Most of the villagers in Chitmu are margis, but the two most important and most respected were Nirwaran Gurai and Terapada Gurai. They were both teachers but they were not related. They were the ones who organized the reception. On the day that Baba was expected they would go out to the road accompanied by a crowd of margis from the village and remain there until Baba arrived, with no care as to the time. They would erect a beautiful gate and they wouldn't allow any traffic to pass without their permission. The inhabitants of Chitmu are tribal people, so naturally they would beat drums and dance the whole day long until Baba showed up; it didn't matter how many hours they had to wait. Nirwaran and Terapada Gurai were such strong devotees that when Baba arrived they would shout out their welcome and then go up to talk to him as if he were theirs and theirs alone. No one else could talk to Baba. Only they had the right, so vehement was their devotional sentiment. It was wonderful to see, really very inspiring. Baba used to stop and talk to them for some time. Baba saved both of them on numerous occasions from cases lodged by the CPM and from murder attempts also. One of them would have hanged if Baba had not saved him. They are still alive. I still see them whenever we have any program here; they are very attached to me. Whenever I see them I always remember them waiting for us with their drums and their devotion on the road to Anandanagar.

1981

Baba's Nephew, Dr. Samar Bose

BABA USED TO suffer occasionally from piles before going to jail, but they got much worse after the poisoning. They were also exacerbated by sitting for many hours and doing intellectual work. Once, while we were traveling, his piles started bothering him and the usual medicines that his doctors had prescribed weren't providing much relief. "Why don't you ask Samar to come and treat me?" Baba told me. "After all, he is my nephew." I didn't know Samar very well at the time. I had met him briefly when he dropped his mother off in Patna the day before Baba got out of jail, and then again at his mother's house when we visited her and her family on the way back from Anandanagar. So I called Hiraprabha's house and talked to his elder brother Amal, who is an engineer. He told me that Samar was at the office but that he would give him the message when he got home. At the time Samar was a director in the health department for the state of West Bengal. He was living in Chinsurah but he would commute to Calcutta each morning by train and return home in the evening. Amal conveyed the message and the next morning, on his way to work, Samar stopped at Lake Gardens while Baba was having breakfast.

It was Baba's instruction that whenever any family member came to see him they should only be given time during meals, either breakfast, lunch, or dinner. The rest of Baba's day was reserved for organizational work. If they came at any other time they would have to wait until Baba's next meal. Before taking his food, Baba would ask me if anybody had come. If any family member had arrived he would ask me to send them in. We used to keep a table in Baba's room and he would generally take his meals there. If there was no family member present, then I would remain in the room with Baba and the cook would stand just outside the door in case Baba needed anything else. I would also keep some dada outside the room, in case Baba wanted to talk to someone. Most often this was Dada Vijayananda, though there were certain other dadas who were regulars as well. They would be ready with their notebooks in case Baba wanted to dictate something or make corrections to his books. I would always keep the door ajar so they could hear what Baba was saying. I would ask Baba if he wanted me to send them in, but usually he would say, "No, they can hear very well from the door." But whenever any family member came, I would close the door so that Baba could have some privacy for his family talks. Sometimes he would scold them also.

I told Baba that Dr. Samar had come. Then I sent him into Baba's room and left them alone. When it was time for Samar to leave, Baba called me and asked me to give him some toffee. There was a certain kind of toffee that Baba particularly liked and large quantities of it were piling up in the cabinet. A couple of years earlier one margi from Singapore had given Baba a box of this toffee when he arrived back at the house from field walk. I took it up to his room and afterward Baba asked me what was written on the package.

"Baba, it is written here that this toffee helps to sooth the throat, and that if anyone has to speak for a long time, such as an orator, they will not get hoarse or suffer from a sore throat if they take this toffee."

"Is that so?" Baba said. "This will be good for me then, since I have to speak a lot. I can take it when I am in the car."

After that I used to keep a package of this toffee in the car, and from time to time Baba would take a piece, especially when he had to give a discourse after his field walk. When I saw that Baba liked it, I gave a sample to one dada who was working in Singapore and asked him to bring more. Eventually the word got around and other workers and margis started bringing it for Baba. Once it started accumulating in our cabinets, Baba began giving it as gifts to his family members and sometimes to certain margis.

After I gave Samar the toffee—initially I gave him one package but Baba told me to give him three—he touched Baba's feet and left for his office. In accordance with the Bengali system, non-margis like Samar would touch Baba's feet and then give namaskar; they would not do sastaunga pranam as Baba's margi disciples would. After he left, I asked Baba if he had had a chance to examine him.

"Yes, I have conveyed my problem to him and he has told me that he will consult with some of his colleagues. He will return after two or three days with some medicine."

Samar consulted with his colleagues, emphasizing that his uncle was a strict vegetarian, and returned after three days with a month's supply of medicine. When he brought the medicine, Baba's first question was if he had liked the toffee. Not only had he liked it, but he had given it to his family members and some friends and they had all liked it. "Very good," Baba said, pleased with his answer. "Ramananda, give him some more packages of that toffee."

The medicine helped and thereafter Samar started coming every month or two to visit Baba and to check on his condition and bring him more medicine. Since the CPM government was in power at that time—they were very antagonistic toward Ananda Marga—he would come at certain hours when he was unlikely to be observed. Baba counselled him to take these precautions, warning him that he would run into difficulties with the government if they knew he was visiting Baba. He would bring Baba news of the family during these visits and Baba would always send him off loaded with toffee.

1981

Baba Gives Me His Cane

*D*URING DHARMA SAMIKSHA, Baba would punish as many as 150 disciples in a single day in order to cleanse them of their negative samskaras and thus elevate their minds. He would receive the margis all morning long in Jodhpur Park, and then after lunch he would tell me that we had to go back so that he could finish his work. Again he would spent many hours in the afternoon conducting Dharma Samiksha. As a result of meting out so much punishment, Baba's hands and shoulders became affected. He had so much pain in the evenings that I had to keep two or three persons on call to massage him so that he could have some relief.

When Dharma Samiksha ended, I felt I needed to say something. Up until then I had kept silent. I told Baba that it wasn't good for him to keep punishing the workers and margis in this way because it was affecting his health. And really, he was in so much pain sometimes that it seemed inhuman that he should have to endure it.

"But if I stop, who will do my work?" Baba said.

"Baba, you will have to decide on the proper alternative. But I can see with my own eyes that it is too much for you."

The next morning Baba called me and asked me if I was ready to take up this responsibility. When I said that I was, Baba said, "Don't worry, I will guide you. I will tell you how much punishment the person requires and when you should stop. I'll let you know how hard you should punish him and where."

After that, Baba began taking my help during collective reporting sessions. He would hand me the stick and tell me how much punishment to give to a particular dada. If only light punishment was necessary he would tell me to do brooming work. If he wanted me to strike harder, he would tell me so. "This person has done very bad things," he would say, "so he requires strong punishment." I would close my eyes and hit the person harder.

Baba also stopped fasting because of my request. For the first three or four months after he came out of prison he was still weak. But even so, he began fasting four times a month, just as he had before he had begun his protest fast. I was very adamant when I approached Baba. "Baba, you don't need to fast anymore," I told him. "The whole world knows that you have fasted for five years, four months, and two days. From now on, please take something on fasting days."

Baba agreed, and from then on he began taking juice and milk on fasting days.

1981

Reporting

*W*HEN BABA WOULD come for reporting, the workers would stand up and they would generally remain standing throughout the reporting session. Sometimes, if it went on too long, Baba would ask them to sit. Once Baba was ready, he would ask me who was going to be reporting that day. There was a fixed order: first ERAWS, then SDM, PU, Seva Dal, and finally the different departments. Baba would ask them questions and invariably he would catch those workers who had violated the rules and expose them in front of everyone. Then he would give them punishment—or rather, I would give them punishment under his direction. Everyone has some shortcomings so there was always somebody who was punished for his misdeeds. Those who hadn't completed their work would have to give in writing that they would complete their work within a certain period of time, usually not more than one day.

There was also a certain etiquette while Baba was talking. I will give you one example. It was the rule that if Baba was speaking to someone then no one should interrupt. You should only speak if he indicated that you should speak. Once, Baba was asking a certain overseas dada for the English verb that is used when one mixes flour and water and prepares the dough for making chapattis, unleavened bread. Baba asked him several times but this dada couldn't remember the word. Then one Indian dada volunteered the word. "Baba, the word is 'knead.'" Baba immediately got angry. "I didn't ask you. I asked this boy. I wanted to teach him something. It is his language. He knows the word but he was unable to remember it. Why did you interrupt?" Baba had me punish him for quite some time for violating the system. "Beat him harder," he told me. "Beat him harder."

But reporting sessions were full of levity as well. Baba would often tell stories and cut jokes. For example, one time Baba told a story about a lazy student who could not bring himself to study for his exam. When he sat for his exam he was unable to copy from his classmates because the examiner had people walking up and down in the exam hall to prevent copying. So the student wrote the same answer for all five questions on his exam paper: *harazo ki kismat teri hathonme hai; jara pass kar do to kya bhat hai.* It is a couplet from a Hindi poem; it means, "my life's fate is in your hands; I request you to declare me passed."

The examiner is supposed to write his comments next to the student's answers and give him a grade. So this examiner wrote the following comment after each of the student's answers: *kitabon ki kunji teri hathonme hai; jara yad kar lo to kya bhat hai,* which means, "the key of the book is in your hand; if you remember what it says then you will be declared passed."

1981

Prabhakar and Subhadra Sandhu

PRABHAKAR SANDHU AND his wife, Subhadra Didi, were a very devoted couple from Mumbai. They used to attend the DMCs with great regularity. Baba used to encourage margis to bring their families when they came for DMC, and Prabhakar and his wife faithfully followed this instruction, always bringing their children to the programs. Prabhakar was in medical manufacturing. He would bring medicines for Baba from his company whenever he came to visit, along with detailed instructions on how to administer them.

Prabhakar and his wife would never leave after the DMC without seeking Baba's permission—they were very good sadhakas, both of them, with glowing faces. Baba used to tell them, "Don't say that you are leaving. Say that you are coming. This means that you are going to return."

Once, when they came to Baba to get permission to leave, Subhadra Didi prostrated in front of Baba and said, "I don't want to leave you, I don't want to leave. We have come from so far away. We don't want to go back." She was crying profusely and so was Prabhakar. Then Baba said, "Whenever you do your dhyana you will find me there. Don't think that I am only in Calcutta. I am always with you, inside of you. I don't want to see you crying when you leave. I want to see you laughing."

Prabhakar said, "Baba, when we leave you it creates such strong feelings of separation. That is why we come to Calcutta to see you, so that we don't feel that separation."

"That is fine, Prabhakar," Baba said, "but even so, I don't want to see you crying like this. I want my sons and daughters to laugh. I want to see them always laughing."

1982

The Colour of Buckets

ANY TIMES I saw how nothing could be hidden from Baba. I remember one afternoon in Tiljala, Baba was taking reports from bhukti pradhans and ACB members from different parts of India. These reporting sessions with the margis were similar in style to the reporting sessions with the wholetimers. Baba would often expose the faults of the margis and take steps to rectify them, just as he did with the wholetimers.

As usual I accompanied Baba from his room to the reporting hall and took my seat next to his cot. Typically Baba would ask the general secretary to read out the names of those who were slated to give their reports on that day. The GS would then announce the names, such as SS Manila Sector, if it was sectorial reporting, or BP Hooghly, if it was bhukti pradhan reporting, as in this case. Normally the dadas in charge of reporting would select those persons who had done good work so that Baba would be pleased. In this case the GS called the bhukti pradhan of Hooghly District to give his report, since he was an active, hard-working BP. But Baba intervened.

"No, no, no," he said. "I know you have chosen those BPs who have done good work. I know this man. He is very good, so I don't want to take his report. All the BPs are good but some have not been doing satisfactory work. This time I will personally select the people. You will not call the people. Where is the bhukti pradhan of Bareilly?" Bareilly is an important city near Lucknow, in Uttar Pradesh.

The bhukti pradhan of Bareilly came forward and started giving his report, enumerating the different things he had done for the different departments: school, prachar, and so on.

"Yes, yes," Baba said. "I know you have done good work but I want to know what work you did on one particular Monday between the hours of nine and two."

Baba gave the date but this margi looked puzzled. Obviously, he could not remember what he had done that day. But Baba kept prodding him. "Go on, tell, tell, what were you doing on that Monday between the hours of nine and two?"

Slowly a light dawned in his mind. "Baba, I went to the shop that morning to buy buckets for the school. The dada in charge of the school came by that morning to borrow some buckets so I told him that I would go to the market and buy him some and bring them over myself."

"That was before nine o'clock. What I want to know is what happened between nine o'clock and two. Should I tell everyone?"

"No, Baba, please."

"Then tell me what happened."

The margi hesitated at first but after a few moments he said, "Baba, I quarrelled with my wife."

"And what was the reason for your quarrel?

"It was about the buckets, Baba."

"Was it only about the buckets, or was there more to it than that? Will you tell what happened or do I have to?"

"No, Baba, please don't tell. It was over the colour of the buckets."

"Yes, it was over the colour of the buckets, but it didn't end there, did it?"

"No, Baba."

Gradually, between this man telling the story under Baba's prodding and Baba adding further details, the story came out. That morning, before going to the shop, his wife had asked him to buy orange buckets and mugs for the school. Since the dadas wear orange, the colour of renunciation, she thought they would prefer to have orange buckets. The man went to several shops looking for orange buckets, but when he didn't find any he bought green buckets and mugs instead, thinking that the colour didn't really matter. But when he returned home with the buckets, his wife became upset. She asked him to take them back and get orange buckets and mugs. He wouldn't do it and thus a quarrel broke out and it lasted a full five hours, from nine in the morning until two in the afternoon.

At this point, the man said, "Baba, please stop. I will take punishment and I promise that in the future I won't waste a single moment of my life in such quarrels. I will only think about you."

"You will always think about me, you say, but on that day you wasted five hours of your life quarrelling with your wife."

"I understand, Baba. It was my mistake. I should have compromised. I promise again, from now on I won't waste a single second."

"Very well. You have done some other improper things but I won't reveal them. They will remain between you and me. Since you have promised, it means you will be moving in the right direction. I have pointed out your defects because this is RDS and you are my son—it is the platform for that—but I am also pointing out the solution. From now on you should strive to be an ideal man, and to be an ideal man you should not waste a single second of your life. Is it okay?"

"Yes, Baba."

Baba then looked around the room and said, "This doesn't only apply to him. It applies to every single person in this room."

In the end Baba did not punish him. He said that he had already received punishment enough.

1982

Vanamali's Daughter

*V*ANAMALI SARKAR WAS an administrative officer at the Calcutta police headquarters in Lal Bazar. He was a good sadhaka, short in stature and admired throughout the police force for his simplicity, his honesty, and his personal integrity. He did not come often to see Baba but he was a devoted margi.

Once, after his daughter attempted to commit suicide, he discussed it with his wife and they decided they should tell Baba about it. He came to Lake Gardens and asked me for permission to see Baba. I agreed and he met Baba at the door to Baba's room as Baba was getting ready to go on field walk. As soon as he began to tell Baba what had happened, Baba stopped him. "No need to say anything," he said. "I know what happened. She has already been saved twice. Go and tell her that you talked to me. Then do a one-hour kirtan with her in the morning. Once she does the kirtan, she will never be tempted to do such a thing again. And don't worry about her marriage. It will be solemnized within five months and the boy will be very good. From now on you should not worry about your daughter. I will take care."

Everything happened as Baba foretold. His daughter's marriage was solemnized and she went on to have children and lead a happy family life.

1982

The Police Do Pranam

*D*URING THE YEARS that Baba lived in Calcutta there were certain frequent destinations where we would take him for field walk, such as the botanical gardens or the Sundarbans. The blue photo, for example, where Baba is sitting inside a room in a boat, was taken while crossing the Hooghly river on our way to the botanical gardens. If the place was a little far, like the Sundarbans, we would have to inform Baba one day earlier and get his permission. But our most frequent destination was Rabindra Sarobar, a large lake near Gol Park encircled by a shaded walking path. It was only a short distance from the Lake Gardens house and it was a pleasant place to walk, especially at night when we had less time at our disposal and thus could only take him to nearby areas.

Due to Vanamali Sarkar, Baba used to enjoy the special protection of the local traffic police. At that time there were four main crossings between Lake Gardens and Rabindra Sarobar. Whenever the traffic officers would see Baba's car coming—our car was easy to spot because of the distinctive Ananda Marga flag that flew from the hood—they used to stop the converging traffic so that the car could pass by without hindrance. The same was true when Baba was walking around the lake. Once a white-uniformed officer rushed up to our party. We all stopped, including Baba. I thought that perhaps we had violated some traffic rule, but it turned out that he wanted to touch Baba's feet. He was having some family difficulty and since he had heard from Vanamali Sarkar about Baba, he had come to seek his blessing. This was not uncommon. Vanamali Sarkar was highly respected in the Calcutta police force and he used to tell his fellow officers that if they had any serious problem in their life all they had to do was to go before Baba and do namaskar and their problem would be solved. It became a common occurrence for us to see a small party of police officers approaching us. They would do namaskar to Baba from a respectful distance and then disappear as quietly as they came. Like everyone else, these policemen had their fair share of problems. One of them had a son who was admitted to the hospital with a serious illness; the mother of a traffic constable on motorcycle duty fell mortally ill; another officer's wife had developed a malignant cancer. Their problems were solved when they got Baba's blessings and they communicated this to their fellow officers. Thus Baba was always very safe in Calcutta. From time to time, some officer, pressured by the CBI, would create problems for one of our schools but this was very rare in comparison to the great number of officers who treated Baba with the utmost honour and respect. The organization had to face problems due to the CPM government but Baba never had to directly face such problems.

1982

Uma Shankar of Muzaffarpur

*U*MA SHANKAR WAS a homoeopathic doctor who attributed his cures more to the power of second lesson than to the medicines he used. Homoeopathy has the great advantage of being free from side effects, unlike allopathy, and Baba used to take homoeopathic medicines from time to time.

Uma Shankar rarely got a chance to meet Baba face to face. Baba was always busy with organizational activities and the security people made it difficult sometimes for ordinary margis to be close to him, especially once the organization became very large. Uma Shankar was a jovial man but he felt unfortunate because he couldn't get close to Baba. So he started thinking of some means by which he could hear Baba say his name. That was all he wanted. He felt sure that if he could hear Baba say his name just once then he would know that he was truly blessed; it would mean that Baba knew him and remembered him. Now in every DMC there is a tandava demonstration in front of Baba, both tandava and kaoshiki. One day during the annual New Year's DMC, he went to the dada in charge of the tandava demonstration and asked for permission to be included among the dancers. Generally Baba would make some comment after the demonstration—this was more or less obligatory—and he thought that if he could be in the first row of dancers then Baba might very well look at him and might even say his name. He was a stout man, impressive looking in his own way, and this dada agreed to place him in the front row. He took the red and blue dress from the dada and got ready to dance. Baba reached the stage and the dada made the announcement: "Fifty brothers for tandava. Ready. One, two, three, jump!" Uma Shankar jumped and began dancing tandava to the best of his ability. As he was dancing he could see Baba looking directly at him and he became even more inspired. Finally, when the dada halted the dance, Baba looked at him and said, "I think you are Uma Shankar.

Very good performance, excellent!" Only it wasn't excellent, to say the least. Because of his bodily limitation, he could barely lift his legs more than a foot off the ground. But Baba complimented him and for the rest of his life he would tell people how Baba had praised his tandava.

That evening Baba told me, "You know I had to say something to him; otherwise he would have become disheartened. He is a good person and a good devotee, but the dadas do not give him a chance to come near me. He was hoping that by dancing tandava Baba would speak to him, and I could not disappoint him."

After that, Uma Shankar would dance tandava in every New Year's DMC and Baba would often compliment him on his performance.

1982

Shiva Liila and Krishna Liila

IN BABA'S HOUSE in Lake Gardens there are two works of art that are especially worth mentioning. One is a set of twelve paintings depicting the life of Lord Shiva; the other is a series of some fifteen or sixteen glass cases with miniature scenes from the life of Lord Krishna. Both were commissioned by Baba.

The paintings of Lord Shiva's life came first. Rina-di knew an art professor at Rabindra Bharati University, Manik Bandopadhyaya, a very sentient person and a talented artist. When Baba told me that he wanted the Shiva Liila in his house, I approached her, and she and her husband, Amitabha Sen, took me to meet this professor. He was quite interested in the commission but he said that he would need to have a clear idea of what we wanted. "Don't worry," I said. "We will take you to meet such a person as you have never seen in your life. He will give you all the ideas you require, and you will be very happy that you had a chance to meet him."

He was very much intrigued by the idea of meeting a spiritual guru. A few days later we brought him to Lake Gardens and Baba met him in the hall where he used to hold reporting sessions. Baba asked for a chair to be brought for him but the professor preferred to sit on the ground. He was very humble. He said that it wasn't right for him to sit on a chair in front of such a personality. I told Baba that he was an art professor and an excellent painter, and Rina-di also had many nice things to say about him. Baba was in a smiling mood. He complimented the professor and then started explaining about the life of Shiva and the various episodes that he wanted depicted, such as Shiva sitting in the middle of his *ganadhars*, his *ganadhars* doing Rudra tandava, and so on. It took more than forty-five minutes for Baba to complete his explanation; thus his routine was pushed back. Finally he asked the professor if he had understood.

"Yes, Baba," he said. "I understand, but I need your grace and blessings to be able to do it."

"Don't worry," Baba said. "Since I have explained what I want, it means that you have my blessings."

It took Professor Bandopadhyaya five months to complete the paintings. He framed them himself and brought them to Lake Gardens. Baba was very pleased with the paintings and we hung them in a nearby room.

Sometime later Baba told me that he wanted to commission a pictorial representation of the life of Shrii Krishna. Once again Rina-di came to my aid. She knew a young artist in Krishnagar, Kanchan Karmakar, who had won many prizes for his miniatures of different gods and goddesses. He was only seventeen or eighteen at the time but he had a God-given talent. He could look at the painting of any god or goddess and reproduce the scene in a three-dimensional clay model inside of a glass case. I requested her to bring the boy to Calcutta and we took him to meet Baba. Baba was sitting on a chair and myself, Rina-di, and Kanchan were sitting on the ground in front of him. One by one, Baba described the episodes he wanted, such as Krishna stealing the clothes of the gopis, Krishna in the forest, Krishna killing the demons, and so on. The boy picked up Baba's ideas without any difficulty and he was able to finish the boxes within three to four months. When he presented them to Baba, Baba was effusive in his praise: "What? Such a small boy is capable of doing such great work?" This made Kanchan Karmakar very happy.

We set up the boxes on the first floor, to the left of Baba's door as you come out of his room. I stayed in that room for many years, sleeping just outside Baba's door. All the museum articles from the different countries were stored and displayed in that room. When Baba began giving his garden demonstrations, he would normally end the tour there. He would say a few things about the two liilas. "Now you will see with your own eyes different events from the lives of Shiva and Krishna." Then he would go into his room to take rest and I would finish the tour by showing the Krishna Liila and Shiva Liila to the tour participants.

1982

Garden Demonstration

*I*N 1982 BABA began conducting a tour of his garden and museum twice a month for interested persons. It was the DPS's duty to arrange the participants. Baba wanted highly qualified people who were interested in plants, animals, fossils, and such things. The number could not exceed sixteen but if the DPS had difficulty finding enough suitable people it sometimes fell as low as ten. He would take a few days to make his selection—they were mostly margis but sometimes non-margis were also included—and about half an hour or forty-five minutes before the tour was scheduled to begin he would read out the names to Baba, who would either approve or disapprove the names. If the DPS hadn't been able to find enough suitable candidates then Baba would scold him and threaten to cancel the tour. When that happened we would rush to add one or two margis from those who were present in the compound, and this would usually satisfy Baba. Sometimes he would also suggest certain names—his neighbours or other known people.

Generally the tour would take place after morning field walk—though it sometimes replaced the field walk—and it usually lasted about an hour and a half, sometimes as long as two hours. We would start downstairs, from the left side as you face the house, near the statue of Rabindranath Tagore. First we would move toward Krishna Kunj—*kunj* means "garden". After that we would come to Shiva Kunj, then the water lily pond, and then the room where the fossils were kept—most of the fossils came from Anandanagar. As we walked, Baba would point out certain plants and talk about their origin, their history, their different characteristics, how they should be cultivated, and so on. People would ask questions and in this way an enlightening conversation would continue throughout the tour. Those academics who attended, especially the non-margis, would be astounded at the vast scope of Baba's knowledge. He would also give instructions to the gardeners as he walked, sometimes inquiring if such and such a plant had been given water yet, and so on.

When the circuit was complete, Baba would lead everyone up to the roof to show them the greenhouse with the brahma kamal and the other cold-weather plants. Then we would come downstairs to the first-floor room where most of the museum items were kept in glass cases, including some of the most interesting fossils. At that point Baba would sit down and accept a glass of coconut water. He would chat for a few more minutes with his guests, inquiring whether or not they enjoyed the tour. Then he would ask me to show them the Krishna Liila and Shiva Liila displays, after which he would retire to his room to take rest.

1982

Mr. Maithy and the Agri Horticultural Society of India

*A*T ONE POINT Baba suggested that I become a member of the Agri Horticultural Society of India on Alipore Road, which had been founded in Calcutta early in the nineteenth century. They had a massive collection of plants and as a member it would be easy for me to obtain specific plants that Baba wanted for his various gardens—Anandanagar, Tiljala, Lake Gardens, and so on. I did as Baba asked and soon developed a fine rapport with Mr. Maithy, the assistant manager of the society. He became intrigued by the orders for plants that he would periodically help me with and especially by the information that I was able to give him about the different plants we were ordering, information that had come directly from Baba, who gave a great deal of attention to these orders. Over time Mr. Maithy developed a strong desire to meet Baba, so one day in February he asked me if Baba would be willing to visit their botanical gardens. It was the time of their annual three-day flower show, and he assured me that if Baba was able to come during the exposition he would personally show Baba many rare and wonderful plants.

When I conveyed this to Baba he was enthusiastic. "Why not?" he said. "I go out for field walk every day. Why not go on field walk to the society's botanical gardens?" This was in the morning. I called Mr. Maithy and gave him the message that Baba would be able to visit the gardens that evening.

We were six persons: myself, Baba, and four margis. Mr. Maithy was waiting for us with six entrance passes when we arrived. He touched Baba's feet, gave him namaskar, and then escorted us on a tour through the gardens. The society's gardens were very impressive, and Mr. Maithy was an excellent host, pointing out this flower and that as we walked. Baba also commented on the flowers, telling their history, expressing his concern for the plants, asking which ones were tropical or sub-tropical, which were of Indian origin, and so on. It went on for a full hour, full of fascinating information about the world of plants, and flowers in particular.

When the tour was finished, Mr. Maithy told Baba that he would like to visit his garden, if it were possible. Baba agreed immediately, though he didn't generally invite non-margis to visit. Mr. Maithy came to Lake Gardens a few days later with other important persons from the Agri Horticultural Society, and they were quite impressed with Baba's garden and the way he ran it. Over the course of time we purchased a great number of plants and cuttings from them at very good rates and we always maintained a very cordial relationship with them.

1982

A Children's Home Boy in Baba's Garden

D URING THE YEARS that Baba was in Lake Gardens we always kept a gardener there to assist the garden-in-charge. He would water the plants and do other such daily tasks. Sometimes the gardener was a wholetimer, but most often he was an interested margi or LFT (Local Full-Timer). Once, the gardener let several plants die in the space of a few days. Afraid of how Baba might react, he left Calcutta without informing anyone and this put us in a fix. We needed a new gardener right away but we didn't want to burden Baba with this problem, so Asimananda hit on the solution of bringing a boy from the children's home in Anandanagar and training him to take care of the plants. One boy arrived within a few days—his name was Amrita Deva—and we got him acclimated to his duties as quickly as possible.

A day or two after Amrita Deva's arrival, Baba went up to the greenhouse to see how the cold-weather plants were doing and he saw the new boy watering them. He didn't say anything but when he came downstairs he started inquiring. "I saw a new person this morning watering the plants in the greenhouse. What happened to the gardener?"

"Baba, a few plants died and he could not face the situation," I said, "so he ran away."

"It was not only a few plants. He killed many plants. So who is this boy?"

"Baba, he is from Anandanagar Central Children's Home."

"Is he qualified for the job?"

"Yes, Baba."

Baba didn't say anything else but the next morning he went to the greenhouse and talked to the boy himself. "How do you like this work?" he asked.

"I like it, Baba …"

"But it is not your first choice."

"No, Baba. I wanted to go for higher studies but the dadas sent me here."

Later that morning, Baba called the garden-in-charge and the education-in-charge and rebuked them. "How dare you send this boy here! I made our children's homes for the physical, mental, and spiritual welfare of the children who live there. This boy wants to go for higher studies and you have interrupted his education for your own convenience! Not only that, you did this without my permission or my knowledge. Send him back to Anandanagar this very second! I want a responsible person to accompany him to Anandanagar and then come back here immediately to bring me confirmation that he has arrived safely. In the meantime you people will take over his duties until you can find a suitable person."

The in-charges had to manage for a couple of months until they were able to get an LFT from Chhattisgarh, a hardworking young man who was interested in plants. He later married and established his own nursery.

1982

Acharya Keshav

O N April 11, 1982, in Calcutta, Baba gave his first talk on Shivology, the first in a series of talks that would eventually become the book *Namah Shiva Shantaya*. In the beginning of June we went to Patna and stayed there for nine weeks, where Baba continued the series. When the talks were nearing their conclusion, Baba asked us where we thought would be the best place to finish this work. I said that even though we didn't believe in Hindu mythology, this was a book on Shiva, so the most suitable place would be Varanasi—according to Hindu mythology Varanasi is situated on the *trishula*, or trident, of Shiva. Other workers supported the idea and Baba agreed, so on 12 August we left Patna for Varanasi.

As usual the word spread like wildfire that Baba would be traveling that day by car en route to Varanasi, and the local margis turned out at various points along the way to receive Baba and get his blessings. The biggest of these receptions was in Gazipur, which is home to many margis. Gazipur is on the border of Bihar and Uttar Pradesh. It is a historic place that has been visited by many saints. Vivekananda spent some time in Gazipur and Tagore wrote *Naoka Dubi* there while staying at his brother's house. To get there from Patna you have to cross the Ganges at Buxar and then pass through Balia. In the past, when Baba would stay overnight in Gazipur, he would usually stay in Acharya Keshav's house. We have a big school in Gazipur where margis can stay but it is not really suitable for Baba. So when the margis learned that Baba would be passing through Gazipur that day, they urged Acharya Keshav to invite him to spend the night. "We will stop the car," they said, "and you invite him. If you ask him, Baba won't be able to say no."

Acharya Keshav protested. "How can I get my house ready for Baba on such short notice? He may be here within a couple of hours. I don't want to take that responsibility." But the margis continued to pressure him and finally he agreed, mostly because he was sure that Baba wouldn't accept.

Hundreds of margis assembled on the main highway, where the road bifurcates shortly before reaching the city. When the entourage arrived they brought their garlands to Baba and received his blessings. Baba was very happy to see them. They pushed Acharya Keshav to the front and he invited Baba to spend the night. To his surprise, and ours also, Baba accepted his invitation without any hesitation. Soon our three cars— one car was for the security people and another for the workers—were heading toward his house, about a kilometre from where the margis had gathered to receive us.

When we reached the house, Acharya Keshav's daughter-in-law was a little tense, since they had not had time to purchase new bedsheets and towels or to properly prepare the room. But Baba was very gracious. He asked what room he would be staying in, and when they showed it to him he was very happy with the arrangements. Still, the family was worried that Baba would be inconvenienced, since they had not had time to prepare the house as they usually did when they knew in advance that Baba would be coming.

In the morning, when we were leaving, Keshavji, his son, and his daughter-in-law all started crying, apologizing to Baba for the lack of preparation and the great inconvenience they had caused him. But Baba was quite happy. "When I am your father and you are my children," he said, "then how can you say this? I have come to my own house. When I come to my own house, do my children come and apologize for the inconvenience I have to suffer? You are my son and I am in my own house. I felt completely comfortable. I had no trouble at all. Do you understand?"

"Yes, Baba."

That evening in Varanasi Baba gave the final talk on Shivology, the final chapter in the book *Namah Shiva Shantaya*.

August 1982

Lobin Mahato

*I*N 1981 OUR regular driver had some legal problem so I began driving Baba's car when we went on tour. This included our trips to Anandanagar for the biannual DMCs. Most often we would travel to Anandanagar from Calcutta, sometimes stopping along the way to spend the night at Baba's quarters in Vishnupur, but on this occasion we were traveling from Ranchi. Baba's schedule was not confirmed before we left, so we were not able to get information to the margis a day or two ahead of time as we normally did so they would be able to see Baba as he passed through their respective places. It was only when we were getting ready to leave that I was able to call one or two people. One of these was Lobin Mahato, a retired teacher who lived in Kita, a town about halfway between Ranchi and Anandanagar. Lobin was a highly educated person and a good sadhaka whom Baba loved very much. His house was near the main road, not far from the station. It was flanked on either side by orchards, and whenever Baba would pass through Kita, Lobin would call the local margis and they would rush to his place to prepare a reception for Baba. Baba was well aware of this. As we were getting into the car he asked me if I had informed Lobin that we would be passing through Kita. When I told him that I had only just called due to my uncertainty about our travel arrangements, Baba said, "You should have told him earlier. How will he have time now to prepare a reception?"

But much to my surprise, there was a huge crowd waiting for us when we reached Kita. When Baba saw the commotion, he said, "Oh, there is a very big crowd here. Slow down the car. Where are we?"

I told Baba that it was Kita and that the crowd was composed of margis and a few government officials. He smiled and reminded me that we were on a tight schedule—a lot of important work was waiting for him in Anandanagar—but he cautioned me that I should be sensitive to the sentiments of the people. When we stopped the car, Lobin was the first to greet us. Usually a volunteer would open Baba's door when we stopped, but this time Baba opened the door himself. When he saw Lobin smiling and holding a garland in his hands, he said, "Lobin, you are here? How did you know I was coming? Did anybody inform you?"

"Baba, you yourself informed me last night."

"Did I?"

"Yes, Baba. You came in my meditation last night and told me that you would be coming. Dada called me a couple of hours ago to inform me but I had already told the margis that you would be coming and we had already organized your reception."

Lobin took Baba's permission to garland him and then told the margis to line up so they could give their garlands to Baba one by one. "Everyone will be able to give their garlands to Baba," he called out.

It turned out that when he informed the margis that Baba would be coming, he had also instructed them to bring garlands and had promised them that he would request Baba to allow everyone to have an opportunity to garland him. So now he was directing traffic so that all could come and place their garlands around Baba's neck. I was in a quandary what to do. Baba was on a tight schedule. There was a lot of work to be done, and in the past Baba had instructed me to be very strict with his time in such situations. But Baba had just told me that I should be sensitive to the sentiments of the people. And here was Lobin Mahato telling the margis that everyone would have a chance to garland Baba. Baba was just standing there with folded hands, smiling, giving his namaskar to everyone and accepting their garlands. So I waited until everyone had their chance—it took a full twenty minutes—and then hurried Baba back into the car so we could start moving. But just after we started moving, an old man with a garland ran after the car shouting, "Baba, Baba, Baba."

"Wait, stop the car," Baba said. "I hear something." So I stopped the car. Lobin Mahato caught the old man by the hand and brought him to the car. Baba got out, patted the old man on the cheek, and accepted his garland. "Are you happy now?" he said. "Are you very, very happy?" The old man was thrilled and Lobin was also smiling from ear to ear, though his eyes were full of tears. He told Baba that he would be reaching Anandanagar in two to three hours with a large contingent of margis.

This was not the first reception that Lobin had organized but it was really very unique. Nowadays, whenever he comes to Anandanagar for some program, or when a worker from Anandanagar goes to his house, he invariably starts recalling those beautiful days. He has many Baba stories. I have heard him narrate many incidents when he avoided serious accidents and other calamities by doing guru dhyana. Baba would appear to him and tell him not to go to such and such a place. He is a special person indeed, very sentient. His son is a tattvika.

1982

Parameshvar Dreams of Baba

IN 1982 A margi couple from New Zealand, Parameshvar and Prabha, came to see Baba along with their nineteen-year-old son, Amarendra. Prabha was a hospital nurse and Parameshvar was a chemistry professor. They had been initiated a few years earlier and had heard many stories about Baba and his miracles, so they arranged a leave of ten days and came to Calcutta. They took a room in the Grand Hotel and each day they came with garlands to Lake Gardens, hoping to have a chance to garland Baba and talk to him, but each day they were frustrated in their desire. There were large crowds around Baba in those days wherever he went, and it always seemed that there were other devotees in front of them. Each day, while going to his car for field walk or coming back, Baba would stop and give namaskar to the devotees who were gathered there and accept a few garlands from those closest to him. He would usually chat for a few minutes with the margis but no matter how much they tried, Parameshvar and Prabha could never get close enough to Baba to give him their garlands.

A week passed and the date was fast approaching for them to catch their return flight. Naturally, they felt disheartened; it appeared unlikely that they would have a chance to fulfil their desire. But the day before they were to leave, Baba himself told me about them. "Some people have come from New Zealand to see me," he said. "I would like very much to see them but my time is very short. Can you arrange it so I can see them?"

"Yes, Baba," I said. "The only possible time would be after field walk. If they are here, then I can arrange it."

"Then make sure they are here. If need be, call them at their hotel."

They had given me their contact number, so I had someone call them and tell them that Baba was asking about them and that they should come right away. They got in a cab and rushed to Lake Gardens as soon as they got the call, buying garlands on the way.

When they arrived Baba was out on field walk. "Baba will be back soon," I told them. "He told me personally that he wanted to see you, so this is what you will do: Go and stand by the statue of Rabindranath Tagore, to the left of the gate, the three of you. You will be the only ones there. I will also be there to make sure that you have your chance, and I will let security know that no one else should be allowed to stand on that side of the gate. When Baba gets out of his car he will get down on your side of the gate, so he will see you as soon as he gets down. Then you can do namaskar and give him your garlands."

When Baba came back from field walk he got down in front of these three margis. Very innocently, he asked, "Oh, from where have you come?" As if he were surprised to see them.

"From New Zealand, Baba."

"Very good. And how are you doing?"

"We are fine, Baba, by your grace." They were smiling from ear to ear now. They garlanded Baba and he handed the garlands to me and told me to keep two of them in my room and to give the other one back to them so they could bring it back with them to New Zealand.

When Baba turned back to them he said, "You wanted to give these garlands to me. Are you happy now? You shouldn't think that Baba isn't thinking of you. You wanted to see me; I also wanted to see you."

Baba started talking about the Maoris in New Zealand, how they were being exploited and neglected and how they should do some good work to help the Maori community. Baba talked to them for nearly ten minutes, which was quite uncommon.

One very curious thing happened before Baba went into the house. After this brother took initiation he had dreamed several times of Baba, and in these dreams he had always seen Baba without his glasses. As Baba was talking, he was wondering if this was the same Baba he had seen in his dreams, since he had never seen Baba in real life without his specs. But at that moment Baba took off his specs and started cleaning them. This by itself was highly unusual. I used to clean Baba's glasses every morning and evening with a special liquid that some overseas margis had sent me. I had cleaned his glasses that morning and they were shining when he had gone out for field walk. Nevertheless, he took them off and started cleaning them. Then he looked at Parameshvar without his glasses and said, "Is this the same Baba or is it another Baba?" Just as Parameshvar was wondering the very same thing. Then Baba smiled and put on his glasses.

Afterward Parameshvar told me the story of his dreams and how Baba had graced him by removing his glasses.

1982

Prabhat Samgiita

THERE WERE A number of margis and acharyas in Ananda Marga who used to compose devotional songs and sing them in front of Baba: for example, Kshitij, Natkat Kedar, Muphlish, and several workers, such as Nityasatyananda. At some point Baba began saying that Ananda Marga should have its own system or school of music, its own *gharana*. In the present age, he'd say, music has gone in the wrong direction; it has become distorted. He told this to me on a number of occasions and to others also.

Then in September 1982 we went to Deoghar to spent a few weeks in the MG quarters. It is a beautiful place, about one kilometre from the main town and in full view of the mountains and forests—Baba used to like that house very much. The land was donated by Sudanshu's parents—Sudanshu is presently the BP of Ranchi—and Bhagatji helped to construct the house, as did Dr. Patra, the father of a very devoted family of Deoghar. Patraji gave three children to the mission as wholetimers, two daughters and one son, Cetanananda, who was in the Prabhat Samgiita party for some time—he is a fine singer. Baba used to give extra time to those families that had donated sons or daughters to the mission, so Dr. Patra and his wife used to come often to invite Baba to Deoghar, and Baba enjoyed going there. Deoghar is a temple town by the banks of the Ganges. It is considered by the Hindus to be the place of Lord Shiva. Many saints have frequented Deoghar, so it is sometimes called Baba Dham. It is also host to a one-month spiritual festival in August, attended by hundreds of thousands of people.

Early one morning—it was September 14—Baba came out of his room and asked me to gather some good singers, those who were knowledgeable about music, and have them ready when he called. "I will give you half an hour to bring them," he said. It was barely 4:30 but I managed to round up four or five people whom I knew to be good singers. Devatmananda was one. Didi Ananda Gita was another. Baba was still in his room but the door was partially open and I could hear him humming a melody. Then he came out and sat down. "I want to say something about songs," he said. "Many margis are singing devotional songs but they do so without any acknowledged system. For this reason, I am thinking of introducing a new *gharana*, which I think will benefit everyone. But first I want your advice. Do you think that there will be any interest in this?"

We were all very enthusiastic in our response. We knew how much the margis would appreciate it and we told Baba so.

"Then let us go ahead. Let it be introduced from here, from Deoghar."

Baba started singing the melody that he had been humming in his room. Then he asked those workers to sing the melody back to him. When he was satisfied that they had memorized the melody correctly, he sang it with the words and they noted them down and then sang the song in front of him.

When they were done, he asked, "How do you like this song? Should it remain and become the first Prabhat Samgiita?"

"Yes, Baba, it is very beautiful, both words and music."

"Are you sure? If you don't like it, then I will cancel it."

"No, Baba, don't cancel it. We love the song."

"Okay then. If you approve of it, then let the song remain."

That was how the first Prabhat Samgiita, *bandu he niye calo,* was given.

We stayed in Deoghar for another fifteen days and Baba continued to give new songs, a practice he kept up until his mahaprayana. I used to keep four or five workers nearby who were good in singing. At some point I would hear Baba humming a tune in the bathroom and then I knew that he was going to give a Prabhat Samgiita. He would say, "Ramananda, call the kirtan party. I am ready." Once the kirtan party was ready he would start singing the tune. Most of the time he would be in his room, sometimes in the bathroom. If the door to his room was closed, they would have to put their ears to the ground so they could hear him from underneath the door. When he was in the bathroom they could hear him through the bathroom window. Sometimes he would ask them to come inside the room but mostly they would sit outside and listen. Baba had a gravelly voice but he sang very clearly and never went out of tune. He would sing the melody and they would have to sing it back to him. If they missed any notes, he would correct them. Once he was satisfied that they had picked up the tune correctly, he would give the words. They would go and practice and later Baba would call them to sing the song for him. Sometimes in Lake Gardens he would ask them to sing the song when he went downstairs to inspect his garden. Once they were able to sing the song successfully, both words and melody, Baba would ask them if they liked it or if he should cancel it. Everybody had to say how much they liked it. There was a kind of competition among the workers in this regard. It wasn't enough to say it was good. You had to say, "It is a thousand times good! It's tremendous, incredible!" Then Baba would be happy. He used to ask me every time what I thought of the song, and I would always try to come up with new ways to tell Baba how much I liked it.

Later, when Baba started giving more classical tunes, it became difficult for the people in the kirtan party to keep up. Sometimes it would take them a day or two before they could properly reproduce the melody, and until they got it right there would be no more songs. Baba would say, "If you are not able to sing it correctly, then I will scratch this song," and they would say, "No, Baba, please. We will rehearse it again." He would not let them off until they got it right. Once he was sure they had it right, they would take it for notation and recording.

After two or three years, people started commenting that everybody sang Prabhat Samgiita in front of Baba except Ramananda. "Everyday the kirtan party learns the new songs and sings them for Baba," they would say, "but we never hear Ramananda singing!" They even made this comment in front of Baba and he defended me. "Ramananda doesn't try," he said, "but if he tries he can sing." One day in Lake Gardens Baba put me in a fix. A number of workers were there in his room and he said, "Now I want Ramananda to sing one song." What could I do? I had to sing. So I began singing a song that Baba had given three or four days earlier: *hiya re majhare, nirava prahare, ke go deke gane jay, gane ra bhashaye.* It was a relatively simple song. I sang it all the way through and when I finished, Baba said, "Who says that Ramananda doesn't know how to sing. You see, he can sing if he tries." Later he told me that everybody was saying I couldn't sing. So he had asked me to sing in front of them so that they would know I could.

September 1982

Leaving Baba's Bag

THE ATMOSPHERE IN Deoghar was really quite unique, very devotional. The margis wept and cried much of the time that Baba was there, as if we had entered an entirely different world. Finally, though, it came time to leave for Patna. When everything was prepared I informed Baba that we were ready to depart.

"Have you checked the bathroom?" Baba asked. "You've gotten everything?"

"Yes, Baba."

"What about the bedroom?"

"Yes, Baba, everything is taken care of."

"So we can leave now?"

"Yes, Baba."

Baba came out of his room and went to the car, giving his namaskar to the margis who were waiting to see him off. I was at the wheel, with a security person next to me and one margi in the back seat next to Baba. An hour or two after we left Deoghar it suddenly dawned on me that I had left behind the bag in which I used to keep Baba's glasses, his dentures, some emergency money, and the alarm clock that I kept on the night table by his bed, set to 3:15, the hour that Baba would get up each morning. I was quite upset, as you might imagine, but I didn't say anything. I took Baba's name and continued on to his quarters in Patna.

As soon as we pulled in, I called two devoted local margis, Braj Bihari and Acharya Raj Mohan, and took them into my confidence. We tried calling Deoghar but we couldn't get anyone on the line. Baba was taking rest but he soon asked me why I hadn't put these items out. I had to admit that I had left them in Deoghar.

"Let this be a lesson to you," Baba said. "In the future you should not do anything with undue haste. I know that when I ask you to do something you are always eager to get it done, but whenever you finish any task you should ask yourself in a calm and serene state of mind whether or not everything has been done properly. Only then should you go ahead and say, 'Yes, Baba, everything is ready.' Anyhow, there is no need for you to worry. One margi will bring the bag here within three hours, with nothing missing. In the meantime, I will not face any problem."

That margi was Sudanshuji. He had checked my room and found the bag, and well before we arrived in Patna—it was a five-hour drive—he had left Deoghar to bring it to us. When he arrived, less than three hours after us, I took him to Baba's room, and Baba gave him the same advice he had given me. And indeed, it was true, I had been a little impatient. It was a lesson well learned.

29 September 1982

A Lady Loses Her Specs

ONE AGED SISTER from Nagpur, Mrs. Kale, used to help our whole-timer didis as much as she could. Her husband held a good position as Chief Executive Engineer in the Maharashtra State Electricity Board, so they were well off, which allowed her to be of great service to the mission. Once Mrs. Kale brought a friend of hers to the New Year's DMC. This lady was newly initiated but very devotional by nature. During the daily darshans she made sure to come early so she could sit in front and pay her respects to Baba as he was entering and leaving the dais. On the DMC night, however, she was dismayed to find that she had misplaced her glasses. How will I be able to see Baba's *varabhaya mudra*? she thought. She became so disheartened that she started weeping copiously. Mrs. Kale brought her to me at Baba's house and explained the problem. I was sorry to hear it—the lady was weeping in front of me, obviously very distraught. "I have lost my specs, how can I see Baba's *mudra*?" she kept saying, but I didn't know what I could do to help her. "It is not possible at this late hour to go to the city to buy a new pair," I said. "You would miss the DMC. You will have to rely on Baba's grace."

It was in this pained state of mind that she returned to her place among the margis. Baba and I reached the dais a short time later. Baba greeted the margis and gave his DMC talk, followed by his varabhaya mudra. Later she told me that she saw everything that night by some sort of unknown special vision. In fact, she said, Baba's mudra was clearer to her than it would have been had she been wearing her glasses. Baba had graced her with the power to see.

1 January 1983

Eye Operation

*W*HEN BABA WAS poisoned in the jail he developed three serious symptoms: high blood pressure, diabetes, and problems with his eyes—his eyes would water regularly and get red and his sight was badly affected. At intervals I had to change the prescription for his glasses. So while we were at Anandanagar for the 1983 New Years DMC, the doctors from Ranchi, Dr. Ramesh and Dr. Chakravarty, requested Baba to have his eyes operated on in Ranchi. We were already planning to take Baba to Ranchi for a month or so for rest—Ranchi is about ninety kilometres from Anandanagar and due to its elevation it possesses a very pleasant climate—so we told them that Baba could decide while he was there.

At that time the Ranchi quarters were not as built up as they are now. There was a room for Baba, a room for his PA, a veranda, and a kitchen with a couple of small adjoining rooms where other people could stay. After we arrived, the doctors consulted with Baba and he agreed to the operations, one on each eye. But before an operation can be conducted the patient has to undergo a series of tests. When the tests revealed that Baba suffered from diabetes, the doctors told him that he would have to start taking insulin injections. Baba would not agree, however, because insulin was non-vegetarian. He had first told me about the diabetes a few months after his poisoning but until then he had not taken any medicine for it. I made some inquiries and found a source for vegetarian insulin in the United States but it would take some time before our margi doctors in the States could send us a supply. Fortunately the doctors knew of some tablets that were available in Calcutta with which Baba's diabetes could be controlled. We had to wait for them to arrive before the operation could be scheduled.

When the eye tests were conducted, the doctors told us that the left eye was significantly worse than the right eye, so they recommended operating first on the left eye and then on the right, with a gap of one day between the two operations. We informed Baba and he agreed to the doctor's proposal. My room was chosen as the operation theatre. But while Baba was being administered a local anaesthetic, the medical team—four doctors and the chief eye surgeon—started discussing among themselves in Baba's presence, and the eye surgeon decided that he would operate on the right eye instead. When Baba heard this he said, "No. Why are they changing their mind?"

Dr. Ramesh asked the doctors to leave the room—he did not want them discussing the matter any further in front of Baba and thus disturbing him. Once they were outside, the head eye surgeon, Dr. Kashap, told Ramesh that Baba had lost his sight in his left eye. "Look," he said, "I don't know what my colleagues have told you but the eyesight in his left eye is completely gone. There is no point in operating on it."

"I understand," Ramesh said, "but you have to understand that Baba never goes back on his word. He agreed to operate on his left eye today, so the left eye it will have to be."

After a short discussion Dr. Kashap agreed. He operated on Baba's left eye that day and came back the following day to operate on Baba's right eye. They removed grey cataracts from Baba's eyes. According to the eye surgeon, grey cataracts are very rare and were almost certainly caused by poisoning. Dr. Chakravarty has preserved those cataracts in a special liquid.

For the next two or three days I had to help Baba move around the room, go to the bathroom, take his bath, and so on, until the bandages came off and Baba was able to start doing things by himself.

About a week later, Dr. Chakravarty was giving Baba a checkup—he used to monitor Baba's health—and Baba asked him why the doctors had changed their mind. He hesitated before answering, but finally he admitted that the doctors had discovered that Baba didn't have any sight in his left eye.

"Oh, so that was the reason," Baba said. "Chakravarty, do one thing. You are a doctor. Stand next to me while I cover my right eye with my hand. Ramananda, stand over there and hold up a newspaper. We will see whether or not I can read it with my left eye."

I got a newspaper and held it up about three feet away. Baba told me to move back until I was about six feet away. Then he started reading the headlines, one by one, without a single mistake. When Dr. Chakravarty saw this he fell to the floor and caught hold of Baba's feet.

Baba said, "Where medical science fails, spiritual science succeeds. They have failed in their science, though they have done their duty as best they could. When it comes to me, you people know far better. You understand the spiritual science."

After the operation Baba's eyesight improved. He still had some difficulty in his left eye but he was able to see with it.

Baba's teeth were also affected by the poisoning. Before he went to jail they were very strong—in fact, a dentist had once said after an examination that he had never seen such strong teeth—but after the poisoning they became quite weak. He began having pain while chewing. A dental surgeon also came to examine Baba while he was in Ranchi and he recommended that he have a set of dentures made. His teeth were filed down and the dentures were fitted during the five or six weeks that we were there. After that we went to Ananda Shiila for a change of climate.

January 1983

Rina

IN CALCUTTA THERE is one very devoted family, Rina and Amitabh Singh. They used to come to Lake Gardens almost every morning to see Baba before going to the office, especially Rina-di. One morning—it was most likely in 1983—she arrived a little later than usual and learned that Baba had already finished his morning walk. How can I go to the office without seeing Baba? she thought, feeling heartbroken that she had missed him. Rina decided that she couldn't go to the office without seeing Baba so she insisted on seeing me to ask me if I could allow her to see him. They told her I was busy but she kept insisting so Parimal, Baba's bodyguard, came and told me what she wanted. "How can she see Baba now?" I said. "He is in his room taking rest, and after his rest he has another program. Tell her to come back in the evening. She can see Baba then." Parimal conveyed my message but she still insisted on talking to me directly. "Okay," I said, when he came back upstairs to tell me. "Let her come up."

I used to stay in the room right outside Baba's door. That way, if he needed anything I would be there. At night I would sleep right in front of his door. She came up to my room and told me how sad she was that she hadn't seen Baba that morning, how she could not bring herself to go to the office without having his darshan. There were a couple of other workers in the room, as I remember, and also Baba's cook. Baba's door was ajar and there was a curtain in front of it; Baba was resting on his cot with a shawl over his body. While she was talking I could see how strong and sincere her desire was, so I decided I should do something to alleviate her anguish. Sometimes the job of being Baba's PA was a thankless one—thankless in the sense that if I had to deter someone from their wish then they would sometimes react against me and I had to bear the brunt of their displeasure. But sometimes it was very inspiring, especially when I was able to help a sincere sadhaka fulfil his desire. This was one of those times. Indeed, I felt that Baba had created this drama just to please his devotee. I could see her devotion and I thought that even if Baba scolded me I should help her get her wish. So I asked her if a glimpse of Baba would be enough. Her face immediately lit up. "Yes, Dada," she said. "It will be more than enough." I pushed the curtain aside and opened the door a little further. When I did this, the door creaked a little. Baba called out, "Ke? Ki korcho?" Who is there? What are you doing? I told Baba that the door was open and I was closing it. He said okay and returned to his rest. Thus Rina-di got to see Baba through the crack for a few moments, and that was enough to satisfy her desire. She left for the office with a blissful smile on her face, happy that she had seen her Baba.

That evening, before Baba bolted the door for the night, I did sas-taunga pranam as I always did before Baba went to bed. When I got up he said, "I want to visit Rina and Amitabh's house tomorrow. Do you have their address?"

I didn't have the address but I told Baba I would get it.

"Okay," he said, "but don't tell anyone where we are going."

Sometimes Baba would make surprise visits. He would visit a school or a press or sometimes the house of some margi. On such occasions Baba would give strict instructions that no one was to know of his plans. He wanted his visit to be a complete surprise.

I knew that someone would have to be taken into my confidence to get the address so I asked Parimal, since he would be coming anyway as Baba's bodyguard. Fortunately he knew the address. The next morning before field walk Baba asked me if everything was arranged. I informed him that it was. After greeting the margis, we got in the car and drove to Rina's house—on this occasion I also accompanied Baba. Dilip was Baba's driver and Parimal gave him directions. When we located the house, myself, Baba, and Parimal got out. Rina and Amitabh lived on the first floor—the ground floor was rented out—so I led Baba up the stairs and Parimal followed behind him. The security people, who had come in a separate car, remained downstairs at my instructions. When I rang the bell, Rina-di's son opened the door. He was about fifteen then; now he lives in Chicago. He saw me and called out, "Ma, Ramananda has come." She was doing meditation in a bedroom in front of an altar with Baba's photo and a garland. Amitabh had already left for the office. The son brought a chair for Baba, and when Rina-di came out of the bedroom she cried out "Baba" and ran to catch his feet. When she got up, Baba said, "Now, tell me, is there any need to see Baba through the curtain? If you have a strong desire to see me, then I am always there."

"Baba, I knew you would come," she said with tears in her eyes. "I knew you would come and visit me."

"You see?" Baba said. "There was no need to see me through the curtain. Whenever any devotee has a strong desire to see me, I am always there. Whenever you need me, whenever you want, I will come personally. Is it okay now? Have I done my duty for you?"

She went and brought some sweets. Baba touched them and blessed them. He took a little and then we went for our regular field walk.

1983

Dafliwali Didi

$\mathcal{I}$N SAMASTIPUR DISTRICT of Bihar there is a well-known town called Pusa; it is home to Rajendra Agricultural University and an important branch of the Indian Agricultural Research Institute. It is also home to two well-known acharyas, Acharya Vishvambar and his wife, who is popularly known as Dafliwali Didi, because wherever she goes she always carries a *dafli*, a large tambourine. People even say that she sleeps with it at night. This story is about how she became an acharya.

Vishvambar was an acharya from the early days, He was highly respected in Ananda Marga. His wife was also very popular but since she was illiterate she never thought she could become an acharya. But even though she wasn't an acharya, she was in no way inferior to her husband in prachar. On the weekends they would go together to the villages and while Vishvambar gave lectures she would go door to door and meet the women. On weekdays, while her husband was working, she would pack her lunch and spend the day doing prachar. Her specialty was music and she would sing kirtan and devotional songs wherever she went, accompanying herself on the *dafli*, and everyone would dance and get swept away by her devotional fervour. Through her devotional songs she would attract the womenfolk to Ananda Marga. She even formed a kirtan team with other margi women and they would often accompany her. Whenever any Ananda Marga unit in the area held a kirtan you could be sure that Dafliwali Didi would be there to lead the chanting. When Baba started composing Prabhat Samgiita she added his songs to her repertoire and thereafter the margis would always request her to sing Prabhat Samgiita wherever she went.

She would always show up at the biannual DMCs with a large group of margis from her area, and during these times she would often express her desire to become an acharya. "Baba will never make me an acharya," she would say, "because I cannot read and write. They are very strict about the qualifications so I have left it up to him. If he doesn't want, he doesn't want." And then she would sing in front of Baba during the programs.

One day in 1983 Baba decided to bend the rules. "She is doing so much prachar," he said. "I hardly see any acharya doing as much prachar as she. Why should she not also have the chance to become an acharya?" Since Baba's desire was clear, we called her for acharya training. She filled out the application and attended the training. But when she was called for the acharya exam she failed. She knew the philosophy but it was just too difficult for an illiterate person to pass the exam. But when the trainees who had passed the exam were presented to Baba, he asked the dadas why she was not among them. When they informed him that she hadn't passed the exam, he was not pleased. "You do not know her inner feeling and her devotion," he said. "She is feeling very sad now. Send for her. I want to see her."

When they brought her in front of Baba he declared her passed in devotion and prachar. Then he signed her acharya certificate.

1983

Shankar Bhattavyal

ONE MORNING IN the early eighties a gentleman by the name of Shankar Bhattavyal appeared at the gate of the Lake Gardens house and told the security that he wished to see Baba. It was the duty of the security to vet anyone who came to the gate, so they asked the usual questions: What is your name? When were you initiated? Who is your acharya? And so on. "I don't have an acharya," the man replied, "but Baba knows me and he will want to see me. Please inform him that I am here." This didn't satisfy the security. They asked him if he were a relative and he said no, so they kept him waiting outside the gate. Only margis and Baba's relatives were allowed inside, and since he obviously wasn't a margi they didn't let him in. After repeating his request to inform Baba of his presence, he took a seat in front of a neighbour's house. He ended up waiting there for nearly three hours. After a new shift came on, he asked one of the new volunteers to go upstairs and inform someone that he had been waiting a long time to see Baba. This volunteer came and conveyed his request to me.

When I heard his description of the man and what he had said, I remembered that time in Patna when a similar stranger had made just such a request and Baba had told me that there were some people doing his work who were not in Ananda Marga and who might come to see him from time to time. He had even told me how I would be able to recognize them. Remembering this I went down to the gate. I saw a very refined gentleman who appeared to be Bengali, though he spoke Hindi, English, and Bengali equally well. But what was most striking about him was his face: it was glowing like I had hardly ever seen before, like Pranay's when I first came to Ananda Marga, and I knew right away that he was an elevated sadhaka. So I brought him inside and apologized for the way the security had treated him, though he wasn't offended at all. I asked him to wait on the ground floor while I went upstairs to inform Baba.

Baba was just putting on his shirt for breakfast when I reached his room. I did sastaunga pranam, and when I got up Baba asked me if there was any news, if anyone had come. I told him that one Shankar Bhattavyal was asking to see him.

"Shankar has come? Did he just arrive?"

"Yes, Baba, just now." How could I tell Baba that the security people had kept him waiting for three hours?

"Tell Sudhar to set my breakfast aside. I will take it later. Go downstairs and get Shankar. I have very urgent work with him, and he has to leave as soon as we are done. Be quick."

I brought him to Baba's room and stood by while he did sastaunga pranam and then sat in front of Baba's cot. Baba turned to me and said, "Ramananda, wait outside. I want to speak privately with Shankar. Please close the door on your way out."

I closed the door but I kept my ear glued to it, trying to hear what they were saying. Baba began by scolding him roundly. I wondered why, since he appeared to be such a gentleman, such a saintly personality. Then they began speaking in low voices, but I still managed to hear some of what they said. I heard Shankar say, "By your grace the work is done." A little later I heard Baba say, "You have the capacity to do this work; you have all the necessary qualities. Why do you feel that you don't have the capacity?" Then I heard him reply, "Yes, Baba, I will do it." Later I heard Baba explain why he had punished him. He also told him how much he loved him.

By the time the door opened, Shankar had been with Baba for more than an hour. Baba then told me to escort him personally to the gate. "Don't let anyone talk to him or disturb him," he said. "Once he is out of the gate your duty is done. But before he goes, ask him if he wants to eat anything." But Shankar wouldn't take anything. "I have come only for this purpose," he said, "and now my mission is complete." While I escorted him downstairs, I apologized again for the behaviour of the volunteers. I told him that once they had detained Baba's brother Manas for an hour and a half because the volunteers were new and didn't recognize him, and on another occasion they had done the same with Baba's other brother, Himanshu, and his wife Kalyani, but again he told me that it was nothing.

It was only when I left him in the street and came back upstairs that Baba sat for breakfast. He did not go on field walk that morning.

1983

Baba Teaches Me How to Open the Buttonholes

ONCE IN 1984 a margi brought a new outfit for Baba consisting of a dhoti, a punjabi shirt, and an T-shirt. This was a common occurrence, and whenever I put out any dress for Baba he would ask me if it had been bought by the organization or if it was a present from some margi. He would make an effort to wear any presents in public at least once so that the margi who sent it would feel happy that Baba had worn his dress. That evening I laid out the new dress for him before he went to bed so that he could put it on in the morning when he finished his practices, and I told him who had given it.

In the morning Baba called me when he was finished getting ready. I went into his room and did sastaunga pranam. When I got up he asked me if I had checked the shirt to make sure that it was ready to wear. I didn't understand what he meant.

"I want to teach you something," he said. "Whenever anyone gives me any gift, especially clothes, then you should check it to see if it is ready for use. You see this shirt. It is a new shirt; thus the buttonholes are still partially closed. If you try to pass the button through the hole you will have to struggle to get it through and your time gets wasted. I am not scolding you but teaching you. In the future you should see that my time does not get wasted. If anyone offers anything to me you should check it thoroughly. Did you check the buttonholes?"

"No, Baba."

Baba took out a pen and pushed it through one of the holes. "When someone gives me a new shirt you should check the buttonholes. If you find they are not open then just take a pen and widen them like this. Then I won't have any difficulty. That is why I called you."

1984

Betiah

 $\mathcal{B}$ ETWEEN JANUARY AND April of 1984, Baba gave a DMC every Sunday in a different place, seventeen in all: Anandanagar, Deoghar, Patna, Betiah, Gorakhpur, Allahabad, Kanpur, Agra, Delhi, Jammu, Jaipur, Kota, Gwalior, Varanasi, Daltonganj, Tatanagar, and Ranchi. Throughout the tour Baba travelled by car, and in each place he was taken for field walk to historic local sites where he talked about the history of those places. Some of his talks were published in the book *P. R. Sarkar on History*. Originally Betiah was not on the list. The margis there are very poor and holding DMC means a great expense for the local margis: a pandal has to be erected; you have to make sleeping arrangements for thousands of people; you have to feed them; then there is Baba's entourage to take care of—all the local dadas and didis are required to attend; a suitable place has to be arranged for Baba to stay, along with everything that is needed to make him comfortable. It is no small task. For this reason Betiah was not included in the tour. But when we arrived in Patna, Baba told us that he would like to hold a DMC in Betiah as well. "My children there are not getting the chance because they are poor," he said, "but I want them to have this chance. Can it be arranged?" So I asked the DPS and the local dada to contact the bhukti pradhan and other margis there to see if it could be arranged. DPS left in the morning for Betiah—it is 250 kilometres from Patna to Betiah—and in the evening he arrived back in Patna with the BP, Khublal.

Khublal was very well known to Baba. His daughter is an avadhutika, Ananda Sambuddha, and he always brought gifts for Baba whenever he came to visit, especially mangos if they were in season. Baba would have me repack them and send them as gifts to different workers and margis, as well as his relatives. When Khublal arrived, I sent him into Baba's room to formally invite Baba to Betiah for DMC. Now when Baba asked if everything was ready for his visit you had to say yes, even if it wasn't. So we instructed him what to say, and when Baba asked him if everything was ready, if all the conditions had been met, he said yes, even though, technically speaking, it was a lie. "Very good," Baba said. "Talk to Ramananda and to DPS to fix the details of the program."

Before Baba would hold DMC in any place there were so many requirements that had to be met: Baba's quarters, school, press, master unit, and so on. This was most likely Tuesday, so they had four days to meet the conditions and get everything ready for the program. At that time there was a school in Betiah but no Baba's quarters and no land for a master unit, but Khublal promised me that they would arrange some land by the time Baba arrived, and we thought that this would be enough to satisfy Baba. Khublal returned to Betiah and he and the local margis and workers started whirlwind preparations for Baba's visit.

In those days I had to take care of everything for Baba, from cutting his hair to polishing his shoes to arranging his dress and organizing his travel. Sometimes I also served as his driver, as on this tour. When we left Patna for Betiah we had to pass through a number of towns where there were many margis. This was Bihar and practically every town in Bihar was full of margis. All along the way, the margis erected arches to welcome Baba, and they turned out by the thousands to greet him and give him their garlands. At each place I would stop at the arch and Baba would give the margis his namaskar and accept their garlands. Then we would continue on to the next town. In this way we covered the 250 kilometres with margis crowding round Baba in each succeeding town—singing kirtan, laughing and crying. It was a beautiful scene that repeated itself over and over again.

When we reached Betiah, we were taken to the school, which had been prepared for Baba's stay. It was quite comfortable and had been nicely decorated. The margis had done a wonderful job getting everything ready in a very short time. The pandal, lodgings for the workers and margis, food arrangements—everything was excellent. Betiah is famous for its yoghurt mixed with beaten rice, so Khublal commandeered all the yoghurt from the surrounding villages, and the margis who attended had all the yoghurt and beaten rice they could eat, and of the highest quality.

In the morning Baba chatted a little with the margis. Then he called me and asked me to verify if the conditions for DMC had been met. "See if Baba's quarters have been completed or not," he said. "I will take a bath now and when I come out you will tell me if the conditions have been met."

While Baba was in the bathroom, I talked to Khublal and the other important margis of Betiah. They told me that they had obtained some land for the master unit but of course they didn't have any Baba's quarters. "Do one thing," I told them. "Organize some margis to bring some bricks and cement and set them on the land. That way I can tell Baba that the construction has started and it will be completed very soon." They left immediately to purchase some bricks and cement.

When Baba came out for breakfast, he called me to the table. The margis were just outside. "Ramananda," he said, "did you go and see if my quarters are ready?"

"Baba, the work is in full swing," I said. "Your quarters should be completed very soon."

"I did not ask that. I asked if my quarters were ready or not."

"No, Baba, they are not ready."

"Then there will be no DMC here. Get my car ready. We are going back to Patna."

There was nothing more I could do at that point. Naturally, the news spread through the pandal like wildfire: Baba will not sit for DMC! There will be no varabhaya mudra! Everybody was stunned. Thousands of margis had turned out to see Baba's varabhaya mudra. Young and old, they rushed to where Baba was staying. "We won't allow Baba to go without giving DMC," they kept saying. "He must give his varabhaya mudra. How can he go without giving DMC?" They started prostrating on the road for as much as a full kilometre, determined not to let Baba's car pass. When I saw this I told Baba.

"Ramananda," he said, "do as per my instructions. Don't waste time thinking unnecessarily or worrying about what will happen. Just follow my instructions and watch what happens. Now pack my things and put them in the car."

While I was packing Baba's things into the car, he came out and the margis crowded around him, pleading with him and crying piteously. "We may be liars, Baba," they said, "but we are your sons and daughters. We have the right to keep you here. You can't let down your own children." One aged family acharya, Sarju Prasad, was crying unabashedly. He said, "Baba, we are very poor. We did everything we could, and only by your grace. Be kind to us."

By this time I was also crying. Everybody was. Finally Baba asked for the bhukti pradhan. Baba was standing in front of the car, and the road was covered with margis who were determined not to let his car leave. But Khublal was not there. He was inside Baba's room, unwilling to show his face to the margis. How can I, he was thinking, when I let everybody down so badly? Then Baba himself said, "He might be in my room. Send somebody to bring him." We brought him and he came and did sastaunga pranam.

When he got up, Baba said, "What does my bhukti pradhan say? Should there be DMC today?"

"Yes, Baba."

"Okay. Ramananda, since the bhukti pradhan says that there should be DMC, then we will not leave. There will be DMC."

Then Baba told Khublal, "I know what happened. These dadas taught you to lie to me when you put your request for DMC. But telling a lie in order to see the Lord is also the truth. You said that you had fulfilled the conditions when you had not, but you did this just to bring me to your house. So I had to come."

And actually, so much was accomplished due to that DMC. The land was obtained, Baba's quarters were constructed, and so many other things as well. Wherever Baba went he would inspire the margis to work for the mission, and they would accomplish more than they ever thought possible.

22 January 1984

Arun Gupta

MOST OF THE arrangements for the Kanpur DMC were made by Arun Gupta. Baba stayed in a *dak* bungalow, a guest house for travellers—the DMC also took place there—and Arun's wife prepared Baba's food with the help of some other margi sisters and brought it to his room at meal times. Just after we arrived, Arun confided to me that he wanted to get Baba's blessing for his business. He asked my advice on how to go about it. Arun was the head of the family business, which consisted of quarrying stone in the Jaipur stone mines and manufacturing various items from that stone, such as stone flooring, cups, plates and so on. He and his brother had bought two mountains for quarrying and they had become millionaires in the process. Arun was a good margi— he and his family helped to support the organization financially—and I wanted to help him, but I had to be very careful about approaching Baba for something of this nature. I suggested that he show Baba something manufactured by him but it had to be done at exactly the right moment. The best time, I said, would be while Baba was taking his meal, but I knew that if Baba wasn't in the right mood then he might get annoyed. So I told Arun that we would have to be alert. We would have to wait until Baba was in a light, talkative mood. I had to be careful, you see, since it was my job to ensure that Baba was in a relaxed mood when he ate. I couldn't allow anything that might upset him.

For two days the right opportunity didn't present itself, and Arun was getting anxious. But then on the last day, when Baba sat for his meal, I saw that he was in a jovial mood. So I signalled to Arun that the time had come. Arun's wife had prepared some sweet rice for Baba and Arun served it to him in one of the cups that he manufactured. He mentioned to Baba that the cup was his own fabrication and this was enough. Baba complimented him on the workmanship and started talking about the Jaipur mines and the stone business and so on. "Go ahead with your work," Baba told him. "It is very good." Arun was thrilled. He got his blessing, and he and his brother enjoyed great success in the stone business in the years that followed. Over the years they have given a lot of help to the organization.

February 1984

Mahavir Prasad Jain

*T*HE 1984 TOUR was a busy time for us. Many interesting things happened, too many to recount or even remember. Before the tour began, Mahavir Prasad Jain, a rich businessman and a devoted margi, came to Calcutta to invite Baba to hold DMC in Delhi as part of the tour. At that time there was no Baba's quarters in Delhi, and for a number of years the margis there had faced great difficulties securing accommodations for Baba whenever he came to visit, due to the intense pressure from the CBI that had been going on since 1971. Whenever the margis tried to rent lodgings for Baba, whether a hotel or guesthouse or private house, the CBI would pressure the owners, threatening them to the point that they usually became afraid to offer us the lodgings. By this time the Delhi margis had developed a strong sentiment to have their own Baba's quarters, somewhere where they would no longer have to put up with the intimidation of the CBI. Of course they knew about Baba's conditions for holding DMC—the area had to have its own Baba's quarters, as well as a school, press, and other conditions—and they had decided that the time had come. Mahavir gave Baba his personal guarantee that they would have a Baba's quarters in Delhi by the time of the DMC. On that condition, Baba accepted the invitation and told DPS to confer with Mahavir about the dates, which were fixed for 20-26 February. He also changed Mahavir's name to Ishitamukh, "always smiling."

Mahavir returned to Delhi and he and the local margis began looking for a suitable property. But while they were considering their options, the weeks sped by and they had nothing to show for it. We celebrated DMC in Agra on the nineteenth and from there we proceeded to Delhi by car. When we reached the outskirts of the city, the prominent margis of Delhi were there to receive us. After accepting their gestures of welcome, Baba asked if everything was ready for the DMC. They said yes but actually the most important thing of all was left undone: there was no Baba's quarters. When they took him to the guesthouse that they had arranged for his stay, Baba got angry. "Where have you brought me! These people told me I would be staying in my own house. Liars, cheaters, worthless good-for-nothing scoundrels! Ramananda, we are going back to Calcutta. I won't stay in this place. But first call the people who have cheated me by bringing me here under false pretexts." And Baba continued to use such language about them that it would have singed the ears of a street brawler.

When Mahavir and the others presented themselves in front of Baba, he demanded to know why they had lied to him? When they remained silent, he said, "Ramananda, tell them that if they want me to remain here for DMC, they have twelve hours to fulfil their word and secure a Baba's quarters. Otherwise I am going back to Calcutta. It is too late for us to leave today but tell them that they must have the Baba's quarters in their hands first thing tomorrow morning or else we are leaving."

Amazingly, it didn't even take twelve hours. By nine o'clock that night they had the deed in their hands. They found the place, flew in the money from different areas, paid the seller nine hundred thousand rupees, and signed the deed.

When Baba came out of his room after his morning practices he was in no mood for breakfast. All he wanted to know was whether or not they had secured a suitable Baba's quarters. The margis were already assembled there, waiting to take Baba to the new MG Quarters at Gadaipur. When we arrived there, Baba sat down on a chair, surrounded by waving fields of wheat. He was able to see for himself the results of the intense pressure he had applied so that the margis would increase their output for the mission. That Sunday Baba held the DMC in front of the new MG Quarters, on the land the margis had purchased.

26 February 1984

Apple Bread

*U*NA IS A city and also a district in the state of Himachal Pradesh, in the mountains of northern India. Once in 1981 a margi family from Una came to Calcutta to invite Baba to go there. Baba was extremely busy in organizational activities in those days but he accepted their invitation and told them that he would try to visit Una when the appropriate occasion arose. Before they left, the wife said, "Baba, when you come we will make apple bread for you."

I was surprised to hear this. I had never heard of apple bread. Baba seemed equally surprised. "Apple bread?" he said.

"Yes, Baba. I will prepare it myself."

The 1984 DMC tour took us through Himachal Pradesh on the way to Jammu. We travelled exclusively by car during that tour due to the tandava case. Margis were getting arrested when they did tandava in the airports while receiving Baba, and since he didn't want to see his children being arrested in front of his own eyes, he decided that he would not travel by plane. I was Baba's driver up until Delhi, but for the mountains of Himachal Pradesh and Jammu I hired a professional driver from the International Tourist Department, someone who knew the area well and was experienced in driving the tortuous Himalayan roads. Our route took us through The Punjab, Chandighar, and then into Himachal Pradesh, where our first scheduled stop was in Vilaspur—we were scheduled to have lunch with the margis there on our way to Jammu. Una was not on our itinerary, but it was on the way and this same margi family, along with other margis from Una, were waiting for us at a bifurcation with flags in their hands.

As we approached the fork in the road, I saw this small group of people with flags. Baba turned to me and said, "Ramananda, there is a bifurcation coming up. It is better we stop there and ask for directions so that we don't run the risk of taking a wrong turn."

"Baba, there seem to be some margis there. I recognize our flag."

"Really? What is this place?"

"Let us ask them, Baba. Anyway, they are the only people on the road."

When we stopped, I recognized the same family that had invited Baba to visit Una three years earlier, and I asked them the way to Vilaspur. "Dada, this is the main road to Vilaspur. It's a bigger road but it will take you longer. That road is smaller, but it is shorter and there is less traffic, so it will take you less time. You should take Baba by that road."

Baba was sitting in the back with the window open listening to our conversation. When he heard what they said he became enthusiastic. "If it will take less time," he said, "then why should we not take the smaller road?"

Then the husband said, "Baba, when we came to Calcutta we invited you to come to Una and take apple bread. The apple bread is ready. Una is only seven kilometres from here on this same road. We have arranged a guesthouse for you and my wife has prepared fresh apple bread. Please come. You must come."

"When you came to Calcutta I promised you," Baba said, "so I must keep my promise."

We took the smaller road, which took us by the circuit house of the Block Development Office, where the husband was employed as an engineer. The family had booked the government bungalow that day to receive Baba.

Baba did not go in but he accepted the devotees' offering. "I promised you I would come, even though it was not on my itinerary," he said, "and I have kept my promise. I wanted to try your apple bread. But it will be better if you bring it to me here. I will make it prasad and then you can give it to the members of my entourage."

"Baba, please sanctify Una by touching the ground with your feet. Then we will be happy."

Baba motioned for a security person to open the door so he could touch his feet to the ground. He accepted some apple bread and ate it while he sat there, commenting on how delicious it was. It was the first time he had ever eaten apple bread, and the margis were very happy that Baba had fulfilled their desire.

1 March 1984

Vilaspur

WHILE BABA WAS in Delhi for the DMC program, Ram Svarup, an aged but extremely fit margi from Himachal Pradesh came to Delhi to invite Baba to visit Himachal. We arranged for him to do sastaunga pranam in front of Baba when Baba was coming from his room so that he would have a chance to put his request. When he did sastaunga, Baba asked me who he was.

"Baba, he is Ram Svarup from Himachal Pradesh."

"Oh, I know him. He is the man who sends me some bushels of apples every year, is it not?"

"Yes, Baba."

Ram Svarup had an apple orchard in Himachal and every year before selling his crop he would pack up nine or ten bushels of apples and send them to Baba—he was a very devoted margi. Baba would distribute the apples to workers and margis and relatives. When Ram Svarup got up from his prostration, he told Baba that he had come along with two or three other margis to invite Baba to visit Himachal.

"I have no objection," Baba said, "but you must ask these people. They have organized my schedule."

The workers who were there immediately said, "No, Baba, there is no time. Your schedule is full."

Then Baba said to them, "Do one thing. Since we are going by road we have to pass through Himachal on our way to Jammu. See if there is any place along the way where I can stop and meet the margis. There should be no detour involved but if it is on our way then something can be arranged. Perhaps in Vilaspur. It is on the way."

We consulted with the driver as well as with the margis and he confirmed that the most convenient route would take us through Vilaspur, so we made arrangements for Baba to take his lunch there with the margis before continuing on to Jammu.

Some fifty or sixty margis of Himachal Pradesh came to Vilaspur along with their families to meet Baba in a guest house that they reserved for the occasion. This was after leaving Una. Baba took his lunch there and gave a short darshan. Ram Svarup sat near Baba during the darshan and at one point Baba said, "Ram Svarup, I didn't come here only because I love you, you know. I came because I love all the margis here and because of how much they love me. The mountain people of Himachal are very simple and pure-minded, so I was very pleased that I could come here. Are you all happy now?"

The margis sang some songs and chants in their local language while wearing their traditional mountain dress, which was very beautiful. They also came to Jammu to attend the DMC.

1 March 1984

Chandra Lekha Saigal

C. L. SAIGAL was the director of the Jammu and Kashmir government handicrafts enterprise, and he and his wife used to attend most of the DMCs. Nowadays they live in Delhi with one of their sons, a high-ranking army officer. Saigalji had a sunny disposition and he was a very good cook; he was especially known for his *rajma* pulse, a Kashmiri dish that he used to prepare sometimes for Baba. He led a very simple life and for that reason he is still in very good health, though he is long since retired.

During the 1984 tour, Saigalji joined us in Patna and travelled with Baba's entourage until Jammu, attending all the DMCs on the way—he had taken two months' leave for this purpose. There were five or six cars in our entourage to accommodate the security people, the workers, a few margis, and the Prabhat Samgiita party—Baba used to stop the car at unforeseen moments and call them over to take dictation; Baba gave many Prabhat Samgiitas while we were on the road during those months. From time to time, Baba would ask me about the people who were traveling with us. After Patna, I told Baba that one margi, C. L. Saigal, had joined the tour. "C. L. Saigal?" Baba said. "Why don't you use his proper name?" I had to admit that I didn't know his full name. Baba told me that his name was Chandra Lekha. He always used to insist on using a person's proper name. Baba then asked me why he wanted to attend all these DMCs. "Baba, it was his plan to attend all the DMCs this year," I replied.

"But *why* is he so interested? What is the reason?"

As I had nothing else to offer, I said, "It is because he loves you, Baba, and he wants to receive your blessing."

"He loves me, that's true, but there may be some other reason as well." Baba left it at that, but of course he was quite correct.

Saigalji was with us when we drove to Jammu for DMC, stopping along the way at Una and Vilaspur. We arrived in Jammu earlier than planned and the house that had been arranged for Baba's stay was not yet ready. It belonged to the relatives of some margis and there had been a wedding there so it needed to be cleaned; nor did it have AC, so that also had to be installed. All this took time and the owners hadn't yet finished the preparations, so there was no alternative but to take Baba to a guest house. I telephoned Acharya Kishun and Maharaj Kishan, two important local margis, and Kishan's wife told me that the Jammu margis had gone to Vilaspur to welcome Baba and accompany him to Jammu. We had somehow passed them on the way. I informed Baba of this and he told me to let him know when the margis arrived.

They arrived in the night. When they located the guest house, they apologized to Baba for not having been there to receive him, but Baba was in a jovial mood. He told them that he had come early so that he could receive them. The house they had arranged for his stay was ready by then and they asked him to shift there but Baba told them that he was quite comfortable at the moment and would shift there in the morning after field walk.

The next day they took Baba to a riverside temple for his morning walk and when he came back we moved to the house in Trikutnagar. There Saigalji approached me and asked me to allow him to meet individually with Baba—he had put the same request to me a number of times during our previous stops, but as Baba was always very busy during the tour I had found it very difficult to accommodate his request. I told him I would try, so as not to deflate his hopes, but I didn't think Baba would have time.

We remained in Jammu for three days. After the DMC discourse, when Baba came back to the house to take his food and change his dress, I went looking for someone to give him a massage. He usually liked to talk to somebody after the DMC, to see what they thought of his discourse, but there were only two or three security volunteers in the house, no dada or reliable margi. Baba called me and said, "Ramananda, I am feeling a bit tired. Is there anyone you can send to give me a massage?" I mentioned one of the volunteers but Baba said, "No, no, he doesn't know massage."

"Baba, there is no one else here at the moment. I will send someone to the pandal for a worker; it won't take long." The DMC pandal was a little distance from the house where we were staying. I mentioned one or two names, workers who I knew were good at massage but Baba said, "No, don't send anyone. They are busy in meetings and organizing prachar for this area. I don't want to disturb them. If someone is already here in the compound who can do massage, that would be better."

"Baba, I already checked. There are only the volunteers. I will send one of them to the pandal to bring someone."

"No, no, don't send anyone. If there is someone here who can do massage then it is fine; otherwise, leave it. I don't want to disturb them."

At this point I got the hint. I knew there must be somebody nearby whom I hadn't seen when I checked. So I went out and made a circuit of the house. That's when I spotted Saigalji sitting out back meditating. I had not seen him earlier. I rushed back to Baba and told him that Saigalji was in the compound.

"Oh, he is here, so late at night?" It was nearing midnight by then. "What is he doing?"

"Baba, he is meditating. I don't know if he knows massage but I will ask him."

I rushed back to Saigalji, took my second lesson, and disturbed his meditation. When he told me that he was good at massage, I brought him to Baba's room.

"Does he know massage?" Baba asked.

"Yes, Baba."

"Okay, then send him in."

I asked him to go in and then I was able to relax a little outside Baba's door. When Saigalji did sastaunga pranam there was a sound of something hard hitting the tiles and Baba asked him if he had something in his pocket.

"Yes, Baba. I haven't told anyone but I've been carrying a bottle of pure Ganges water with me from Gangotri, the source of the Ganges where the sun melts the snow and the river begins. When it reaches the plains, the water becomes dirty and the government spends lots of money cleaning it. But this water is pure. For many years I've dreamed of getting a chance to wash your feet with pure Ganges water. Before the tour began I travelled five days to Gangotri to get it. Since then I've been waiting for my chance. I requested Dada many times to give me time. He said he would find an opportunity but each time I asked him he said you were busy."

"I see. Okay, first the massage. Only ten or fifteen minutes because it is getting late and you also have to rest. Then I will go to the bathroom. While I am in the bathroom you can make the arrangements."

After the massage, Baba went to the bathroom and Saigal prepared a basin and some towels. When Baba came out of the bathroom he washed his feet in pure Ganges water. Later, after Saigalji had left and some workers had come, Baba called me into his room. He told me how Saigalji had been waiting the whole tour to have a chance to wash his feet with the water he had brought from Gangotri. Then he showed me his hands. They were red. "You know," he said, "in the north, people are very robust, very healthy and very strong also. Chandra Lekha's intentions were good—that's why I permitted him—but he is very strong and Baba's body is like butter. You can see the result: I am red all over. But don't tell him. He massaged me with much love. Still, next time you should be more careful. Check to see if the person you are sending really knows massage or not."

Afterward I suggested to Saigalji that he learn massage well so that he might have more opportunities in the future to massage Baba. He told me that he had been trained in massage by his father, who had taught him that a good masseuse should apply force so as to get rid of any tiredness that the person might be feeling, and that he was quite adept at it. But actually Baba's body was so delicate, so soft and sensitive, that a different type of massage was required. Baba satisfied his desire, but he had to suffer to do so.

Saigalji saved the water he used to wash Baba's feet. He mixed it with mineral water and kept it in the family meditation room. Whenever any sick person would visit he would give him a few drops and he would be miraculously cured. When he told this to Baba, Baba said, "I did this for you, not for others. But you have done good deeds with it. If it is your desire, you may continue to give it to margis but not to people at large; otherwise, they will come to you in crowds and your work will be hampered."

4 March 1984

Daulat Singh

THIS INCIDENT TOOK place in March 1984 in Jaipur. Jaipur means "the place of kings," and it is famous for its palaces and forts. There are also many strong margis in Jaipur, such as Surendra Sharma, Mangal Bihari, and Major Daulat Singh, who was a very good margi from the early days. Whenever Baba would visit north India he would generally visit two places in Rajasthan—Jaipur and Kota—and whenever he visited those places Daulat Singh would be his driver. In fact, Baba gave him the title "Parthasarathi," which was the name attributed to Krishna when he served as Arjuna's charioteer. "Partha" means "Arjuna" and *sarathi* is "charioteer" or "driver." Baba also stayed in his house on at least one occasion in the sixties. He was a tall, towering personality, very well known in Rajasthan.

Prior to our visit, Baba had given him the duty to help the local Ananda Marga schools. Whether didi school or dada school, it didn't matter. When we arrived, Baba asked me to verify if he had done his duty. In every DMC place there was a checklist of things that had to be completed—jagriti, school, children's home, press, and so on, in addition to the arrangements for Baba's stay. For each of these, a certain person or persons was responsible, and I had to verify whether or not they had done their duty. I gathered that information from the local workers and told Baba that he had helped but that his work was not up to the mark. In their estimation, he should have done more.

Baba was not happy with my answer. "I don't want to scold him," he said, "but when a person takes a responsibility he should fulfil that responsibility. Daulat has much love and affection for me and I also love him. That is why I gave him the title Parthasarathi. But only those people who have done satisfactory work should come to me. Every time I come to Jaipur he drives my car but that is a privilege that has to be earned. He has promised to do some work for the mission. Has he accomplished that work?"

"No Baba, at least not as well as he could have."

"Then why should he be allowed to drive my car?"

"I will find someone else, Baba."

I asked the bhukti pradhan to select a different driver for Baba's car. He objected—everyone knew that Daulat was Baba's driver—but I made it clear that he had no choice in the matter, so he went to find someone else. When the time approached for field walk, I told Daulat that I had relieved him of his duty as Baba's driver and explained why. Within a short time he was a basket case. He started weeping and crying pitifully. This went on for several hours. When Baba went for field walk, Daulat took his own car and drove to the Jaigarh fort in Amer where they had taken Baba for his walk, a place renowned for its beautiful gardens. While Baba was walking with the margis—there were some fifteen or twenty margis on field walk that day—Daulat remained nearby but he did not approach Baba, nor did Baba acknowledge his presence. He was weeping silently the entire time in great anguish, though he was a rich man and very well respected in the society.

When Baba came back, he told me to call him. "He has realized his mistake now," he said.

Daulat came running and promised Baba that he would complete his duty within two weeks. "You have my word as a gentleman," he said.

Baba reinstated him as his driver. Daulat was euphoric. He kept saying, *mil gaya, mil gaya*, I got it, I got it, meaning his old post as Baba's driver. This was how Baba would rectify his disciples.

10 March 1984

Dr. Gilani

DOCTOR GILANI LIVED in Mahasamund, a town about two hundred kilometres from Jaipur. His wife and daughter are also doctors and good devotees. Whenever Baba came to Jaipur, the whole family would attend DMC. He used to do medical camps for the mission on his own every three to four months, and he was especially helpful to the wholetimers in that area. He was one of the driving forces in arranging the master unit. Sometimes he would just stop on the road, get out his medicines, and start checking patients. Baba was his mission, and Baba used to show him much affection and invite him to go on field walk with him.

Dr. Gilani was not properly informed about Baba's 1984 visit to Jaipur; he only found out about it at the last minute. As soon as he got the news, he boarded a train and arrived some hours later at Jaipur station. It was evening by then, and when he arrived at the DMC site he was told that Baba had already left for field walk. He got the address and went straight there, hoping to join Baba for the last portion of the walk, but when he got there the dada who was in charge of security held him back. He would not let him join the walk unless he agreed to give a sizable dona-tion to his department. Dr. Gilani gave him whatever money he had on him but this Dada was not satisfied, not even when he promised to give him more later, as soon as he could manage. "I've given you all I have," he kept saying, but the dada kept on insisting that he give him more.

Dr. Gilani started weeping, "Baba, Baba, Baba," in his despair. They were a good distance from where Baba was walking with the margis, but Baba still heard him. He turned and asked who was there.

Dr. Gilani told Baba who he was and Baba said, "Good, you have come. But why are you way over there? Come and walk with me."

"Baba, Dada is not letting me pass."

"No, no, there is no restriction for you. Let him pass."

That night Dr. Gilani attended the DMC and the next morning Baba told me to bring him to his room.

After he did sastaunga pranam, Baba said, "Don't worry about arriving late. I know it was not your fault. The information was not communicated to you."

"Yes, Baba. When I heard that you had come, I knew I couldn't go without seeing you."

"You had a strong desire and your desire was fulfilled. Are you happy now?

"Yes, Baba."

"In the future you can come with me on field walk whenever you like. Ramananda, see to it that he is allowed."

After he left the room, Baba asked me the name of the dada who had held him back the previous evening and told me to find out the reason why. I made some inquiries and informed Baba that the dada had been pressurizing him for money. He had me call that dada and Baba began scolding him like anything. "Do you know how good this man is, how much he helps the acharyas and margis without being asked? He helps beyond his limits." Baba punished that dada and made him promise that he would never do anything like that again.

11 March 1984

Balaram Singh

*F*ROM JAIPUR WE went to Kota, then to Gwalior, and then to Varanasi. When we arrived in Varanasi, Nigamananda and the rest of the organizing committee took us to the Upavan Guest House, a well-known hotel that they had arranged for Baba's stay—at that time we did not have our own quarters in Varanasi. But Baba never liked staying in hotels. He always preferred a margi's house, however humble, to a hotel, no matter how luxurious that hotel might be. So when the car pulled up in front of the hotel he was not at all pleased.

"What is this place?" he demanded. "Where have you brought me?" When the reception committee, headed by Nigamananda, told him that they had arranged the hotel for his stay, he refused to get out of the car. He started scolding them left and right, to the point that no one dared open his mouth. "Ramananda," Baba said, "who booked this place? Don't these people know that a hotel is not the place for me? If there is no proper place for us to stay then let us continue on to Daltonganj. There I have my own room, my own quarters. Why should we remain here any longer?"

Naturally, I had to support Baba in this drama—he had coached me as to what I should say in such situations. I also scolded the margis and said that it would be better if we left this place. When the margis heard that Baba was going to leave without giving DMC they became distraught. Nigamananda didn't know what to do. But there was one margi in the reception committee by the name of Balaram Singh, the deputy director of agriculture in Uttar Pradesh. When he heard that Baba was threatening to leave Varanasi he came forward and offered his house for Baba's stay.

"Baba, you shouldn't go," he said. "You can stay in my house. It has a nice garden and a pleasant climate. There is no air conditioning but I can get it installed within three hours. It is your house, Baba."

It took a little more convincing but Baba finally agreed. Baba had to wait on the veranda of Balaram's house while his room was being prepared and the air conditioning installed, but the margis gave him refreshments and kept him engaged with pleasant conversation. Baba was very happy with the arrangements. The DMC was held nearby, and when Baba was leaving he thanked the margis for all the inconveniences and struggles they had gone through on his behalf. Balaram then told Baba how blessed he was that the Lord had come and stayed in his house.

28 March 1984

Rishikundu

RISHIKUNDU WAS A devoted margi who lived in the Bhavanipur area of Calcutta, where he earned his living by running a popular general store. One morning he came to me in Lake Gardens and said, "Dada, I have heard that Baba is very fond of kulfi. I would like to bring him some, either for his breakfast or for his evening meal. Could you please ask him when I should bring it. It takes three to four hours to prepare, so I will need to know in advance, and I would like to be present when Baba takes it, if that is possible."

In the middle of our conversation Baba rang the call bell. I rushed to his room and did sastaunga pranam. When I got up he asked if everything was ready for field walk and if any margis had come. I told him that Rishi-da was outside. "Rishi has come?" he said. "He has left his business on a weekday and come all this way? What did he say?" Since it was time for Baba to leave for field walk I didn't mention the kulfi, thinking that I would wait for a more appropriate moment to broach the subject. When Baba came out he greeted Rishi effusively. "Rishi, my boy, you are here so early? Come along then. Come with me on field walk."

Baba kept everyone busy with his talks during the walk, so Rishi didn't get a chance to say anything about the kulfi. Perhaps he thought that he should wait for me to bring up the matter with Baba. When Baba came back from his walk, he was immediately swept up in reporting and PCs, which continued for several hours, so I didn't get any scope to ask him about the kulfi. In the evening, before Baba's dinner, Rishi arrived again, but this time he was carrying a tiffin carrier that he handled with great care. I knew right away what was inside, so when it was time for Baba to take his evening meal I told him that Rishi had brought a special dish for him. "Oh, has he brought it?" Baba exclaimed. "Call him."

I brought Rishi to Baba's room. When he opened the tiffin carrier, it contained a very high-quality kulfi, which is a kind of Indian ice cream.

Baba asked him to sit beside him, and while Rishi put some of it on Baba's plate, Baba narrated the history of kulfi. When he finished his story, Baba ate a little and asked that the rest be kept as prasad. "Never in my life have I eaten such delicious kulfi," he said. "Tell me, Rishi, who has prepared this kulfi? Really, it is quite wonderful."

"Baba, by your grace, it was prepared by a close friend of mine who is an expert in kulfi preparation. I told him that it would be served to my gurudeva and that he had to think of you while he was preparing it. He made it with much reverence and love."

Baba was pleased to hear this. They were both laughing, and it was obvious that Rishi was beside himself with joy because he had been able to please his guru.

1984

Pi Pu Phi Shu

BABA WANTED THE ideology to be established through the sincere efforts of his sons and daughters, and for this he wanted them to be active. Generally they were, but sometimes Baba had to create external pressure in order to motivate them. One Sunday evening, the DPS and the GS came to me and asked me to request Baba to sit for General Darshan. This was in the Lake Gardens house. He used to sit for darshan in the downstairs hall, where the upper walls are decorated with the verses of *Ananda Sutram* written out in Bengali script. Baba would give General Darshan there every Sunday evening as long as there were sufficient margis. Before coming out for darshan he would ask the DPS and GS to inform him if enough margis had come. It was his standing instruction that if there was a crowd then he would come and sit, but if it were only a few people then he wouldn't. The margis knew this and there was invariably a good-sized crowd. So I took their message to Baba and informed him that a big crowd had gathered.

"No, these are all worthless people," he said, "wasting my time. They don't do any work, so I don't want to see them. Tell them there will be no General Darshan today."

Baba was sitting on his cot dressed in a lungi and t-shirt. He had just finished getting a massage. After a few minutes the DPS, Tapeshvarananda, appeared in the doorway. It was getting late and the margis were getting restless. "Baba," he said, "so many margis have come to see you. Won't you come out for General Darshan?"

"Worthless fellow! Get out of here!"

There were some workers that Baba scolded more than others and Tapeshvarananda was one of them, so I also told him to get out of Baba's room. Sarvatmananda, the GS, was standing far enough behind Tapeshvarananda that Baba wouldn't see him—he knew better than to stand in the line of fire. I went out to talk to them.

After a few minutes I went back to Baba and requested him on their behalf to give General Darshan.

"Why are you pressurizing me?" Baba said. "These margis in Bengal are worthless people. They don't do any work for the organization, and yet every Sunday they come here and insist that I sit for General Darshan. I am not going."

Again I left Baba alone in his room. Next Jagadishvarananda came to request Baba but I told him it was better he not go in Baba's room. Jagadishvarananda was another of those people whom Baba liked to scold, and since Baba was already in an angry mood I didn't want Jagadishvarananda upsetting him any further. Instead, I advised him to select a group of margis to come and request Baba. Jagadishvarananda was the public relations secretary and the controller of Amra Bengali, so I told him that it was his job to select the persons and he agreed.

In the meantime the rumour spread among the margis that Baba was angry and was not coming for that reason. They realized right away that he must be angry because they were not working to his satisfaction. So they selected seven persons among the seventy or so that were in the hall, including Shankar Gangully, Shanti Rainjan, Shankar Ghosh, Ritin Ghosh, and Sailen Sarkar, and Jagadishvarananda brought them upstairs. Then Baba called for me. "Have the margis gone home?" he asked.

"No, Baba," I answered. "But there are a few margis waiting outside who would like to talk to you." Baba kept silent, so I asked Shankar Gangully to come inside the room. I told the others to wait outside the door, which I left open.

He came in and did sastaunga pranam. When he got up, he said, "Baba, tell us what we should do. We will do whatever you ask of us."

"No. You are all worthless people, lazy people, sleeping all the time. I cannot even call you lazy. Even lazy people do something, but you don't do anything. To call you lazy would be an insult to lazy people the world over."

"Baba, you are right," he said. "We are not working properly. We have not shown enough energy in our activities. I take full responsibility for this. But we are ready to change. We will all take the responsibility." Shankar then called out to the other six: "Will you all promise that from now on you will work with full energy and speed?"

Collectively they promised that from then on they would give maximum effort and maximum time to Baba's work. After that Baba agreed to go for General Darshan. He came downstairs, received the garlands the margis had brought, and listened to some Prabhat Samgiita. After the songs, he told the following story:

"Once there was a king who decided to give a prize to the laziest person in his realm. He selected a group of ministers to search the length and breadth of his kingdom for the laziest person. After some time, they found a beggar who seemed to qualify. He spent his entire day sitting on a chair. But after observing him they discovered that at times he left his coat on the chair and went out to beg; thus he could not qualify as the laziest person. They continued their search but they were frustrated in their efforts. Finally the king got fed up and decided to go with them. After a while they came across two men who were lying down, seemingly awake but totally motionless. The king called to them but they didn't answer, and it appeared as if they were too lazy to speak. The king's ministers made some inquiries and found out from the locals that they had been lying there for days doing absolutely nothing. If somebody fed them they ate, but if no one gave them food they made no effort to get some. 'It appears as if these are truly the laziest people in my kingdom,' the king said, 'but we must test them to make sure. Do one thing. Light a fire near them. Let us see if we can get them to say something.'

"Soon the flames got so hot that they had no alternative but to speak. But even then they used abbreviations so that they wouldn't have to expend the energy to say complete phrases. The first one said, *pi po*, short for *pith porche*, 'back is burning.' His companion answered *phi shu*, short for *phire shuye jao*, 'turn to your other side.' The king was so impressed he awarded them the prize."

Then Baba said, "The Calcutta margis are *pipo phishu*, but I will not award them for their laziness like that king."

"No, Baba," the margis protested, "we are not *pipo phishu*. We promise, we will work hard."

Everyone laughed, including Baba. The margis had learned their lesson.

1984

My Transfer

*I*N SEPTEMBER OF 1984 I started suffering once again from head pains due to the torture I had received at the hands of the CBI during the emergency, but I didn't tell Baba about it. However, when the pain got to the point that it was hampering my work, I had no choice but to tell him that I needed to ask someone to help me with my duties. At first I was reluctant to say why—I only said that I was having some difficulties attending to him properly—but finally I told him that the head pains had come back. Baba took it very seriously. He relieved me of my duties that very same day so that I could get medical treatment and put Dada Pranavananda in my place. That was the seventeenth or eighteenth of October. I took a day or two to train him; then Baba sent me to Lakshadweep for prachar with instructions to stop in Madras first to see the doctors. The pain got worse by the time I got there so I stayed in Shiva Bhagawan's house for one month while I received treatment. During those weeks Baba insisted on receiving daily reports of my condition. Later on, I was sent to the All-India Institute of Medical Science in Delhi, where the doctors found some clotting in my brain.

October 1984

The Bhopal Gas Tragedy

OUT OF SENTIMENT I had kept the ten one-hundred-rupee notes that Baba had given me during the time of the Contai floods. After his gesture, I had been able to collect sufficient funds and I couldn't bring myself to part with those notes. But when I was sent to Bhopal to do relief work after the gas tragedy in December 1984, I thought that I should not be so sentimental about those notes. People were dying there and the money could be used to help them. So I went to the market and used them to buy food. I took the food to the Hamidia Government Hospital, to the second floor where many of the worst cases were. It was very crowded. They had put cots out but even then many people were lying on the floor and I could see that they were in bad shape. There must have been at least three hundred patients lying on that floor. After taking permission from the hospital director, I started distributing the food I had brought: bananas, oranges, bread, biscuits, milk packets, and so on. Later in the day, I received a draft from Bombay. I was also able to collect money from the Bhopal margis—in all it came to about fifty thousand rupees—and the next day I returned to the hospital in a truck filled with food. The director was sitting in his office along with another doctor. When I saw him he said to the other doctor, "This swamiji came yesterday. I don't know what medicine he has given, but all the patients he tended to yesterday have recovered."

I was surprised. "How can that be?" I said. "I saw so many patients in serious condition yesterday."

"What medicine did you give them?" he asked.

"No medicine, just fruits. I have a truck downstairs filled with fruits and other foodstuffs and some people to help me. I came to ask permission to distribute the food to the other floors as well, and to the people in the camp."

"But surely you must have given them some medicine."

"No, sir, no medicine, just fruits and other foods."

I realized that it must have been due to Baba's money. After that we started distributing to different locations.

December 1984

Jaganath of Ludhiana

*J*AGANATH OF LUDHIANA was practically illiterate—he could write his
name but little more. That was no impediment, however, when it came
to devotion. I have seen few people with such single-minded devotion
for Baba. But first, let me tell you a little about him. Jaganath was from
the Punjab, where the people are very strong and healthy compared to
the people of Bihar and Bengal. He was in the dairy business—he used
to collect milk from different dairy farmers and prepare cheese, yoghurt,
butter, and other dairy products—and because he consumed so many
milk products, he grew very stout and strong. Whenever anyone would
go to his house, he would welcome them with a huge glass of lassi—in the
Punjab the lassis are very thick and the glasses very tall. Baba generally
didn't drink lassi. In those days he would take a small glass of yoghurt
water after lunch. But when he went to Ludhiana for DMC, Jaganath
prepared one of these giant lassis for him, and he would not let Baba
leave without drinking it. When Baba saw the glass, he was surprised.
"What is this?" he asked.

"Baba, this is a Punjabi lassi," Jaganath told him. "If you drink it you
will become very healthy."

"I am already healthy, Jaganath, though not as healthy as you. But
how can I possibly drink so much? I have never seen such a huge glass
in my life."

"No, Baba, you have to drink it. If you only drink a little, then everyone
will know that you are not from the Punjab."

They went back and forth like this for a while. Finally Baba took a
few sips and distributed the rest as prasad. Jaganath was very happy that
Baba had tasted his lassi.

In 1982 Jaganath came to Calcutta for Dharma Samiksha. In Dharma
Samiksha, Baba would review the practices of his disciples and give them
punishment in order to remove their negative samskaras. Oftentimes

he would ask a couple of dadas to hold the person up so that they didn't move while he beat them with his cane. But not in Jaganath's case. "There is no need to hold me," Jaganath told the dadas. "The only reason I have come here is so that I can receive a beating from Baba. That way all my sins will disappear." Baba laughed and told the dadas not to touch him. Jaganath stood there with a blissful smile on his face while Baba beat him on his side. The more Baba beat him, the bigger his smile became.

In 1985, Baba selected Jaganath for *microvita* sadhana. When he went into Baba's room to learn the sadhana, Baba asked him about his meditation lessons. "Baba, I don't know any lessons," he replied. "I only know you." So Baba sent him to Shraddhananda to get his lessons reviewed. Three times he came back to Baba's room and three times he told Baba that he didn't know any lessons. The third time, Baba asked Jaganath to tell him exactly what he had learned when his acharya had taught him how to meditate.

"Baba, I just remember you," he said. "You are my mantra, you are my lesson. I just think of you and that is why I am always happy."

Then Baba gave him *microvita* sadhana. He was such a simple man. There was no impurity in him. Never have I seen such a person.

1985

Baba's Love for Birds

*I*N 1986 I was working in the relief department. One day in the SS meeting Baba started talking about the ostrich and its history. He told us how in ancient times soldiers used to fight on ostriches, that they were capable of running faster than horses, nearly eighty kilometres per hour. "Sadly," he said, "a day will come when this species will disappear from the earth. We should make every effort to save these birds so that future generations will have a chance to see them."

After the meeting, Baba expressed his desire to obtain some ostriches. SS Nairobi was given the duty and he contacted an African dada who was working in South Africa. This dada was originally from Botswana, where his father was the minister of environment, wildlife, and tourism. He informed the SS that the exportation of ostriches from Botswana was not permitted but that he would try to obtain a pair through his father. I was in Delhi at the time, and when we got word that he had been successful, Baba sent me to Bombay to receive the birds.

When I arrived in Bombay I contacted one margi veterinarian and hired a carpenter to make me a pair of strong boxes so I could take the birds with me by flight to Calcutta. This veterinarian used to go often to the airport to certify that incoming animals were free of disease, so he knew exactly what to do to get the birds released from quarantine. When the birds arrived we went to the airport and he secured their release. They were young birds, one male, one female—adult birds were too large to make the trip. I brought the birds to our office in Andheri and from there to our Ghatkopar office, where we have a school and a children's home. The next day we boarded our flight to Calcutta.

In the meantime, the Indian wildlife authorities found out that two ostriches from Botswana had been imported into India and released to Ananda Marga. This was a rare variety of ostrich, an endangered variety, and since there was no such ostrich in any Indian zoo they began searching for us so that they could take possession of the birds. By the time they came to Ghatkopar, however, I had already left for Calcutta with the two ostriches.

When we landed in Calcutta there were four or five dadas there to receive us. We packed the two boxes in a van and brought them to Baba's house in Tiljala. An area had been fenced off for the ostriches behind where the memorial is now, so we brought them there and when Baba came out for field walk he came to see the birds. He was very happy to see them. "Yes, these are the birds I wanted to save," he said. After praising me and the other workers for managing to bring them, he sat there for some time and watched them while he talked to us. He told us that they had been human beings in their past life and that they had conceived a samskara to see him. "I wanted to see them and they also wanted to see me," he said. He also emphasized that they should be given special attention.

A short time later, the wildlife authorities appeared at the gate with the police. They told us that they had come to take the birds to a zoo where they could be properly cared for. "We have information that this variety of ostrich is on the verge of extinction," they said. "You will not be able to care properly for them. This is our responsibility. It is a very prestigious bird. It belongs in an Indian zoo where everyone will have a chance to see it."

When we informed Baba that they were at the gate, demanding to take possession of the birds, he told us to protest. "What right do they have to take these birds?" he said. "They did nothing to bring them here. We have all the proper documents. Don't let them enter."

The authorities kept bothering us but eventually they gave up. After that the local people used to come regularly to see the ostriches. In Bengali they are called *ont pakhi*. The birds remained in Tiljala for some time but once they grew to their adult size, Baba sent them to Pashaka, the wildlife sanctuary in Anandanagar, so that they would have sufficient room to roam. He did not want them to be caged.

1986

Baba's Birthday Present

*A*ROUND THIS SAME time I again went to Madras for some treatment and stayed in Shiva Bhagawan Goenka's house. While I was there a group of margis and workers decided to give Baba a new car for his birthday. His old DeSoto was deteriorating and everyone wanted Baba to have a more modern, more comfortable car. After some deliberation they decided to get Baba a Standard 2000, the same car that is now in the museum in Calcutta. It was one of the most comfortable cars in India, designed in Japan and assembled in Chennai. They were not available in Calcutta, however, so we contacted the dealer in Chennai, but unfortunately the company had only one car left and it had been reserved by a famous film star, Rajanikant. The next car would not be ready for at least a month, which meant that we could not have it in time for Baba's birthday. Fortunately Shiva Bhagawan knew Rajanikant, who was then shooting on location in Assam. He contacted him by telephone and asked him if he would allow us to go ahead of him in the queue. Rajanikant was happy to oblige. He telephoned the showroom and authorized us to buy the car that was being held for him. A quick collection was taken up and L. C. Ananda flew in from Bombay with the money. There was just one problem: we were putting the car in Baba's name and the buyer had to have a local address, but at the time margis were reluctant to allow us to use their address due to the CBI harassment that they were sure to face as a consequence. I made some inquiries and approached Hemaji, the sister of Acharya Yatishvarananda, and she came forward without any hesitation. "Dada," she said, "it will be a privilege to have my address associated with Baba's name."

Thus we were able to successfully purchase the car. The company provided us with a driver to take the car to Calcutta and Baba sent word that I was to accompany him. L. C. Ananda and his wife were the other two passengers. Before starting off, the margis performed a special South

Indian ceremony. They broke open a green coconut, poured the water on the ground, and garlanded the car. They also bought two special South Indian garlands made of rose flowers to send to Baba along with their namaskar. One was from Shiva Bhagawan and his family; the other was the combined gift of six different margis. Since it was a two-day trip to Calcutta, they had the garland makers pack them in special ice chests, which they put in the trunk, and asked me to personally give them to Baba and to tell him who they were from and how much they loved him.

When we arrived at Lake Gardens, Baba was just coming down the stairs with Keshavananda, his PA, and Pratap, his bodyguard. Keshavananda saw me and told Baba that Anandaji and I had come. Baba asked me how I was. After I told him that I was okay, Anandaji told him that we had brought this car for him, which we wanted to present to him on his birthday, the following day.

"That I know," he said, "but you have also brought something else for me, haven't you?"

Then I remembered the garlands. "Yes, Baba," I said. "We have brought two special South Indian garlands for you."

"Yes, I was asking about the garlands."

In the meantime somebody brought the two chests. I took out one garland and held it out in front of Baba and Anandaji held out the other. They were huge garlands, very beautiful and very sweet smelling.

"Do you want me to put them on here," Baba asked, "or inside the hall when I sit for General Darshan?" At that moment we were in the antechamber near the bottom of the stairs, where the paintings of various artists are hung.

I said, "Baba, it will be very nice if you put them on here."

"Should I enter the hall wearing the garlands, then?"

"Yes, Baba, the margis will like that very much."

Baba inclined his head and I put one garland around his neck; Anandaji put the other. The garlands were so long that they were touching Baba's feet. In order for him to walk we had to hold up the bottom of the garlands.

Baba then asked me who had sent them.

"Baba, one is from Shiva Bhagawan. The other is a collective gift of several margis. One is Hemaji. The car is in her address. The others …" But I couldn't remember who the other margis were. Maybe I remembered one other.

"Did they not specifically ask you to tell me their names?"

"Yes, Baba, but I have forgotten the rest of the names."

"Then I will tell you their names." One by one he counted off the other names. "The garlands are much more important than the car," he continued. "They sent these garlands with so much love and affection." Then I remembered to tell Baba what they had told me when giving me the garlands, to give him their namaskar and to convey how much they loved him. Baba accepted their namaskars and sent them his pranam.

Later those same margis telephoned Lake Gardens. I told them how I had forgotten their names and how Baba had said their names himself and sent them his pranam. I cannot describe how much joy they felt when they heard this, and when they heard how Baba had entered the darshan hall wearing their garlands, with myself and Anandaji holding them up so that Baba could walk.

I also spoke with Shiva Bhagawan and related to him Baba's comment: "Ramananda, these garlands are heavier than I am!"

1988

Dhanjoo Ghista

*A*CHARYA DHANJOO GHISTA has been very devoted to Baba since the early days. He received his PC in Cochin during the fall 1971 DMC tour, shortly after I became PA, but even before then he had written to Baba about what he wanted to do in his life and Baba wrote him a personal reply in which he instructed Dhanjoo to serve humanity with a loving heart wherever he lived. In 1973, while Dhanjoo was a professor at Indian Institute of Technology-Madras, he had a memorable visit with Baba in Bankipur Jail.

While we were in Jamaica in 1979, Dhanjoo's wife, Garda, cooked for Baba—the family was then living in the US—and I arranged for him to go on daily field walk. When we were leaving, Baba stopped in front of him and asked, "What do you want?" After Dhanjoo replied, Baba paused for a moment and then said, "You will have it."

In the 1980s, Dhanjoo and his family used to visit Baba every year from Canada, where he worked as a professor, and Baba gave them much love and attention. I also arranged for him to go on field walk. He and his family used to garland Baba during their visits; they also went on Baba's garden tour. In 1982, he and Garda received Dharma Samiksha. During the early years of Prabhat Samgiita, Dhanjoo and his family had the opportunity to sit with Baba in Lake Gardens while Baba would translate the songs. When Baba visited the Calcutta Zoo, I arranged for Dhanjoo to accompany us on the visit, during which Baba inquired about the animals and their well-being.

In 1988, Baba called Dhanjoo to Calcutta to give him microvita sadhana, the landmark event in his life. He has since become a family acharya and Vice Chancellor of Ananda Marga Gurukula and continues to serve the mission, as Baba instructed him so many years ago.

1988

Baba Cures Me

*T*HE HEAD PAINS that I had developed as a result of the tortures I'd received at the hands of the CBI eventually started getting worse. Baba had given me some medicine for the clotting when he came out of jail but I had discontinued it. So finally I went to Delhi for a checkup—this was in late 1987 or perhaps early 1988. They told me that I needed an operation. Then I got a call from M. P. Jain that Baba wanted to see me and that he had an air ticket for me. Baba was in Tiljala at the time. When I got to Tiljala I went to Baba's room and prostrated in front of him. When I got up he asked me where the pain was.

"Baba, I can't locate it exactly. I just know that my head hurts terribly."

"Tell me exactly where it is, as best you can."

I told Baba as best I could. Then he took out his stick and started rubbing those places. He rubbed them for a few minutes and the pain went away.

"Is it okay now?" he asked.

"Yes, Baba."

"Now there is no need for an operation. I told you to take the medicine, didn't I, but you discontinued it."

Then he gave me a mixture of olive oil, camphor, and lavender and told me to rub it regularly on the affected areas. I did as he instructed and since then I have been free of pain. I am so much in debt to him for the way he took care of me, not only then but throughout my life.

1988

Glossary

Akhanda Kirtan: Kirtan done for an extended period of time. *Akhanda* means "endless."

Ananda Marga: The Path of Bliss; the socio-spiritual organization founded by Baba in 1955.

Ananda Vanii: Baba's twice-yearly message to the margis; *vanii* means "message."

ASP: Assistant superintendent of police.

Avadhuta: A senior Ananda Marga monk who is initiated into *kapalik* meditation.

Avadhutika: A senior Ananda Marga nun, also initiated into *kapalik* meditation.

BP: Bhukti pradhan.

Bhukti pradhan: The district secretary of Ananda Marga.

CBI: Central Bureau of Investigation.

CPM: Communist Party of India (Marxist).

Darshan: Literally, "the sight of the guru." Often used to refer to Baba's talks.

DPS: Dharma prachar secretary.

DSP: Deputy superintendent of police.

Dharmamahachakra: "The great circle of Dharma"; gatherings during which Baba would address the margis and give his varabhaya mudra.

Dhoti: A long piece of white cloth that is worn by Indian males from the waist down as their traditional dress.

Dhyana: Meditation.

DMC: Dharmamahachakra.

Ekadashi: The eleventh day of the lunar fortnight; traditionally yogis fast on this day.

General Darshan: Baba's non-DMC talks.

Guru Dakshina: An offering to the guru, typically made at the time of initiation.

Guru Dhyana: Meditation on the guru.

IG: Inspector General.

Ista: A devotee's personal conception of God.

Jagriti: Spiritual centre or ashram. Literally, "a place of awakening."

Kirtan: Chanting or singing of mantras, often combined with a traditional dance.

Kitchuri: An Indian dish with rice, lentils, and vegetables cooked together.

Kurta: A Indian dress shirt.

Lakh: One hundred thousand.

Local Fulltimer: A non-monastic fulltime volunteer worker.

Lungi: A piece of cloth of any colour or pattern used as informal dress by Indian males; also known as a sarong.

Mahaprayana: Death; literally, "great passage."

Mandap: Altar.

Microvita sadhana: A special meditation technique that Baba taught to a small number of select disciples.

MG quarters: Baba's quarters. MG is short for Marga Guru.

PA: Personal assistant.

Pandal: A huge tent that is erected as a shelter for large gatherings.

Prachar: The effort to spread the philosophy and teachings; literally, "propagation."

Pranam: Respectful greetings.

Prasad: A sacred offering, typically consisting of food that is later shared by the devotees.

Pratik: The symbol of Ananda Marga.

RM: Rector master.

Sadhaka: Spiritual aspirant.

Sadhana: Spiritual practice or meditation; literally, "the effort to complete."

Sastaunga pranam: Full prostration.

Shloka: Sanskrit verse.

Shraddha: Funeral ceremony.

SP: Superintendent of Police.

SS: Sectorial secretary.

Svadhyaya: The study of spiritual books.

Tandava: A vigorous dance taught by Baba to his male disciples, attributed to Lord Shiva.

Tattvika: A designation used in Ananda Marga for those who have shown their mastery of the philosophy by passing the tattvika exam.

Trikuti: The midpoint between the two eyebrows, sometimes known as the "third eye"; it is associated with the sixth chakra.

Varabhaya Mudra: A special gesture through which Baba emanated his spiritual force at the end of certain gatherings, principally DMCs.

Vishesh Yoga: An advanced system of spiritual practices or meditation.

Wholetimer: A full-time worker of Ananda Marga; an Ananda Marga monk or nun.

Worker: Short for whole-time worker or wholetimer.

www.ingramcontent.com/pod-product-compliance
Lightning Source LLC
Chambersburg PA
CBHW020437130626
46549CB00001B/177